EASTERN EUROPE AND THE USSR

Commission of the European Communities

EASTERN EUROPE AND THE USSR
THE CHALLENGE OF FREEDOM

GILES MERRITT

Office for Official Publications of the European Community

Kogan Page is the UK member of the Euro Business Publishing Network.
The European members are: Les Editions d'Organisation, France; Verlag Moderne Industrie, West Germany; Liber, Sweden; Franco Angeli, Italy; and Deusto, Spain.
The Network has been established in response to the growing demand for international business information and to make the work of Network authors available in other European languages.

First published in 1991

Kogan Page Limited
120 Pentonville Road
London N1 9JN

British Library Cataloguing in Publication Data

A CIP record for this book is available from the British Library.

ISBN 0 7494 0516 3 – Paperback

Typeset by Saxon Printing Ltd, Derby

Printed in England by Clays Ltd, St Ives plc

Contents

List of Plates   7

Foreword   9

Acknowledgements   11

Chapter 1   After Communism: Redrawing the Map of Europe   13

Chapter 2   The EC Dimension: From the Atlantic to the Urals, and Perhaps to Vladivostock   31

Chapter 3   Economic Integration: The Long Hard Road to the Free Market   47

Chapter 4   Industry: Could the Eastern Europeans be Tomorrow's 'Technology Tigers'?   77

Chapter 5   Trade: Comecon's Collapse – Putting Humpty Dumpty Together Again   91

Chapter 6   Investment: Getting Capital to Flow Eastwards   113

Chapter 7 Immigration: The Spectre of Mass
Migration from the East   **137**

Chapter 8 Agriculture: The East Could Become the
Granary of Europe   **151**

Chapter 9 Energy: The Key to a New
East-West Partnership   **169**

Chapter 10 Environment: Cleaning Eastern
Europe's Augean Stables   **191**

Chapter 11 Debt: Avoiding the Latin America Debt
Path   **211**

Chapter 12 Assistance: A 'Marshall Plan' for
Eastern Europe?   **235**

List of Plates

1 ' Kommunism' is dismantled in Prague, 1989
   Photo L Hajsky – Ceteka

2 Hungary's brief foretaste of freedom: Stalin's statue in
   Budapest is broken up during the uprising of 1956
   Photo Popperfoto

3 **Days of the Iron Curtain**: Frontier guard on the Czechoslovak/
   Austrian border, 1968...
   Photo Popperfoto

4 ... the barriers are rolled back between Austria and
   Czechoslovakia, December 1989
   Photo Ceteka

5 **About turn**: Soviet tanks enter Prague, August 1968...
   Photo Popperfoto

6 ... and withdraw from the Czechoslovak town of Frenstat,
   February 1990
   Photo Kurz-Schuh – Contrast/Gamma

7 Greenpeace protests against unsafe Czechoslovak nuclear
   plant in Bohunice
   Photo E Schuh – Contrast/Gamma

8 School children wearing protective masks in the polluted
   Czechoslovak city of Mezihori
   Photo V Cech – Gamma

9 Industrial pollution in Estonia
   Photo F Mayer – Magnum

10 Pollution road: A horse drawn cart passes a rubber dyeing
   factory in Copsa Mica, Romania
   Photo P Dejong – Associated Press

11 Romanian refugees make camp at Tourville-La-Riviere,
France
Photo G Saussier – Gamma

12 Demonstrators against the construction of the Gabcikova –
Nagymaros power plant over the Danube form a human chain
Photo Matusz/Interfoto MTI

13 Window shopping: A Polish farmer ponders the latest in
agricultural machinery
Photo E de Keerle – Gamma

14 Towards a high-tech future: Sigma M5000 computer assembly
line in Vilnius, Lithuania
Photo A Uloziavitchus – Gamma

15 Potato picking in present-day Poland
Photo F Lochan – Gamma

16 International Herald Tribune, December 1990
Cartoonist Reisinger

17 Walesa and Delors raise their glasses to the future, Brussels,
March 1991
Photo EC

18 Havel and Dubček celebrate Civic Forum's success, December
1989
Photo I Berry – Magnum

Foreword

Czech philosopher Ladislav Hejdánek once wrote that 'any attempt to solve the situation in Central and Eastern Europe is an attempt to find its solution in a pan-European framework'. I am glad that as well-informed and perceptive an analyst as Giles Merritt has come to the same conclusion in this book.

Central and Eastern Europe has not just changed of late, it has been literally turned upside down in both a political and economic sense. The events we have recently witnessed – for instance the withdrawal of Soviet troops, the dissolution of the Warsaw Pact and German unification – are those that most of us predicted would take place only in the distant future.

The changes in Central and Eastern Europe, intensified by the recent dramatic events in the USSR, represent a 'challenge of freedom', not only for this region but also for the West, and thus for the European Community, as a pole of economic prosperity and political stability.

The Association Agreements between the Czech and Slovak Federal Republic, Poland and Hungary and the European Community will be a milestone in the gradual incorporation of these three Central European 'Troika' countries into the integration process now being developed within the framework of the EC 'Twelve'.

But the EC's concern with Central and Eastern Europe should not keep it from pursuing the aims it has set itself; namely the creation of the European Single Market and after that economic and monetary union and political union. At the same time, cooperation with Czechoslovakia, Poland and Hungary in the fields of trade and economic policy should be radically improved.

We fully realize that Czechoslovakia will not achieve membership of the EC through any adroitness at the negotiating table. We know that we will only achieve it by hard work, and by adapting ourselves to the norms and standards of the 'Twelve', and above all by complying with the two fundamental conditions of democratic stability and an efficient market economy.

It is in the nature of the systemic changes that we are now resolutely carrying out in Czechoslovakia that practically everything must be done all at the same time. The aim must be to simultaneously develop new political and economic processes. The difficulty is that of reconciling the newly aroused economic expectations of our people with the unpredictable and often painful impact on society of fundamental economic reforms. The major question for us is this: Can a democratically elected government achieve economic change so drastic that it will have a severe impact on its people, and in spite of that remain stable? If we cannot, the risk will be of frustration, stagnation, recession, instability and the danger of nationalistic dictatorships.

That is why we need the help and cooperation of the West in our drive to achieve these fundamental changes. The EC nations cannot replace our own reform effort, but in the spirit of European solidarity they should share with us the benefits of their efficient and functioning societies.

Western governments have already provided us with financial and technical assistance and trade concessions. They have eliminated restrictions on technology transfer and supported our integration into international organizations. The more important question, however, is what will be the future response of Western private investors.

The dramatic events in the USSR connected with the attempted coup d'état, vividly underlined the complicated and vulnerable situation in which the new democracies in Central Europe find themselves. They also served to remind us of the way the USSR's internal political and economic problems, and those of its former republics will continue to affect us for many years to come.

Indeed, the situation in the USSR underlines the need for Czechoslovakia and its Central European partners in the 'Troika' to weave new economic, security and political ties with the West.

The help already being given by the Western democracies to Czechoslovakia, Poland and Hungary must also be seen in a security context. It is a well-known truth that free, democratic and prosperous societies are the most peace-loving parts of the international scene. The economic success of the Central European 'Troika' would significantly help democracy in Eastern Europe. The more the West helps to stabilize the democracies of Czechoslovakia, Poland and Hungary, the more effectively it will be supporting democratic forces in the USSR and throughout Central and Eastern Europe.

In March 1947, the then Czechoslovak Minister of Foreign Affairs, Jan Masaryk, expressed his ideas on the international role of Czechoslovakia with these words: 'Neither a curtain, nor a bridge, but a link in the democratic chain spanning the world and holding this planet together.' I am convinced that our integration into the European Community is in keeping with this concept and that it represents a new joining together of the broken links of that chain. It represents our contribution to the creation of a united and democratic Europe.

Jiri Dienstbier
Foreign Minister of the Czech and Slovak Federal Republic
Prague, August 1991

Acknowledgements

The Challenge of Freedom sets out to argue that helping Eastern Europe is of vital self-interest for Western Europe. It has been written with the encouragement and support of the European Commission, but it is not in any sense an official publication. I am most grateful for the privileged access I was given to key EC officials, but the views and interpretations that resulted are entirely my own.

I have attempted to combine within this book a plea for greater Western assistance to Eastern Europe and a snapshot of these countries and their problems as at mid-1991. The problem with such snapshots is that detailed facts and figures soon begin to be overtaken by events. I hope that the reader will agree with me that it is preferable to run that risk than to take refuge in generalities.

I owe a debt of gratitude not only to the European Commission but to the many experts in both Eastern and Western Europe who have given me their time and their help during the preparation of this book. I should particularly like to thank the following: Frans Andriessen, Umberto Agnelli, Sergio Arzeni, Klara Baracs, Nicholas Bayne, Hans Beck, Pablo Benavides, John Birch, Peter Akos Bod, Jorge Braga de Macedo, Simon Broadbent, Margaret Brusasco, Vladimir Chemiatenkov, Milan Cernohuby, Paul Corddry, Mikhailo Crnobrnja, Jiri Dienstbier, Joly Dixon, Huw Evans, Geoffrey Fitchew, John Flemming, Adrian Fortescue, Lawrence Freedman, Tom Garvey, Vlastimil Gejdos, Johannes ter Haar, Carl Hahn, Jan Kulakowski, Istvan Kormendi, Pascal Lamy, Herman de Lange, Michael Leigh, André Leysen, Ivan Lipovecz, John Maddison, Constantinos Maniatopoulos, Janos Martonyi, John Maslen, Karel Matous, Alan Mayhew, Rolf Moehler, Kate Mortimer, Krzysztof Ners, Tom Niles, Mario Nuti, Peter Palecka, Michael Palmer, Antonino Pitrone, Zdenek Pirek, Richard Portes, Paul Rayment, Sir Adam Ridley, James Rollo, Bob Simmons, Norman Scott, Antony Steiner, Susan Strange, Ivan Szasz, Eugen Szekely, Jan Truszczynski, Jaroslav Ungerman, Peter Vadasz, Jozef van Brabant, Costas Velentyas, Christian Waeterloos, Tom Weston, Christopher Wilkinson, David Michael Wilson and Alan Winters.

This book is being published in five languages, thanks in large part to the backing of the European Commission. I am especially grateful to Richard Lewis of the Commission's Secretariat General for his enthusiasm and unstinting support. I should also like to thank Johanna Maas and her colleague Nicola Bellieni for their help with many aspects of this project, not least their efforts to smooth my way through the labyrinths of the EC bureaucracy. My sincere thanks, too, to Miranda Rhys-Williams who undertook the task of picture research, and to distinguished journalists Harald Hotze and Yves Benoit, who not only translated my text into German and French respectively but who also gave me much valuable advice.

The greatest debt of all, however, is that which I owe to my wife Pamela for her encouragement and constructive criticism. Without her advice this book would have been much the poorer.

Giles Merritt,
August 1991

1

After Communism:

Redrawing the Map of Europe

The old order changeth — Why Eastern Europe is a Western problem — Eastern European flashpoints and the Balkan powder keg — Latin American parallels: from the USSR's 'Pinochet Option' to Poland's Peronism — Western responses; the launching of G-24 — The double-edged sword of conditionality — Filling the security vacuum — Practical steps the West can take

---

The powder train of revolution that flared across Eastern Europe in the autumn of 1989 brought with it the end of an era. The toppling of the Berlin Wall and the downfall of the hard-faced communist regimes that had ruled Eastern Europe for almost half a century was an upheaval that gripped the attention of the world.

The significance of those events is only now becoming clearer. The signs are that the whole of Europe will be touched. The end of the Cold War and the reintegration of the USSR and its former satellites into a wider Europe promises to be a process of global importance.

If it goes well, the effect could be to create a wider political and economic framework on such a scale as to redress Europe's declining weight in the world. If it goes wrong, the whole of Europe may begin to revert to the fragmentation and instability that blighted the first half of the 20th century and caused two world wars.

A glimpse of that nightmare came with the abortive coup in the USSR from 18-21 August 1991. For 60 hours the world held its breath. While President Mikhail Gorbachev languished under house arrest in his Black Sea holiday villa, the USSR teetered on the edge of chaos. The fear was that the coup's attempt to turn back the clock of Soviet reform would either bring about a return to totalitarianism and the Cold War, or it would plunge the country into civil war.

The coup against President Gorbachev has given the West a considerable shock. It has jolted Western governments into reappraisals of their attitudes towards helping the USSR. The coup attempt has raised uncomfortable questions over whether Western refusal to give greater financial aid to the USSR may have helped to precipitate the move to oust President Gorbachev. It came within less than a month of Gorbachev's empty-handed return from the London G-7 summit, at which the leaders of the seven leading industrialized nations had declined to pour billions of dollars into the 'black hole' of the Soviet economy.

The defeat of the coup and the end of communist government is certain to result in greater financial assistance. Russian Federation leader Boris Yeltsin's courageous defence of Soviet democracy, and of President Gorbachev's constitutional right to remain in power, will probably be rewarded with Western generosity on a level unsurpassed since World War II. The ascendency in post-coup Soviet politics of those who, like Yeltsin, believe in the radical reform of the Soviet economy will also overcome Western doubts about the wisdom of giving aid.

In retrospect, it is possible to say that the 60-hour coup came at a providential moment. As well as strengthening Western interest in the USSR, it is also likely to reinvigorate Western support for the process of reform throughout Eastern Europe. The coup raised the spectre of a hostile and backward-looking régime in the Kremlin just as Western public opinion seemed to be flagging in its commitment to helping the peoples of Eastern Europe.

By mid-1991, the early and enthusiastic commitment of the peoples of Western Europe and the United States to aiding Eastern Europe seemed in danger of melting away. The lessening of public interest was in turn beginning to ease the pressure on Western governments to mount a massive rescue operation to re-launch the Eastern European economies.

Thanks to the coup against Mikhail Gorbechev, however, the importance of helping the USSR and the whole of Eastern Europe is once again clear to all. Few people in the West can now doubt that the coming years are a crucial period for these formerly communist countries. Economic collapse and further political unrest lie ahead unless the industrialized nations respond with financial assistance, technical advice, technological know-how and freer access to Western markets.

The old order changeth

In years to come, historians may well characterize the Cold War as a period of calm and stability. Between the early 1960s, when the Cuba missile crisis showed that nuclear war between the US and USSR was indeed unthinkable, and the late 1980s, Western Europe did not need to spare more than a passing thought for Eastern Europe.

It was as if an invisible wall separated the two Europes. Other than the occasional bout of sabre-rattling by Nato or the Warsaw Pact, the countries of Eastern Europe scarcely impinged on the politics of Western Europe. The main thrust of European politics – the development of the European Community – was aimed at ensuring that Germany and France would never again go to war, not at averting a threat from the USSR.

Suddenly, the invisible wall known as the Iron Curtain has been removed. But Western Europeans may before long look back on the Cold War period as 'the good old days'. The 'victory' of capitalism over communism is genuine enough, yet it may turn out to be a hollow one. The disintegration of the Soviet bloc, and quite possibly of much of the USSR itself, will impose new strains and challenges on the West.

The lifting of the Iron Curtain will have far-reaching political effects. The debate among Western Europeans over political and economic union will be significantly changed. The discussion over whether the European Community should be 'deepened' or 'widened' – meaning whether the 12 should unite more closely before taking on new members – will soon be yesterday's debate.

Even deepening *and* widening, in which some of the EFTA countries join a more federal-style EC, will be much less central to the debate on the future of Europe. The Western Europeans' focus on their internal political arrangements is likely to be eclipsed by the new uncertainties crowding in from the East.

Why Eastern Europe is a Western problem

The Eastern European nations, and above all the USSR, are loose cannon that could endanger the EC ship. Unless secured by both political links and some strong economic ties, they risk plunging through the sides of the ship and might even cause it to sink. Put another way, the political and social instability that could spread through Eastern Europe if its problems are not addressed might easily undermine the European Community's unity and sense of purpose.

Neither the EC nor the West as a whole has woken to this sea-change in European politics. Eastern Europe is being treated as if it were yet another Third World development problem. Until the coup attempt, the USSR was regarded more as a fractious and undisciplined child that was refusing to face up to the reality of communism's failure.

It is perhaps inevitable that Western nations whose experience over the past 25 years and more has been confined to giving development aid to Asian, African and Latin American countries should try to apply the same techniques to Eastern Europe. But it is not a sound basis for building a wider Europe. The policies of aid tied to export contracts and development loans that become a crippling debt burden have not been a success in the Third World and are totally unsuited to the economic transformation of Eastern Europe.

The fundamental difference between Eastern Europe and the Third World is, of course, that Eastern Europe is on the

West's doorstep. Economic collapse in the USSR would send serious shock waves into the EC. Unrest in the Balkans, leading to violence between rival ethnic communities, could spark a conflagration that might easily involve one EC member state – Greece – and would thus concern the whole of the European Community.

Eastern European flashpoints and the Balkan powder keg

The focus of Europe's security concern has shifted from the nuclear stand-off between two superpowers to the mosaic of ethnic tensions that threaten peace in Eastern Europe. Now that these communities are no longer frozen into the Soviet bloc, their economic development and prosperity will be vital if these flashpoints are to be defused.

There are half a dozen potential border disputes and 14 significant ethnic pockets in Eastern Europe, many of them the result of the post-World War I settlements reached at the Trianon peace conference, and others of the Yalta settlement secured by Stalin in 1944. Greek minorities live in tense circumstances in Albania, Yugoslavia and Bulgaria. There are Albanians in Yugoslavia, Turks in Bulgaria and Hungarians in Romania and the Ukraine. There are substantial German communities in Poland, Czechoslovakia, Hungary and Romania.

The Romanians who live in Soviet Moldavia, and who account for two-thirds of its population, are agitating for Moldavia's reunification with Romania. There are also Romanians in the Ukraine. Poland has vociferous minorities who hail originally from the Ukraine and Byelorussia. Hungary has a strongly assertive expatriate community of 2.6 million just across its border with Romania.

Then there are the Soviet republics themselves. The Baltic states of Latvia, Estonia and Lithuania are to leave the USSR as quickly as possible, even though their economic viability as independent countries is questionable.

The Balkans are the most worrying trouble spot of all. The powder keg scenario most often advanced is that Yugoslavia's disintegration could spark a train of events that would engulf the Balkan peninsula in violence.

The nationalism that divides the Yugoslav republics might easily result in the secession of the province of Kosovo, which is 90 per cent inhabited by Albanians. If integrated into Albania, that could rekindle Greek aspirations to secure the return of parts of southern Albania. Greece and Bulgaria also have claims to territory that is now part of Yugoslavia.

Further east, across the Black Sea, there is unrest in the Caucasus region of the USSR. The three trans-Caucasian republics – Georgia, Armenia and Azerbaijan – all have serious ethnic conflicts of their own, and they also have determined separatist movements. Their ambitions to leave the USSR may yet be realized, and their ethnic difficulties would probably then make them even more unstable and prone to violence.

Latin American parallels

The coup that in the early hours of 18 August sought to remove Mikhail Gorbachev from office had long been fore-shadowed. The threat of coming 'dictatorship' was the reason Soviet foreign minister Eduard Shevardnadze gave for resigning in late 1990, and in the months that followed the rumblings of discontent grew louder still from hardliners within the government who blamed the deteriorating Soviet economy on Gorbachev's reform programme.

Only two days before the plotters seized power, a close Gorbachev aide issued a dramatic warning that a 'Stalinist' coup was in the offing. Alexander Yakolev, one of the architects of President Gorbachev's *Perestroika* strategy, used the occasion of his resignation from the Communist Party to publicly warn that a move to oust Gorbachev was imminent.

The idea that the USSR might be threatened by a Latin America-style military-backed coup had been commonplace among Sovietologists for some time. One popular scenario, usually referred to as the 'Pinochet Option', was that a senior Red Army figure akin to Chile's General Augusto Pinochet would emerge to seize the reins of power. Those who warned of the risk of the Pinochet Option saw it as a means of reconciling the USSR's need for stable, indeed authoritarian, government with the Soviet people's hunger for a free market economic system.

Such a coup was usually dismissed as less than credible on the grounds that the Soviet military has no tradition of political interference. That analysis was to be proved only half right. The events of 18-21 August 1991, in which the vacillation of Red Army units helped bring about the coup's collapse, reflected the reluctance of the military to play a political role. But it also marked a turning point in which the Red Army and the KGB moved against the legally constituted government headed by Mikhail Gorbachev.

For the USSR, the threat of succumbing to the dictatorship of a self-appointed junta now seems to be past. But for some Eastern European countries there remains a risk that their newly re-established democracies could become tainted with the sort of politics associated with Latin America.

As Mario Nuti, a noted economist who advises the EC Commission on Eastern European affairs, has pointed out, Poland also has Latin American parallels. 'Latin America-style prospects – hyperinflation, recession, high unemployment, populism – have already emerged in Poland and may appear in some of [the] countries now poised to follow the painful Polish road to stabilization', comments Nuti.[1]

His concern is shared by Hungarian expert Attila Szilassy, who says, 'There is a real fear that under the rule of the dirigist wing of Solidarity, Poland will embrace a European version of Peronism.'

Szilassy emphasizes that this is not a particularly Polish problem, and identifies what he calls 'demagogic hard cores' in Hungary, Romania and the Slovak Republic in Czechoslovakia. He adds: 'A kind of Caudillismo, a personification of power in the hands of charismatic persons, known from Latin America as a substitute for democratic institutions, is emerging in Eastern Europe as a very dangerous phenomenon'.[2]

The threat of Latin America-style politics in Eastern Europe may seem a distant one to many people in the West. But it is closer than it appears. The democratic governments that have been elected in Eastern Europe are a sign of hope rather than a guarantee of change. Their durability cannot be taken for granted, for the democratic political institutions of the Eastern European countries are much less firmly rooted than they appear.

The fragility of Eastern Europe's new-found democracy is striking to Western aid specialists now working on economic assistance programmes. Tom Garvey, who heads the EC's PHARE aid programme, is in no doubt that political stability is still very vulnerable. He says: 'At first, we thought democracy could be quickly achieved. Now we can see the steps needed to implement a democratic system of government, such as dismantling the Nomenklatura, are part of a very long process. For the time being, we have democratic parliaments atop old structures. I think it will take quite a long time before we truly democratize these countries.'

Western responses; the launching of G-24

Western Europe's self-interest, unless it wants to risk turmoil in the East, is to defuse the explosive problems of Eastern Europe as quickly as it can.

Western governments began to recognize during 1990 the potential threat to their security posed by the lifting of the Iron Curtain. The year before, though, they had already set up the mechanisms for channelling economic assistance to Eastern Europe. The West's motives were at that point largely humanitarian. It is fair to say that Western concern also reflected a sense of satisfaction that communism had so demonstrably failed and that the perceived menace of the Soviet-led Warsaw Pact was evaporating.

In mid-1989, the G-7 summit in Paris attended by the leaders of the world's seven leading industrial powers – the United States, Japan, Germany, France, the United Kingdom, Italy and Canada – decided to set up a new structure called the Group of 24 to handle the problem of assisting Eastern Europe.

The G-24 countries were the EC 12 and the dozen non-EC countries grouped in the 'rich man's club' of the Paris-based Organisation for Economic Cooperation and Development. It was decided that the EC Commission would act as coordinator of the G-24 effort because it was already becoming clear that the European Community has a central role to play in Eastern Europe.

The seeds of the Western effort to help Eastern Europe were first sown at a small private luncheon in the White House. Jacques Delors, the president of the EC Commission, was George Bush's guest of honour and the two men soon became deeply engrossed in a discussion of the Polish situation.

The time was May 1989, and food aid for the Polish people was becoming a major preoccupation in Washington. The vociferous Polish-American lobby had seen to that. President Bush was quickly struck by Delors's familiarity and expertise both on the Polish issue and on Eastern European affairs in general.

Delors, a former French finance minister who took over the top EC job in 1985, had in his early years risen through the ranks of the Banque de France. His strong trade union background and his devout catholicism had helped him to forge strong links with the Solidarity leadership.

The discussion over the White House lunch table appears to have left an indelible impression on George Bush. Two months later it prompted the US President to move that the European Commission be appointed to coordinate and run the G-24 effort.

The decision to hand over the running of G-24 to the Brussels Commission came as a surprise to most of the participants at the 'Summit of the Arch' hosted by the French government. Often, national governments jealously guard such responsibilities, so the decision to invite Brussels to take charge of the West's aid effort astonished not only the world's press covering the summit but also many of the hundreds of senior officials taking part.

The Summit of the Arch was an elaborately stage-managed event that France's President Francois Mitterrand had carefully planned to take place on July 14 in order that the world's most powerful leaders should be on hand to celebrate the 200th anniversary of the French Revolution. For all the pomp and circumstance, though, the summit had seemed doomed to failure. The US and France were divided over Western policy towards Eastern Europe.

Tempers had begun to fray during the countdown week before the summit. It had become apparent that the US government was planning to unveil a plan for a Western aid 'consortium' to help Poland and Hungary. French officials were distraught on two counts.

To begin with, the surprise US initiative was more far-reaching and ambitious than the paper being tabled by the summit's French hosts, who were proposing a somewhat humdrum approach in which East-West economic relations would be analyzed first and then ideas for assistance examined at a later date. The French feared they would be upstaged. In the second place, the idea of an aid consortium might eclipse the French government's pet project for the setting up of the European Bank for Reconstruction and Development.

On the eve of a summit which therefore looked as if it might end in acrimony the G-7 leaders, together with Delors, who attends such events as representative of the EC, met during the course of an elaborate banquet. Delors used the opportunity to tell President Bush that he welcomed the US idea of an aid consortium, and Bush responded by suggesting that its running should be placed in Delors's hands.

In the event, the twin proposals were in fact put forward by Germany's Chancellor Helmut Kohl, so drawing the teeth of any French opposition. Thus was G-24 born.

Whether the G-24 mechanism will prove adequate for Eastern Europe's needs remains to be seen. It was devised at a time when Eastern Europe's problems were on a different scale and of a different type than is the case today, two years after the Summit of the Arch.

At that time, the focus was on food aid and technical assistance for two countries – Poland and Hungary – that had loosened the bonds of their communist régimes. Since then, the picture has altered radically. The whole of Eastern Europe is free of the Warsaw Pact and the Comecon trading area, and the Soviet bloc is no more. But so far as the Eastern European economies are concerned, the change is for the worse.

The process of adapting to the free market system will mean a sharp deterioration in the already weakened Eastern European economies. On top of that, there is the overwhelming question of what to do about the USSR itself, against whose economic needs those of Eastern Europe pale into insignificance. The West's aim must be to prevent the USSR from becoming alarmingly unstable, without at the same time pouring billions of dollars into aid that would be used to prop up the country's ramshackle centrally-planned economy.

The double-edged sword of conditionality

The events of August 1991, and particularly the ending of the Communist Party's 73-year régime of power, have opened the way for a new and positive relationship between the USSR and the West. But that sea-change does not necessarily resolve the issue of what conditions the West can and should impose in return for its help.

The doctrine of 'conditionality' has been used by Western governments to ensure that aid is not funnelled towards unsatisfactory projects, nor used to delay rather than accelerate the shift towards a market economy. So far, conditionality has chiefly been applied to Eastern European countries because the assistance given to the USSR has been minimal.

The West's conditionality policies have in the past provoked mixed reactions in Eastern Europe and outright hostility in the USSR. But it is likely that in a new era of Soviet-Western cooperation the setting of conditions by Western governments, the European Community and agencies such as the IMF will be seen as constructive attempts to encourage economic development.

Some Eastern Europeans have actually welcomed conditionality. Czechoslovakia has found that it helps to keep up the momentum of its economic reform process. Others are less enthusiastic. Hungarian officials describe conditionality as 'patronizing' and Poland takes a middle view.

Poland accepts that Western donors, and notably the EC, have the right to see that their economic assistance is properly employed. But it rejects any attempts to tie aid to political developments. 'Political conditionality makes no sense for Poland', says Jan Kulakowski, the Polish ambassador to the EC. 'We think we have demonstrated our commitment to democracy.'

The USSR, not surprisingly, had been the loudest in its rejection of conditionality. 'The USSR will remain a great power, and whatever happens it is impossible for the European Community to try and exercise 'tutelage' on us', remarks Vladimir Chemiatenkov, who was Soviet ambassador to the EC until March 1991. 'Political conditions are our *bête noir*. No foreign governments can decide what is good for us.'

Moscow's prickly attitude towards conditionality is certain to change, following the events of August 1991. President Bush led the West in declaring a form of conditionality that was implacably opposed to the coup – Western assistance would be forthcoming only when the USSR's constitutionally appointed president was restored. That very positive example of Western involvement in Soviet affairs, coupled with the new determination to embark on radical economic reform, could mean that conditionality will be the basis of a new partnership.

The governments of the Western donor nations in any case remain convinced that it is essential to tie strings to their aid in order to force the pace of reform and to underwrite the fledgling democracies of Eastern Europe, and now of the Soviet republics. The terms of Western conditionality are worked out within the G-24 framework and Herman de Lange, a Dutch EC official who runs the G-24 coordination process, argues that building consensus on conditionality has been one of the EC Commission's main achievements.

The G-24 experience with Eastern Europe will be just a modest foretaste of the complexities that await aid donors to the USSR and the republics. Furthermore, the G-24 governments will have to re-focus their present vision of conditionality to meet the fast-changing situation in the USSR. Western assistance and the conditions it will be wrapped in will no longer be conducted solely at the level of central government in Moscow. Aid will also have to be granted and administered at the level of the republics.

Dealing with the USSR, as it disintegrates into some looser confederation, will present the West with problems on a scale that overshadows those of Eastern Europe. The political turmoil in the Soviet republics will demand a much more coherent approach, particularly from the EC member states, to the self-determination of the peoples of the USSR.

The unravelling of the USSR carries with it the risk of serious ethnic conflict, and for the West the doctrine of conditionality therefore risks being a double-edged sword. Any lack of consistent and carefully thought out Western policies on the self-determination of ethnic communities in Eastern Europe and the USSR is liable to aggravate matters.

Many of the secessionist republics have substantial ethnic minorities on their territory who are bitterly opposed to being abandoned to the tender mercies of the nationalist administrations who would take up the reins of government hitherto held by Moscow. The danger is that a wave of secessions from the USSR could also spark widespread civil unrest and violence.

Western conditionality will need to be carefully fashioned if it is to help rather than hinder the peaceful development of the Soviet republics. The EC's involvement in the Yugoslav crisis that erupted into violence in mid-1991 stands as an example of the difficulties of intervening in ethnic disputes.

The scope of Western economic assistance, whatever the future definition of conditionality, will be of crucial importance. In the aftermath of the failed August coup in the USSR, the Western G-7 powers seem prepared to look again at the need to pump economic assistance into the country.

How much aid may be needed to stave off economic collapse and help underwrite the reforms in newly independent or autonomous Soviet republics is anyone's guess. The EC Commission has estimated that the 8 million people in the three breakaway Baltic republics will need up to US$3.5bn over the two years to the end of 1993, and by the standards of the USSR they are both few in number and comparatively rich.

The scale of assistance that may be needed was outlined in the proposals mooted in May 1991 for a 'Grand Bargain' to be struck between the Western nations and Moscow. It proposed a headline figure of US$150bn in emergency aid and technical assistance to the USSR over five years. Prepared by a group of eminent US and Soviet economists based at Harvard University, the plan was for a radical switch to free market conditions that would be backed by between US$15bn and $30bn a year in aid to the USSR over five years.

At that time, the plan was deliberately obstructed by Soviet conservatives, and opposed in the West by hard-headed politicians and business leaders who warned that it would simply enable the USSR to delay economic reforms and cling to the misguided idea of there being a 'middle way' between communism and the free market. Now, perhaps, the way ahead is clearer.

One-third of the money would go towards making the rouble a convertible currency, by supporting it at a reasonable exchange rate. Another one-third would be spent on importing consumer goods and on freeing the USSR from its disastrous arrangements of government-fixed prices. And the final one-third would be spent on the modernization of the USSR's Stone Age telecommunications and transport systems.

The authors of the rescue package, or 'Harvard Plan', argue that although it may sound a lot of money, US$30bn a year is in fact less than 0.2 per cent of the combined GNPs of the world's industrialized nations. The US contribution, stressed the US economists working on the plan, would be just 1 per cent of US military spending, which would be recouped through the savings in defence costs that would stem from greater détente and a peaceful USSR.

Financial assistance to the USSR will, however, be wasted until a number of crucial reforms have been introduced. Until there is a workable system of property rights and contract law there can be no move towards a market economy. Until there are at least the bare bones of a fiscal and monetary policy there can be no question of a market economy that functions. Most of all, until there is a constitutional settlement that clearly establishes the powers of the central government and those of the Soviet republics there can be no stability in which to develop a market economy.

Filling the security vacuum

When Czechoslovakia's President Vaclav Havel became the first Eastern European leader to visit Nato's Brussels headquarters in March 1991, he did not mince his words about the dangers of the security vacuum created by the collapse of the Warsaw Pact. 'Instability, poverty, misfortune and disorder in the countries that have rid themselves of despotic rule could threaten the West just as the arms arsenal of the former despotic governments did', he told a beribboned gathering of Nato top brass, ambassadors and ministers. 'Our countries are dangerously sliding into a political, economic and security vacuum.'

Havel's message was simple. Unless the West somehow incorporates into a new security framework the Eastern European countries who were formerly ranged against it, the consequences could be very serious. It is not only nature that abhors a vacuum. The security vacuum in Europe could be filled by political developments that might set back the integration of the EC.

For the Nato allies, however, the filling of this vacuum is far from straightforward. Poland, Czechoslovakia and Hungary have all indicated that they are seeking a special relationship with Nato, and have even made it clear that if given a chance they would apply for Nato membership. The West's anxiety, though, is that it must avoid antagonizing the USSR.

Although the USSR is withdrawing its troops from Eastern Europe, it is unlikely to want to see its former allies going over to Nato. Moscow has even been doubtful about their ambitions to join the European Community, given the interest among some European countries in developing an EC security dimension.

If the end of communist-led government in the USSR ushers in a new era of friendly relations between Moscow and the West, the security issue will certainly be greatly defused. But even a carefully controlled and harmonious dismembering of the USSR will inevitably create new tensions and security problems in Europe.

The USSR tried during the first half of 1991 to persuade its former satellites to sign 'friendship treaties' that would prevent them from joining any other alliance or grouping of a security nature. With the exception of Romania, all have resisted Moscow's urgings. As a Czechoslovak foreign ministry spokesman put it in May 1991: 'The Soviet military believes that we [the countries of Eastern Europe] are still within their sphere of influence . . . They do not realize this is no longer the case.'

Czechoslovakia's changed view of its position in the East-West security spectrum was underlined by the presence of a unit of 200 Czech troops in the Gulf, but it is nevertheless important that the USSR should not feel threatened by the West. It clearly would do so if it felt that the shield that had been provided by its former Eastern European allies were to be transformed into a sword that was turned against it. Welcoming the ex-Warsaw Pact countries into Nato would not improve the climate of détente.

The Eastern Europeans cannot be left in limbo. They need to be involved in a security framework of some sort. The way to ensure that Eastern Europe's ethnic flashpoints do not explode into violence is to incorporate these countries into a Europe-wide system that would not only discourage ethnic tensions but could also physically intervene to prevent clashes.

In theory, the rules for such a framework exist. The 35-nation Conference on Security and Cooperation in Europe (CSCE) groups the nations of Europe together with the United States and Canada, and provides a structure in which security problems can be resolved. In June 1991 it adopted a set of procedures for dealing with any future disputes and security crises in Europe.

The CSCE mechanism provides rules, but not the means for enforcing them. There is no agreed system under which the peace would be kept in Eastern Europe if armed conflicts were to erupt. There have been a number of proposals for a European intervention force that would be comparable to the UN's blue-helmeted peace-keeping troops, but that would probably require a more muscular organization than the CSCE to run it.

Eastern Europe's security problems in the 1990s clearly require some form of supranational peace-keeping authority. Many of the ethnic tensions involve territorial disputes that could suck in national governments. The problems of policing Eastern Europe's trouble-spots look certain to multiply as the post-communist political thaw continues.

The search for new European security arrangements is made still more complicated by the question marks over Nato's future. The Atlantic alliance was formed in response to the communist takeover in Prague in February 1948, and the continued usefulness of Nato came into question as soon as it became plain that the threat from Soviet-backed communism was in full retreat.

The shock of the August coup attempt in Moscow has, for the time being, strengthened the case of those who argue against any weakening of Nato that would lower the West's guard. In the longer term, however, the absence of a militant and militarily powerful enemy such as that once represented by the Warsaw Pact will rob Nato of its raison d'etre.

The pressure among the EC countries in Nato to develop a more 'European' security framework has created tensions with the US. Washington does not like the idea of any 'Europeans-only' arrangement such as the Western European Union, and warns that the nuclear balance is still a crucial factor in maintaining world peace. The picture is made even more cloudy by France's role, for non-Nato France is urging the need for new security arrangements that will address the problems of Eastern Europe.

A solution to the 'limbo' problem created by Poland, Czechoslovakia and Hungary, now that they are adrift between the USSR and Nato, has been proposed by Francois Heisbourg, who heads the London-based Institute for International Security Studies. Heisbourg suggests a system of 'negative security guarantees' under which the three limbo countries would pledge themselves to permit no foreign troops on their soil.

That might go part of the way towards filling the security vacuum, but it would not resolve the problems of ethnic rivalries. These are addressed, however, in an altogether more ambitious idea drawn up by William H Luers, a former US ambassador to Czechoslovakia. Luers argues that Nato and the European Community should jointly underwrite a new political and economic organization, and says: 'It would stress regional cooperation and concentrate on economic and political development. It would seek to enlarge significantly public and private funds directed to the region. It would be designed to discourage local conflicts and head off Balkanization. And it would include a collective-security component in which the Central European members would provide the defensive military force.

The setting up of such an organization sounds a daunting task, but there are increasing numbers of political leaders in Western Europe who recognize that the post-war institutions are not up to the job of overhauling the economies of Eastern European countries and underpinning their security. Renato Ruggiero, Italy's foreign trade minister, believes there should be a new organization comparable to the Organization for European Economic Cooperation (OEEC) that was set up in the aftermath of World War II.

The OEEC coordinated the US financial assistance being poured into Europe under the Marshall Plan, and Ruggiero sees a similar role for a modern-day version. He says it should produce 'common development programmes' that would link Eastern and Western Europe.

Practical steps the West can take

Whether or not new institutions and bureaucracies offer the answer to Europe's problems threatens to become a matter for unending debate. But Eastern Europe's difficulties are very pressing; there is little time in which to prevent them from developing into full-blown crises, and therefore there remains little time for talk.

The aim of this book is to look at the policy options open to the European Community and other Western nations as they try to mobilize help for Eastern Europe.

Some of the policy options examined here are being translated into action. In areas such as financial aid, technical assistance, energy cooperation, trade liberalization, debt restructuring and investment promotion, Western governments are moving ahead as fast and as far as they are able.

But there remain a number of practical steps that could have a significant impact, and often these are not being given the political support they deserve. In a number of cases, the necessary political support is lacking not so much on the side of the Western nations as on that of the Eastern Europeans themselves. Old rivalries and suspicions are being revived at a time when cohesion and partnership are essential if these countries are to make the transition to becoming democratically stable market economies.

The Eastern Europeans are discovering how naive were their hopes of being able to switch smoothly from socialism to free enterprise. Far from requiring fairly minor adjustments, it is now clear that hugely disruptive structural upheavals are needed in countries where there are no banking systems, no financial markets and no savings to be invested.

The task of relaunching these economies will be made easier, though, if the countries of Eastern Europe cooperate with one another as well as with the West. The leaders of Poland, Czechoslovakia and Hungary met in the small Hungarian town of Visegrad in February 1991 to discuss common policies ranging from security to economic issues, but the Visegrad Declaration that resulted was couched in general terms. The reality is that the Eastern Europeans continue to turn their backs on one another and direct all their efforts towards the West. The West responded promptly and honourably to the events of 1989 and the desire of the people of Eastern Europe to be reunited in a single Europe. But since then, as the scale of Eastern Europe's difficulties has grown more daunting, the interest and commitment of the West has begun to wane.

Western Europe must redouble its efforts, and increase its financial assistance. The alternative is to be embroiled in a deepening Eastern European crisis.

Notes

1. 'Crisis, Reform and Stabilisation in Central Eastern Europe: Prospects and Western Response', by Domenico Mario Nuti. In Jean-Paul Fitoussi (ed) *Eastern Europe: The Transition*, Paris, 1990.

2. *Assistance to Reforms in Eastern Europe*, by Attila Szilassy. Netherlands Institute for International Relations, February 1991.

2

The EC Dimension:

From the Atlantic to the Urals, and Perhaps to Vladivostock

The Eastern Europeans' EC ambitions — The winding trail towards EC membership — The Association Agreements: start of a new phase — Putting the EC's money where its mouth is — The conundrum of the USSR — Bringing Eastern Europe into a durable relationship

In his airy, ultra-modern office at the top of the European Commission, Frans Andriessen is sketching out his ideas for bringing the more advanced Eastern European countries into what might be termed the magnetic field of the EC. The problem, he says, calls for creative thinking.

His solution is 'affiliate' membership, a term that currently has no place in the lexicon of the European Community. Andriessen's proposal is to create a new category of political rather than economic membership. It would not impose the strains of being part of the EC Single Market, but would draw the new democracies of Eastern Europe into the Community's political structure.

Poland, Hungary and Czechoslovakia would send their elected representatives to the European Parliament and would have observers in the Council of Ministers. They would coordinate their foreign policies on those of the Community, and at the same time would prepare for eventual full membership of the EC, with all the economic rigours that would involve for their much weaker economies.

Frans Andriessen is the EC Commissioner responsible for handling foreign relations. A former Dutch finance minister, he is a veteran politician of considerable standing. When at the beginning of 1989 he exchanged his job as EC Farm Commissioner for the external relations portfolio, the future of Eastern Europe was not an issue. Now it looms large.

The Community is the focus of the Eastern European countries' hopes and fears – they hope to become fully-fledged members of the EC as soon as possible, and they fear that anything less will pose a threat to their economic rebirth and their fragile new democracies.

Poland, Hungary and Czechoslovakia are in the forefront, jostling one another brusquely in their efforts to advance their own particular claims. All three are being granted 'associate' status under new association agreements with the Community that could pave the way to EC membership in the year 2002, or thereabouts.

Bulgaria has let it be known that it too would like to be an EC associate, and it seems likely that it will be invited to negotiate an association agreement before long, perhaps during 1992. Romania harbours similar ambitions, even though its transition to democracy is much less certain. Romanian diplomats say that they hope for EC associate status during 1993.

Bringing Eastern European countries into the political framework of the EC would mark a major step forward. It is important that the sense of isolation that has gripped them for so long, both when they were still firmly embedded in the Soviet bloc and even afterwards, should be dispelled as quickly as possible.

Affiliation to the EC would also provide a firmer base for tackling the Eastern Europeans' main structural problems. In areas such as environmental cleaning up and control, transport and communications infrastructure and the building of new energy relationships to replace their dependence on the

USSR, some sort of partial membership would have strong practical advantages.

But whether the EC member states will warm to the idea is uncertain. They are preoccupied with the internal streamlining of the Community and find it hard to lift their gaze beyond the issues of political and monetary union. When they do so, the membership bids of developed countries in the European Free Trade Association – Austria, Sweden and perhaps Norway – seem more pressing.

It would be a mistake if the device of affiliate membership of the EC for Eastern European countries were to be rejected or, more likely, left to gather dust. For the present, though, Frans Andriessen's immediate problems concerning Eastern Europe are strictly economic.

Keeping up the momentum of Western assistance to Eastern Europe is a top priority. The level of financial aid being contributed by the Group of 24 industrial nations that the EC Commission coordinates is encouraging, he says, but it may not last. 'I am very concerned that it may be difficult to continue G-24 assistance at the same level in years to come', Andriessen warns.

In the longer term, Frans Andriessen also reckons that the many different assistance programmes operated by various international agencies will need to be consolidated and strengthened. As well as the Commission itself and G-24 there are the IMF and World Bank, the European Investment Bank and the Bank for European Reconstruction and Development, to name only the main players. 'I am not sure this plethora of aid mechanisms will be sufficient', he says.

The association agreements being concluded between the Community and Poland, Hungary amd Czechoslovakia have highlighted both the economic backwardness of these three countries and the political difficulties that prevent the EC from making the substantial trade concessions that have been demanded.

It has become plain that although EC membership is the goal of these three countries, they still know very little about the European Community. Their governments are slowly finding out about the full range of Community competences and cooperation mechanisms, while the man in the street admits to profound ignorance about the EC. Only 1 per cent of people polled in Czechoslovakia and Poland, and 2 per cent in Hungary, claim to be well informed about the EC, and between three-quarters and four-fifths of people confessed to various levels of ignorance.

Not much is known in the EC about Eastern Europe, either. After all, the Eastern Europeans' interest in joining the Community is a new and unexpected development. Most EC officials and politicians have concentrated their attention on the likelihood that the Community will be enlarged to include the rich Western European nations in EFTA. The possibility that it will also accommodate poor Eastern European countries is likely to take some time to get used to.

The EC Commission's role as the main organizer and coordinator of financial aid to Eastern Europe means that it is rapidly gaining experience of the wider European dimension. The European Parliament, on the other hand, has not yet focused much of its attention on the goals and problems of Eastern Europe. 'The European Parliament has been slow on Eastern Europe', admits Costas Velentyas, who is Secretary General of the parliament's all-party group on Eastern European affairs. 'Our profile has been lower than one would wish.'

Building up interest among the MEPs who have been elected to the European Parliament from constituencies throughout the EC will take time. It will also require the settling down of revolutionary movements such as Civic Forum and Solidarity into more conventional parties if the necessary political ties are to be developed between the parliamentarians of Western and Eastern Europe.

In the meantime, the European Parliament's group of 75 MEPs is hard at work trying to encourage economic cooperation. It is led by French conservative Alain Pompidou, son of Georges Pompidou, General de Gaulle's successor as President of the Republic, and concentrates on such practical areas as technology transfer and tourism development.

The Eastern Europeans' EC ambitions

Attitudes within the Community to the Eastern Europeans

are varied. 'We oscillate between being deeply pessimistic about their economic prospects and taking a much more positive view', comments Jorge Braga de Macedo, a senior Portugese official in the EC Commission's economic and monetary directorate. 'One opinion is that these countries have an industrial culture and are potential success stories like the South East Asians. The other is that they suffer from serious structural difficulties.'

Eastern Europeans, too, are less than consistent. The Hungarian government, for instance, has been strident in its demands that its EC membership ambitions should be taken seriously and that it should not be sidetracked in any way. Prime Minister Joszef Antall at one point even proposed an entry date of 1995. Yet turn to the country's Industry Minister Peter Akos Bod and ask what rapid entry into the EC would mean and his reply is unequivocal: 'If we joined the EC tomorrow it would destroy 90 per cent of our industry.'

The Eastern Europeans have not been very rigorous in analyzing their reasons for wanting to join the EC. They have rather mixed motives. Getting away from their communist pasts seems more important to them than adapting to the very demanding rules that EC member states have to observe.

The new democratically elected governments of Eastern Europe tend to view EC membership as a natural corollary of the revolutions that freed them from communist rule. Much the same goes for their expectations of financial assistance from the EC. 'The Community countries must understand that it is in their interest to help us, and it is also their moral duty', says Zdenko Pirek, the Czechoslovak Vice-Minister of Foreign Affairs in charge of negotiations with the EC.

The three candidate countries are pursuing determinedly separate paths in their bids to become EC members. The rival claims they put forward as they try to outdo one another has come to be known in Brussels as 'the beauty contest'. Yet it is liable to backfire on them. The EC inevitably sees the three Eastern European neighbours as a bloc – sympathetic though it may be to the ex-Soviet satellites' dislike of being lumped together.

If the Eastern Europeans are to strengthen their claims to become EC members they must change tack in a number of important ways. To begin with, they should recognize that their relationship with the Community will be as a group. To Western European eyes, their similarities far outweigh their national peculiarities.

There seems no likelihood at all that one of the three Eastern European candidates will slip through ahead of the others. Hungarian hopes of slipping into the EC on the coat-tails of neighbouring Austria are just a fantasy. So are Czechoslovak claims that its more developed industrial base gives it an edge, or Polish insistence that Solidarity's ten-year struggle and its radical economic reforms make it the best suited to join the Community.

The Eastern Europeans would also be well advised to alter the emphasis of their dealings with the EC. Rather than dwell on the Community's lack of speed and generosity in response to their overtures, the candidate countries would do better to underline the efforts they are making to conform to EC practices. In areas as far apart as accounting practices and industrial standards, the EC needs to be reassured that Eastern Europeans will be taking giant strides to catch up.

The case for bringing Eastern Europe into the stable and prosperous environment of the EC is a good one. It may well be the only way to ensure that they do not become so politically unstable as to endanger the Community itself. But if the EC member states are to accept that, the Eastern Europeans will first have to narrow the gap that separates them – not just economically but also culturally, for there is half a century of mutual ignorance and suspicion to be overcome.

The winding trail towards EC membership

For all their doubts about the Eastern European nations' fitness to join the EC, even if it is ten years or more hence, the European Community's member governments know that in the long run they have little choice.

One overriding consideration makes inevitable the Eastern Europeans' eventual membership of the EC. It is the German factor. EC Commission President Jacques Delors repeatedly emphasizes the point to political leaders across Europe that if the rest of the Community wants Germany to remain firmly anchored inside the EC, Eastern Europe cannot be left outside it.

The turning towards the West of the former Comecon countries marks a fundamental shift in relationships within Europe. Germany, which in spite of its economic strength has long felt on the periphery of an Atlantic-oriented (and French-dominated) EC, is due to become the cultural centre of a reborn *Mittel Europa*. If Germany's EC partners attempted to thwart such a development by denying the Eastern Europeans entry to the Community, Germany would slowly but surely disengage itself from the EC.

The message that Delors has been stressing is that although Western Europeans may be uncertain as to the precise speed and direction of their economic and political integration, the German factor means that Eastern Europe must be part of it. The alternative would be a sharp drop in Germany's commitment to the EC. The drive towards European union would soon run out of steam.

The political imperative is clear cut. But the economic hurdles in the way of the Eastern Europeans are still forbidding. The candidate countries are only at the beginning of a long, winding and arduous trail they must climb if they are to achieve EC membership.

The association agreements: start of a new phase

The association agreements that Poland, Czechoslovakia and Hungary hammered out with EC negotiators during much of 1991 have subtly changed in character since they were first mooted. They originally bore all the hallmarks of agreements that were designed to forestall any premature EC membership applications. But the persistence of the Eastern Europeans has ensured that the agreements do not have 'No Entry' stamped across every page.

In diplomatic jargon, the association pacts are 'second generation' agreements because they follow on from the bilateral trade and economic cooperation ones that the EC had struck with a number of Eastern European countries in the latter 1980s. In many ways, though, they signal a new departure in the Community's relations with Eastern Europe.

Formal economic relationships between the Community and the Comecon nations had been long delayed, of course, by the long-standing refusal of the communist régimes to recognize the EC Commission's authority on trade matters. It was a slight that still rankles with some senior Eurocrats in the Brussels Commission.

Once it had become clear during 1990 that Poland, Hungary and Czechoslovakia were irrevocably launched along the way to becoming democratic market economies, the EC decided that its economic assistance through the G-24 and PHARE efforts should be complemented by a new formal relationship with these countries. A move earlier in the year to extend to them the EC's Generalized System of Preferences, which consists of tariff cuts normally offered to Third World countries, also needed to be formalized into a new and more comprehensive trade agreement.

When the offer of association deals with the three Eastern Europeans was announced in September 1990, it was emphasized by the EC Commission that they would not bring with them automatic entry into the Community. On the contrary, the intention was that they should head off any plans the Eastern Europeans might have to rush into EC membership. As well as covering technical assistance and economic cooperation, Brussels stressed that the pacts also held out the prospect for the Eastern Europeans of being part of a new Europe-wide free trade zone, the European Economic Area.

The negotiations began positively enough, even though there was some muted grumbling among the Eastern Europeans when they discovered that the three outline agreements prepared by the EC Commission as a basis for negotiation were all exactly the same. Given the wide differences between their industrial and agricultural structures, it struck them as either ignorant or insensitive.

By March 1991, however, the high hopes and good intentions that launched the negotiations had turned into recriminations. There were even gloomy forecasts that the

Eastern Europeans might feel forced to walk away from the talks. The main bone of contention was that the EC was denying the Eastern Europeans the access to EC markets that their industries and farmers would need if their economies were to be reborn.

It seemed as if the 'Fortress Europe' that the EC was so anxious to deny not only existed, but was being used to protect pampered European producers against legitimate competition from struggling Eastern Europe. The deal on offer was a ten-year transition to mutual free trade, with the EC offering 'asymmetrical' tariff cuts in the first five years that would help to make it easier for Eastern European goods to penetrate EC markets than vice versa.

The snag was that the EC offer specifically excluded the three sectors that really matter to the Eastern Europeans – steel, textiles and agriculture. Worse, the EC Commission was refusing to write into the association agreements any mention of eventual Community membership. Indeed, it had suddenly taken to calling the pacts 'Europe Agreements' in order to play down the association status that implies the holders' eventual full membership.

The EC Commission's own hands were tied during this first stage of talks by the very strict negotiating mandate that had been drawn up by the EC member governments. In mid-April 1991, Frans Andriessen told EC foreign ministers that unless the Commission was given more room to manoeuvre, the association agreements would collapse in deadlock.

Their response was encouraging. The Council of Ministers agreed to allow the Commission much more flexibility in its negotiations. Concessions on agricultural imports from Eastern Europe could be considered, provided that some sort of reciprocal deal was offered for EC farmers. Quotas limiting steel imports into the EC would go within five years, and tariffs on cheaper Eastern European textiles would be dropped completely within ten years.

This softening also led to the easing of a number of general EC requirements that had smacked of protectionism. Most important of all, it was conceded that eventual membership could be mentioned in the preambles to each association agreement, but with no fixed or automatic time-frame.

The association agreements linking Poland, Hungary and Czechoslovakia to the European Community are more than the EC countries intended to give, and less than the Eastern Europeans had hoped for. That sounds like an acceptable compromise, and to some extent it is. The Eastern Europeans have been disabused of any notions that the EC is a milch cow that will unquestioningly subsidize their economic transition to the free market. For its part, the EC has learned that its commitment to Eastern Europe must go far beyond resounding declarations and some development loans.

The association agreements mark the beginning of a new phase in the Eastern Europeans' relations with the Community. They provide a basis on which trade can be expanded from its present very low base, and that in turn should encourage the foreign investment by Western business that Eastern Europe so desperately lacks.

Putting the EC's money where its mouth is

But there is an important element missing from the association agreements. The financial protocol that the Eastern Europeans had been pressing for, which could have set out levels of future EC financial assistance over the coming decade, has not been granted.

The EC member governments decided in November 1990 that they would not agree to a financial protocol. The argument against it is largely that it would amount to writing a blank cheque. Community governments prefer to spend their own money directly in bilateral tied aid schemes that can be used to boost their industries' exports. The national bureaucracies in any case wish to retain the power and authority that goes with large-scale financial assistance, rather than transfer that power to the European Commission.

A similar fate befell Frans Andriessen's suggestion to the G-24 countries, half of whom are the EC member states, that they should subscribe the funds for a 'general facility'. This would relieve Brussels of the need to take the hat round for each new financing project, and would also enable it to set its project aid into multi-annual programmes. In other words, it would overcome the random, piecemeal approach that has been a feature of Western assistance in Eastern Europe.

National governments' unwillingness to cede responsibility to the EC Commission is understandable, if misguided. The tiny Brussels bureaucracy represents no real challenge to the sprawling ministries of many EC member governments, but it is in a position to bring a more rational and structured approach to assisting Eastern Europe.

The underlying reason for the Western governments' coolness to all suggestions that they should put money into non-specific funds that would then be administered at EC level is that it sounds expensive. The sums of money being discussed, both as long-term investment targets and immediate needs in aid as well as macro-economic support, are beginning to alarm finance ministries throughout the EC.

Hundreds of billions of dollars need to be pumped into Eastern Europe in the years ahead, and it is not a development that EC member governments relish. They felt free to promise their full support when the revolutionary movements of 1989 swept communists from power, but diverting their own taxpayers' funds in order to avert unrest in Eastern Europe is not an enticing prospect.

The 12 EC governments had by mid-1991 subscribed about two-thirds of all the financial assistance being given by the Group of 24. The worry among EC Commission officials is that getting further funding out of the member states is going to be an uphill struggle.

Hans Beck, a German who heads the EC mission in Budapest, is convinced that the enlargement of the Community to include the Eastern Europeans is inevitable. At the same time, he is increasingly concerned that the present EC member states may baulk at the costs involved. 'I don't know if we're financially capable of making the sort of commitment that is needed', comments Beck, 'but if the EC is not ready to make the sort of financial sacrifices that are needed, then enlargement will not be possible.'

The conundrum of the USSR

The process of absorbing Eastern European countries into the

European Community will not be easy, but at least the EC is in no doubt as to its goals. What to do about the USSR is much more problematic.

France's General de Gaulle once spoke, in a celebrated phrase, of a Europe that would stretch from the Atlantic to the Urals. But bringing the Eastern Europeans in and blocking the USSR off would not be easy. Should the EC perhaps be contemplating a Community that will one day stretch from the Atlantic to the Bering Straits?

There are no straightforward answers to the questions about the USSR's future place in Europe. It can neither be left outside the new and enlarged EC nor can it be included. Its dying socialist economy has no place in the Community. That was certainly the case before the attempted coup of August 1991, when hardliners in the Soviet government refused to accept that its centrally-planned economy is doomed, and hung onto the idea that some sort of 'third way' or 'market socialism' could resolve the country's problems. Even in the wake of the coup, with the way clear for radical reforms and the switch to a market economy, the USSR remains a long, long way from being ready for EC membership.

But the USSR is also a superpower whose economy is still tightly linked with the economies of Eastern Europe. The health of those economies during their difficult transitions to free enterprise will depend to a large extent on their ability to continue trading with the USSR.

In order to help Eastern Europe pick up enough momentum to join the Community, therefore, the EC needs to help the USSR. It must ensure that the economic links of the Comecon years do not dissolve. Special aid and trade measures have to be devised that will provide the USSR with the hard currency it needs to resume its traditional level of imports from Eastern Europe.

It is hard to see what sort of formal relationship will evolve between the USSR and the EC. It will continue to be a nuclear superpower, even though its appetite for global influence is much diminished. The security dimension makes it hard to fit its relationship with the EC into a neat new category.

The USSR looks to the EC as a provider of emergency aid and technical assistance, and it also has hopes that a more durable economic relationship with the Community will open the way to massive Western investment in Soviet energy exploration and development. Whether Moscow sees anything more formal seems doubtful, not least because Soviet politicians continue to believe that it is with the larger EC member states that they must deal, not with the Brussels Eurocrats.

The question of whether or not it might ever become a member of the EC was put to the EC's first ambassador to the USSR, Michael Emerson, shortly after he arrived in Moscow in early 1991 to open the Community's new diplomatic mission there. His reply was guarded but interesting. 'Indulging in long-term political speculation', he said, 'I would be more inclined to pursue a vision of two enormous blocs, the EC and the USSR, that would become increasingly convergent in their politico-economic-judicial systems. Both would become single markets and economic and monetary unions with strongly decentralized and democratic constitutions . . . The external relations between the two blocs would become deep and wide-ranging. The stability of this relationship would become a major feature in the political architecture of Europe.'[1]

Bringing Eastern Europe into a durable relationship

'The USSR is chaotic and unpredictable – as are our policies towards it', wryly comments Richard Portes, head of the Centre for Economic Policy Research in London. Something of the sort could be said for the EC nations' policies towards Eastern Europe as a whole.

Establishing a durable and consistent relationship between the EC and the Eastern European countries is essential, but it will not be easy. In both Eastern and Western Europe there are conflicting currents of political opinion that could make it harder for a straightforward new relationship to emerge.

In the first place, there is the pace of events. The speed with which developments have succeeded one another since the autumn of 1989 is dizzying. 'There is nothing static about dealing with Eastern Europe,' remarks Pablo Benavides, the

Spanish EC Commission official who handles negotiations with Eastern Europe. 'In our dealings with Japan, the United States or the EFTA countries, things are fairly stable and it's the nuance that counts. Dealing with Eastern Europe is much faster moving.'

Benavides says that the speed with which the Eastern Europeans' own situation is changing is the key. 'No sooner have you signed an agreement than it emerges that it no longer corresponds with their situation, nor with their needs.' He adds that EC attitudes have to be constantly adjusted, almost from day to day. 'I call it the "Walkman syndrome" - you've got to keep listening while walking.'

The EC handles external trade and economic relations on behalf of its member states, but that does not mean that the EC countries do not each have very pronounced views on the way the Eastern European relationship should develop. While these different national approaches do not cut across any common EC positions, they do not make it any easier to see what sort of 'architecture' will link the Eastern and Western nations of Europe during the rest of the 1990s.

The models being championed include France's idea for a European confederation of the states of Europe and Italy's *Pentagonale* which groups the five countries that were once part of the Austro-Hungarian empire. Both have their limitations. Eastern European leaders are wary of President Mitterrand's confederation because it appears to block out the United States.

The *Pentagonale* has already proved that it has a practical part to play, but is restricted in its scope. Since being formed in late 1989 it has begun to provide a framework in which Italy and Austria are able to transfer resources and know-how to Hungary, Czechoslovakia and Yugoslavia. Its theme has been economic and infrastructural cooperation in the Danube-Adriatic region.

The Eastern Europeans tend to be doubtful about any new political frameworks that they suspect might be used to sidetrack them from their goal of full EC membership. The success of the *Pentagonale* has been due to its obvious limitations. It poses no threat to EC membership ambitions.

But it is unclear what relationship the Eastern Europeans *will* have with the EC in the closing years of this century. Associate status can mean everything or nothing. Turkey has been an associate since 1963, and seems little nearer EC membership after almost 30 years. The Eastern Europeans are worried that they too will find that their association agreements are not passports into the Community.

That conjures up an image of a two-tier Europe, in which the existing 12 members of the EC would be joined by most, if not all, of the rich countries in the European Free Trade Association, leaving the much poorer Eastern Europeans outside. The idea of a Europe of 'concentric circles' that has been described by Jacques Delors, in which the EC will be at the centre with the EFTA countries in the first ring and the Eastern Europeans in the outer ring, does not greatly allay their fears.

It remains to be seen whether the mood in EC countries will permit an enlargement that will involve taking the Eastern Europeans aboard. EC Commission officials themselves reflect the breadth of opinion that exists on the subject. 'I can't imagine a Europe of haves and have nots', says Hans Beck in the offices of his EC mission overlooking the city of Budapest. 'It therefore seems to me that at the end of the day enlargement to include the Eastern Europeans is inevitable.'

Pablo Benavides is more cautious. He suggests that, for the time being, Poland, Czechoslovakia and Hungary are heading for membership of a free trade area that will confer on them three of the EC single market's four freedoms. There will be freedom of movement for capital, services and goods (other than agriculture), but not for people. 'We must prepare for their membership without there being a prejudice in their favour. It's an important nuance', adds Benavides. 'My personal view is that it would be very dangerous to welcome these countries while they are in serious economic difficulties. They must have a minimum of economic health, otherwise no one will gain.'

For the foreseeable future, it looks as if the Eastern European countries will be left outside. Whether they will be offered the affiliate or 'political' membership that Frans

Andriessen is talking of is a matter that the EC member states are unlikely to discuss in any depth until 1992 or even later.

Both the EC countries and the Eastern Europeans will do well to see their relationship as a flexible one that can be improved without further formal ties being necessary. The Eastern Europeans have to work hard to align their new market economies on EC practice and standards, and the EC nations must open the doors to their markets wider still.

Access to the Community marketplace will be of vital importance to the economic recovery of Eastern Europe. Poland's President Lech Walesa summed it up when he visited Brussels in early 1991 and made an impassioned plea to Jacques Delors for more open access for Polish products. 'Having raised the Iron Curtain', said Walesa, 'please don't bring down a silver curtain in its stead.'

Notes

1. *Europe*. The magazine of the EC mission in Washington DC, April 1991.

3

Economic Integration:

The Long Hard Road to the Free Market

The goal is a single European economy — The scale of Eastern Europe's troubles — A patchwork of poor economies, not a rich tapestry — The role of Western assistance — What economic integration with the West would mean

---

The massive building that houses Czechoslovakia's Federal Ministry for Strategic Planning is a monument to Stalinism. Its granite bulk is ornamented with huge bas-reliefs in the 'socialist-realist' style depicting joyful workers of farm and factory. It is an elaborate tombstone to a system that has failed.

In an office high on the fifth floor, a group of worried and perplexed officials are reviewing the country's economic predicament. It is a gloomy discussion made somehow more poignant by the fact that until recently the Ministry was the hub of the country's industrial machine, and these men were its masters. Until the 'velvet revolution' in the autumn of 1989, an élite corps of a thousand senior technocrats ran the country's centrally-planned 'command' economy from this imposing building on a bluff overlooking the city of Prague.

Today their numbers have been cut to a mere 100 and they are a small band of harried men beset by problems to which they see no solutions. 'Our exports to the West are dropping, as well as those to our traditional Comecon customers', says Vlastimil Gejdos, who is in charge of macroeconomic analysis. 'We've had three devaluations since 1989, and in my opinion it has made no difference. Our problems boil down to a lack of familiarity with Western tastes and market conditions.'

The speed with which communism was toppled in Eastern Europe still makes the head whirl. 'What had taken 10 years in Poland and 10 months in Hungary took only 10 weeks in Germany, 10 days in Czechoslovakia and 10 hours in Romania', runs the joke. But political change is one thing, economic change quite another.

Switching from a communist economy to a market economy is going to take a good deal longer. Even in Czechoslovakia, where the government insists that the 'shock therapy' of immediate and radical reform is the answer, the transition could well take until the end of the 1990s.

Elsewhere in Eastern Europe it is also shaping up to be a long haul. The structures of socialism and state ownership cannot be dismantled at the stroke of a pen. Nor can Eastern Europeans easily remove the cultural blinkers that result from years of not having to compete in order to earn a living.

Looming over the process of economic reform in Eastern Europe there is the shadow of the USSR. To all but a few paranoiacs, its menace is no longer military but economic. Until it successfully embarks on the transition towards a free enterprise system, the USSR's economic woes will remain a threat to progress in Eastern Europe. The importance of the Soviet economy of almost 300 million people to the Eastern European countries whose combined population is just over 110 million people will long outlive the death of communism.

Eastern European countries are increasingly anxious that the West should include the USSR in its efforts to re-launch the formerly communist economies. The point that Czechoslovakia's President Vaclav Havel has made repeatedly is that the West can best help Eastern Europe by helping the USSR. If Soviet trade starts to flow again, then the economies of its former partners in the Comecon trading bloc will also benefit. If the Soviet economy collapses, that will deal a savage blow to the whole of Eastern Europe.

The goal is a single European economy

The regeneration of Eastern Europe is of crucial importance to the Western European economy. If the economies of Eastern Europe stagnate, the EC and other Western nations will be burdened with heavy financial transfers. If they begin to flourish, though, Western European industry can look forward to the fillip of sustained demand from tens of millions of new and hungry consumers. The logic is the same as for the EC Single Market and the creation of a 'continental marketplace' for European industry.

But Eastern Europe is an industrial wasteland. The big questions are how long it will take for these countries to be integrated into a wider European market economy, and what policies Western nations should adopt to speed the process.

It is no more than guesswork, but the most popular estimates among the experts are that economic integration will take between 15 and 25 years, depending on the state of particular countries. André Leysen, a Belgian industrialist with much experience of Eastern Europe, and who has the distinction of being the only non-German board member of the *Treuhandanstalt* privatization agency in eastern Germany, reckons, 'five years for East Germany, twenty-five years for Eastern Europe and fifty years for the USSR'.

'Most Eastern European countries seem able to rely on a growth trend of about 4 per cent', French economist Daniel Cohen has commented. He adds, 'About 25 years will be necessary before Eastern Europe can catch up with our current standards.'[1]

Before things get better, though, they are likely to get worse. The shock of dismantling a socialist economy and submitting its industries to the stresses of the free market means that Eastern Europeans are bracing themselves for tough times until the mid-1990s at the earliest. The World Bank has forecast that Poland, Hungary and Czechoslovakia will not regain their 1989 income levels until 1996. The outlook for Romania, Bulgaria and Yugoslavia is even worse.

The strain of adapting to the market economy is made all the greater by the need to perform well in the international financial marketplace. Strong growth will mean that Eastern

Europe's industries suck in imports of Western equipment and products. That, in turn, means that the balance of payments deficits of these countries will grow and their currencies will come under pressure. EC Commission analysts have suggested that if the Eastern European economies grow by 3 per cent in 1991 and 5 per cent in 1992, their combined payments deficit will be US$17bn, but if they attain 6 per cent growth annual rates that payments gap will widen to US$24bn.

The scale of Eastern Europe's troubles

The size of Eastern Europe's economic problems is daunting. The Eastern European countries lag such a long, long way behind Western Europe that it is hard to see the gap being narrowed in the foreseeable future.

To begin with, the six countries of Eastern and Central Europe have a combined GNP that only just manages to equal that of Italy.[2] The foreign trade of the Eastern Europeans and the USSR, both with one another and elsewhere, accounts for 9 per cent of world trade. Although these countries have a combined population of some 400 million, they are largely irrelevant to the global economy.

The private sectors of the Central European countries are tiny. Private enterprise is to be the mainspring of their transition to market economies, but it will have to be carefully nurtured. It is hard to be precise, of course but in both Poland and Hungary about 15 per cent of the economy is made up by privately owned businesses; in Bulgaria the figure is 9 per cent and in Czechoslovakia and Romania it is only 3 per cent. The privatization process has a long way to go.

So far, the Eastern European economies have been contracting, and this is not necessarily a bad sign. If they are slimming down to become leaner and more flexible then they will be able to bounce back in the mid-1990s. The International Monetary Fund (IMF) has calculated that in 1990 the six Eastern European economies shrank by 8.6 per cent, but says that in 1991 the fall will start to level off. The IMF expects a further drop of only 1.5 per cent in their Gross Domestic

Products (GDP) and predicts positive growth of 2.8 per cent in 1992. From 1993 to 1996, which is the furthest the IMF economists can reasonably look ahead, the forecast is for an average growth rate in Eastern Europe of 4.4 per cent.

For the USSR the picture is rather different. The Soviet economy did not shrink as dramatically as did those of the Eastern Europeans in 1990, but is expected to nose-dive in the next few years. The IMF experts see Soviet GDP declining 4.2 per cent in 1991 and 2.1 per cent in 1992.

The major debate in Eastern Europe is over the best way to switch from a socialist 'command' economy to a free market. The two camps are those who urge 'shock therapy' and those who believe a gradualist approach carries less risk.

West Germany's *Wirtschaftswunder* of the 1950s and 1960s is the classic example of shock therapy. In 1948 Ludwig Erhard ignored the views of American experts who were advocating a cautious and gradual return to free market conditions and took a leap into the dark. Today, the advocates of shock therapy for Eastern Europe and the USSR have the examples of Poland, pre-crisis Yugoslavia and, to a lesser extent, Czechoslovakia to point to.

The argument against a 'big bang' such as that taken by Poland, when it suddenly decontrolled prices and wages in January 1990, is that it creates serious economic and political risks. The transition to the free market and even the new-found democracies of Eastern Europe could be jeopardized if the shock tactic backfires, warn the gradualists.

The case for shock therapy is nevertheless more convincing. It is, in sum, that you cannot be half pregnant. Gradualism is often indistinguishable from the 'third way' of 'market socialism' that some Eastern European and Soviet politicians talk wistfully of, but that no Western experts subscribe to.

Paul McCracken, an eminent American economist, has summed up the argument neatly. He says: 'The problem with gradualism is that the economy is kept in a state of macro-disequilibrium. Prices held down by controls cannot serve their function as the economy's communications system. Other procedures for allocation and distribution – that is, the bureaucracy and the black market – must take over.'[3]

Gradualism is not really an economic strategy. On the contrary, it is more likely to be a failure to act. It is human nature not to take the plunge, and it is in the nature of politicians to be cautious about adopting shock therapy policies that risk being deeply unpopular. So it is that the argument between gradualism and shock therapy rages back and forth inside each of the Eastern European governments, and will continue to do so.

The most striking feature of Eastern Europe's economic outlook is that it is very misleading to talk in terms of a regional economy. Each national economy has its own individual character and its very specific strengths and weaknesses. The Eastern Europeans and the USSR will each have to find their salvation along different paths.

A patchwork of poor economies, not a rich tapestry

The USSR

Russians often pride themselves on their black humour, so it would be interesting to know if the following grim joke raises many laughs in Moscow. The backroom boys at Salomon Brothers, a leading Wall Street investment bank, have come up with a novel way of calculating the worth of the Soviet economy.

At the official rate of exchange between the rouble and the dollar in mid-1991, they valued the Soviet economy at US$1,662bn, or 36 per cent of the US economy. Re-jigged slightly on a purchasing power parity basis they put it at 33 per cent of the US economy. Using the commercial rate of exchange for the rouble reduced the Soviet economy to 16 per cent of the US economy, and the tourist exchange rate yanked it right down to 3 per cent of the US economy. Apply the black market rate, however, and the Soviet economy reaches rock bottom; it is worth US$47bn, or 1 per cent of the US economy.

In one sense, it is all nonsense. A superpower of 287 million people, with almost limitless energy reserves and a huge industrial and technological base, cannot be down-valued in so superficial a way, whatever the gravity of its immediate economic problems. In another sense, it is accurate. The nub of the USSR's problem is that its closed and artificial economy has little or no international worth.

Of the many problems that beset the Soviet economy there are two notable evils: a valueless currency and a system of official prices that is a grotesque distortion of human and economic values. The USSR has become a society where a bus driver earns three times as much as a surgeon, and where the roubles earned by either have only a fraction of the purchasing power of a dollar.

When Mikhail Gorbachev came to power in 1985 and announced his now famous twin policies of *glasnost* (openness) and *perestroika* (restructuring), the ills of the Soviet economy seemed manageable and fairly unthreatening. The dinosaur of the communist economy was dying from creeping paralysis, but the message still had not reached its small, faraway brain in Moscow.

Gorbachev's belief was that he could tinker with the USSR's inefficient but impressively large economy. His priority, after all, was to end the nuclear stalemate of the Cold War and bring his country back into the community of nations with the hope of improving living standards and, indeed, the Soviet way of life.

But by 1987 the USSR's economic problems had become a great deal more insistent. The State was paying out far more than it was taking in, so the budget deficit was soaring. Because there is no bond market in a communist economy there is no mechanism through which the government can cover its deficit by borrowing peoples' savings. Soviet government officials say that any budget deficit over 2-3 per cent of the GDP can therefore only be financed by printing more money.

A study by EC Commission economists has predicted that the Soviet budget deficit could reach 20 per cent of GDP by the end of 1991.[4] In 1985 it had been a manageable 2.5 per cent. In 1987 it rose to 8.5 per cent and by 1988 it was at 11 per cent. A plan to sell government bonds to the public was in fact drawn up, but then abandoned. Instead, the printing presses were being run to produce more roubles with which the government could pay its debts, and from 1987 to 1990 the average annual growth in Soviet money supply was 14-15 per cent.[5]

In a market economy such an increase could well have led to serious inflation. Yet in the USSR inflation has been damped down to 5-7 per cent a year, quite simply because there are not enough goods in the shops on which to spend the extra cash. It therefore goes to swell the Soviet peoples' involuntary savings, generally known as the 'rouble overhang'. This is widely reckoned at about roubles 250-300bn, most of it in savings accounts, with probably a further roubles 150bn tucked away under mattresses.

In many ways the problem of the rouble overhang is worse than runaway inflation. Apart from representing a huge and unstable volume of money, it is proof that the Soviet currency has become useless. It no longer buys things. Any product or service that is in short supply can only be purchased with dollars or by barter.

At Moscow's Sheremetyevo airport the taxi drivers will only accept foreign currency or Marlboro cigarettes (no other brand will do) for the ride into the city. Travellers with roubles either take the bus or walk. The dollar has become the only money that really talks, and there is now estimated to be US$2bn in circulation in the USSR.

A worthless and discredited currency which citizens cannot spend is a potentially disastrous basis for economic reform. But that is only half the problem. The USSR's absurd and chaotic system of State-fixed prices is the other half.

The Soviet economic planners seem to have lost control of their own system of price controls and subsidies. Whatever they do, they create even worse anomalies. In the summer of 1990, for instance, the government decided to raise the price of grain by one-third to encourage production, but it neglected to raise cattle prices too, even though grain is a major part of the cost of feeding livestock. Farmers stopped selling beef to the government, so the authorities were forced to raise the official price they pay to the farmers. They decided to leave the retail price of beef unchanged, though, for fear of annoying the consumers.

Prices in the USSR no longer reflect reality. Steel is priced at about a one-seventh of what it costs in Western Europe, but the goods it is transformed into can cost very much more, depending once again on the prices determined by the central planners. A car costs twice as much, a TV set three times, and household items such as food, rent and heating are artificially cheap.

'We are living in an economic kingdom of crooked mirrors', complain two noted Soviet economists, V Popov and N Shmelev, 'where what is big looks small, what is small looks big, what is straight looks distorted and what is distorted looks straight. All price proportions are in a mess.'

Cock-eyed prices are at the root of the USSR's economic difficulties. Because they distort demand they convey no market signals to industry. Instead of relying on sales to decide what volume of goods to manufacture, Soviet factories wait for the planners to set output levels. The result is a ramshackle economic structure in which supply and demand are unrelated.

It is not, in short, an economy that can be finely tuned as it gently adapts to a more free-enterprise culture that will attract foreign investors. It is an economic disaster area that requires radical change. By 1991, with the national income expected to fall by 16 per cent, it had become clear to the Soviet government that *perestroika* was not the answer.

Quentin Peel, the *Financial Times* correspondent in Moscow in April 1991 reported: '*Perestroika* is dead, and that is no bad thing. For it was always doomed. It was an attempt to make the old system work better, to give Soviet socialism an efficient human face. But the old system was so flawed, such a total distortion of the laws of economics and human nature that it could not be simply "restructured". It had to be dismantled. That is what is happening today, whether Mr Gorbachev likes it or not.'

How fast and how drastically the USSR will dismantle communism's economic structures is the key question. During 1990 and the first half of 1991 the economy went into free fall as two rival factions sought to gain the upper hand and dictate economic policy. In the autumn of 1990 a dramatic 500-day dash to make the USSR much more of a market economy was proposed by a group of 13 market economists led by Stanislav Shatalin. His plan had been drawn up with President Gorbachev's backing and that of Russian President Boris Yeltsin.

Within weeks the Shatalin Plan was in tatters. Old guard communist bosses, the powerful Soviet bureaucracy and above all, the military saw it as a dangerous threat and reportedly gave Gorbachev no choice but to drop it. Nikolai Petrakov, who at that time was Mikhail Gorbachev's economic adviser, was stung into telling in public what had happened in private. The conservatives issued Gorbachev with an ultimatum, he said, and 'they had men with guns' standing behind them.

The Shatalin Plan's opponents claimed it would lead to 20 million unemployed, and uncontrollable inflation. The USSR is nevertheless now headed along the road to radical reform. Moscow knows that it cannot resist the pressures from the Soviet republics to introduce greater free market conditions.

Even if a new consensus emerges in the USSR to apply shock therapy to the economy, it will take time to turn the USSR into a viable economic system. The demilitarization of the Soviet economy is shaping up to be a massive undertaking that could take the whole of the 1990s to accomplish.

The USSR's defence industry is the backbone of the industrial structure. It is indivisible from the rest of Soviet industry because defence factories also turn out consumer goods such as refrigerators and TV sets. The trick will be to raise the share of their output that is civil and cut back on their military production. Easier said than done, of course, as the switch requires investment capital.

Abandoning the safety of defence contracts is politically unattractive too. In the Leningrad area, for instance, one job in four relies on the defence industry. The overwhelming size of the industry is hard to believe; it accounts for somewhere between one-third and a half of industrial output.

A programme of defence conversion – *konvertsia* as the Russians have tagged it – is under way and its chief aim is to raise the proportion of civilian goods produced by the defence plants. There are 600 major factories in the *konvertsia* scheme, and the target is to raise their civilian output from 40 per cent of total production to 60 per cent by 1995. It does not add up to sweeping change.

Nor does the Soviet privatization programme. Although it has been billed as the 'world's biggest sell-off', the plan consists largely of privatizing 23,000 shops, restaurants and small service-sector businesses by the end of 1992. Meeting that deadline appears to be an impossibility. Meanwhile, the privatization of Soviet manufacturing industry is a much tougher nut to crack. The republics, instead of the ponderous and hitherto all-powerful Moscow bureaucracy, are due to handle this but that does not resolve such questions as how companies will be valued and sold, to whom and in exchange for what.

The Soviet economy is a wounded bear. During the 1980s it deteriorated from being inefficient but powerful to become an economy that is collapsing in on itself. The most vulnerable aspect of the economy is the system of centrally-planned production that Lenin believed would cut out wasteful duplication. Now it seems tailor-made to create shortages.

In the autumn of 1990 there was the alarming spectacle of the Ukraine banning the 'export' of extra grain shipments to other parts of the USSR, and of the heavy engineering centre of Sverdlovsk in the Urals threatening to halt all deliveries of its goods unless its food supplies were increased. It was an episode that bodes ill for the future.

Poland

In January 1990 the new Solidarity-backed, non-communist Polish government set an example to the rest of Eastern Europe. It introduced the Balcerowicz Plan with the aim of transforming the country into a market economy in a single frantic dash. 'You don't cross a chasm in little hops', is one of the favourite sayings of the plan's author, Poland's youthful deputy premier and finance minister Leszek Balcerowicz. His programme, combining tough austerity measures with the introduction of free market conditions, underlined the point.

The plan, which was drawn up by a team of Polish and American economists and backed by the IMF, devalued the zloty by 58 per cent and at the same time made it partially convertible so that trading companies would have access to foreign exchange. It also freed both prices and wages, but imposed such a savage anti-inflationary squeeze on incomes that real wages fell 35 per cent in 1990.

After 45 years of communism, the Polish economy was in a parlous state. Its industrial base consisted of 7,000 generally inefficient State-run companies with a stranglehold on the Polish economy. They produced 90 per cent of total output. Few of these large and generally old-fashioned companies could claim to be internationally competitive, other than in the protected environment of the Comecon trade bloc.

Although Poland's population of almost 40 million makes it a major European nation, its living standards are closer to those of the Third World. The 1980s and the protracted political tussle between the communist regime and Solidarity depressed the economy, and by 1989 Poland was in the grip of hyperinflation and economic stagnation. The Balcerowicz Plan was a gamble that both the Poles themselves and the country's Western creditors approved of.

It has been hailed as a success. 'Its major achievement was introducing convertibility', says Alan Mayhew, a senior EC Commission official who has been 'lent' to Warsaw as an economic adviser. 'Balcerowicz managed to reverse the "dollarization" of the Polish economy. Now the Poles are able to trust the zloty. Convertibility has also suppressed the need for a black market. Everything is available now . . . at a price.'

The toughness of the Polish austerity plan was also essential to getting the substantial debt relief the country's Western creditors agreed to in March 1991. The willingness of the Poles to suffer drastic cuts in their living standards as they restructured their economy was instrumental in persuading the creditor governments to agree to write off half of Poland's US$33bn 'official' debt by 1994.

The rigours imposed by the Polish programme are considerable. Although the 25 per cent drop in industrial output recorded in 1990 is probably exaggerated (communist factory bosses tended to hype their production figures), Poland has nevertheless suffered a brutal shock. Unemployment soared from virtually zero to 1.5 million, or 7.7 per cent, within 18 months. It would probably have gone to 2.5 million had not Polish companies devised a variety of survival tactics that enabled them to keep workers on at reduced wage levels. As it is, 70 per cent of people questioned in a May 1991 opinion poll reckoned that their job was in danger.

The squeeze on jobs, wages and output has to be set against the rebirth of Poland's private sector. The entrepreneurial spirit is flourishing vigorously and over 100,000 small businesses had sprung into being by mid-1991. The Warsaw stock exchange reopened after 50 years, and fittingly enough was housed in the building previously occupied by the Central Committee of the Communist Party. It began trading in the shares of only five publicly quoted companies, but aims to expand that list quickly.

Poland's exporters also used the much cheaper zloty to good effect and boosted their hard currency exports in 1990 by 43 per cent to some US$11bn. But although there is growing optimism that the country is set on the right path, Poland is far from out of the woods. The political strains of austerity may dictate a softening and slowing down of the Balcerowicz Plan.

In some ways, the Polish dash to become a market economy has failed to pick up the speed that was hoped for. The privatization programme has been notable for its slowness. In 1990 only five companies were sold off to the public in stock offerings, even though Poland had intended to go for an accelerated system of privatization. 'I'm fully conscious that it is so far disappointing', commented Janusz Lewandowski when he took over as minister in charge of privatization in early 1991. 'In one year we sold five companies. That is five out of 8,000. It is very slow, very time-consuming. It would take 100 years to privatize Poland at the speed of 1990.'

Another deep-seated difficulty now being recognized by the Polish government is that the property to be privatised is worth an estimated US$80bn, but the pool of savings in Poland that is available to buy it stands at no more than US$10bn.

Hungary

It used to be said in Eastern Europe, when the Soviet yoke was at its most oppressive: 'Hungary is always the happiest barracks in the camp'. Somehow, the 10 million Hungarians

managed to dilute communist orthodoxy and distance themselves from their Soviet masters.

Hungarians date their transition towards a market economy from the early 1970s, which gives them almost a two
decade headstart over the rest of Eastern Europe. Indeed,
they first embarked on economic reform in 1968, when the
memory of their 1956 uprising and its bloody Soviet repres-
sion was still fresh.

The country is well ahead of its Eastern European neighbours in a number of areas. Its economic liberalization and
privatization programmes are more advanced, its economy is
more flexible and it has a dynamic small-business sector that
is generating new jobs and more wealth at an encouraging
rate. Above all, it is attracting as much Western investment as
the rest of Eastern Europe put together.

Nevertheless, Hungary is finding the road to a market
economy to be long and hard. The collapse of Comecon,
precipitated by the USSR's insistence that trade payments
must be made in dollars, has hit Hungarian industry severely.
Exports to the Comecon area fell 24 per cent in 1990, and the
country's GDP contracted by 5-6 per cent. For 1991 the
damage will probably be greater still and the GDP is likely to
shrink by a further 8-10 per cent.

Coupled to an inflation rate that was 30 per cent in 1990, the
effect has been a setback in living standards. The 1980s were a
time of economic stagnation for Hungary, but so far, for all the
talk of progress towards a free enterprise economy, the 1990s
have been a time of greater hardship.

Yet Hungarians are optimistic. In the first place, they have
achieved the nearest thing to a Western-style two-party
democratic system to be found in Eastern Europe. The
conservative Hungarian Democratic Forum government, led
by Jozsef Antall, that came to power in the spring of 1990 has
chalked up a number of important achievements. They are
not the sort of breakthroughs that will immediately ease the
pain of economic transition, but they are institutional changes
that are crucial to Hungary's future.

The Antall government has both strengthened and set up a
number of key independent institutions, including the

National Bank (central bank), both supreme and constitutional courts and an independent TV and radio service. In addition to that there is the basis of a commercial banking system that was launched in 1987 and there is also a taxation system tailored to the needs of a market economy. The Budapest stock exchange, which was the first to reopen in Eastern Europe, is also developing at an encouraging pace.

The speed with which the private sector develops will determine Hungary's future. By the mid-1990s the government hopes that privately owned business will account for 50 per cent of the economy, but achieving that goal is still a long way away.

No one knows how big the private sector really is. Hungary's thriving black economy could add a further 25-30 per cent to the recorded GDP of some US$70bn. That would certainly help to explain why Hungarians seem to accept the rigours of economic transition with such fortitude.

The legitimate private sector is in any case going from strength to strength. Hungarian analysts say that productivity in the medium-sized private sector businesses that are now an established part of the economy rose by over 20 per cent in 1990. That was for concerns with between 50 and 300 employees; for small businesses employing under 50 people the rise was 250 per cent.

The fly in the ointment is the slowness of Hungary's privatization programme. The Hungarian government prides itself on the fact that its privatization effort consists of genuine sales, rather than the Polish and Czech efforts which some Hungarian officials characterize as 'giveaways'. Perhaps, but it is all taking place at a snail's pace.

'Privatization is far too slow', criticizes Ivan Lipovecz, editor of Budapest's highly successful weekly economic magazine *Heti Vilaggezdesag*. 'It is slow because it is overly bureaucratic. The people who run the programme are very suspicious of profiteering and the government is fixed on the idea of getting top dollar.'

In its first year, 1990, the privatization programme was to have yielded forints 50bn in sell-offs. Of the 10,000 shops and restaurants on its list the government's State Property Agency sold less than 200 and realized a mere forints 6bn. For 1991-94 the government's target is forints 500bn in privatization sales each year, but nobody takes that very seriously. Confusion over land registration and valuation continues to delay the sale of small businesses, and selling off industrial companies is proving to be very difficult indeed.

The Hungarian economy's trump card is foreign investment. The openness of the economy and its sophistication compared to Eastern Europe as a whole have attracted many more investors than Hungary's neighbours.

In the 18 months up to mid-1991 about US$1bn flowed into Hungary, placing the country well on the road to its target of US$2bn a year in foreign investment. It was more than foreign investors had spent in the whole of the previous 18 years. It is little enough for a country whose pre-World War II economy was 35 per cent foreign-owned, but it is an encouraging signpost towards the future.

Czechoslovakia

The economy of the Czech and Slovak Republics, as post-revolutionary Czechoslovakia styles itself, is of course two economies. There is that of the 10 million people in the Czech republic, where industries like automobiles and glassmaking stand a good chance of being successfully modernized, and that of the more rural 5 million-strong Slovak republic to the south, where the ailing defence and textile industries are both concentrated.

The signs are that the years to the mid-1990s may see an alarming rise in Slovakian unemployment. For the country as a whole the shake-out of moving towards a market economy is likely to mean 10 per cent joblessness, and in Slovakia it could go much higher. Often enough, married women work in the region's textile plants and their husbands are employed in armaments. The outlook for both sectors is bleak.

For the present, though, Czechoslovakia is moving purposefully towards its goal of becoming a market economy. Vaclav Klaus, the federal finance minister who leads the faction inside Civic Forum that is committed to a rapid transition away from socialism, is determined that a combination of tight money policies and radical reform represents the country's best hope.

Klaus is a forceful figure who has wasted no time in trying to move Czechoslavakia away from its former Eastern European partners and into the Western community. Within weeks of the 'velvet revolution' that ousted the communists, the new government in Prague was applying for membership of the Organization for Economic Cooperation and Development in Paris, which groups the 24 rich nations of the world. Poland, Hungary and Yugoslavia had sought only associate status, but Czechoslovakia aimed at once for the real thing.

It was an engagingly cheeky action, for the transition to a free enterprise economy has so far been a painful process. Czechoslovak living standards have fallen sharply. How far can perhaps be judged by the 1994 target that government officials say has been set for industrial output to be restored to its 1990 levels. The point is, of course, that it aims to do so with modernized industrial structures that will once again make Czechoslovakia an industrial power to be reckoned with.

Before the disruption caused by its revolution and the abrupt switch away from socialism, Czechoslovakia was a comparatively rich country by Eastern European standards. Its GDP of some US$118bn yielded a *per capita* income of US$7,600, on paper at any rate, that put the country just ahead of the two poorest EC states: Greece and Portugal. Czechoslovakia was one of the earliest cradles of industry in Europe, and in the years before World War II it had become an advanced industrial nation.

Under communism, the industrial base failed to keep up with technological developments elsewhere. The tentacles of State control reached out and made Czechoslovakia almost a carbon copy of the USSR and Albania. The aim was to forge Czechoslovak industry into a single and more coherent industrial machine, but the effect has been to create an industrial time-warp. Czechoslovak factories provide the visitor with an interesting reminder of how mechanical engineering looked before the advent of electronics.

The breadth of State control remains a dominant feature of the Czechoslovak economy. It is striking to contrast the country's *per capita* income with the average monthly wage of US$100. That gives an indication of the share of the economy that is in the hands of the State, and the distance that Czechoslovakia's privatization process has to travel.

When privatization got under way in January 1991 only 3 per cent of the economy lay in private hands. The government's aim is to privatize 50 per cent of the economy and it is handling the process in three phases. The first will be the selling off of small retail businesses, the second is the sale of substantial stakes in companies like Skoda to foreign investors and the third is the transformation of State enterprises into joint-stock companies in which citizens will be offered shares through a voucher scheme.

By mid-1991 several hundred small businesses had been auctioned off, but the future of the voucher system was still unclear. Privatization is a crucial element in Czechoslovakia's transition, but it has not been launched with the same verve and determination that marked the introduction of price liberalization and the semi-convertibility of its koruna currency.

Klaus is something of a Thatcherite. His determination to use free market forces to sweep aside the inefficiencies of socialism is counterbalanced by President Vaclav Havel, who is concerned with limiting the rise in unemployment. Eastern Europe's debate over shock therapy versus gradualism is perhaps conducted at its loudest within the Prague government.

The drying up of Comecon trade and the slow-down that has gripped the Czechoslovak economy threatens major job losses. During 1990 the government found itself forced to put some of its free market policies into reverse to avoid massive industrial closures.

Subsidies paid to bail out loss-making companies were tripled to around US$5bn instead of being cut back by two-thirds. It seems clear that most Czechoslovaks would prefer their brand of capitalism to be modelled more on that of West Germany or the Benelux countries than on that favoured by Margaret Thatcher or Ronald Reagan.

Vaclav Klaus' point is, however, that there is no choice. The radical route is the only one that will regenerate the country's economy. Time is not on Czechoslovakia's side. Industrial output is sagging and could drop by 15 per cent for the whole of 1991, having only slackened by 3 per cent in 1990.

Czechoslovakia needs a dynamic and stable economic environment before it can hope to boost foreign investment from the US$500 million received by mid-1991, and Klaus believes his austerity measures are having that effect. Real wages will have fallen 10 per cent in 1991, curbing inflation and helping to make Czechoslovak industry more competitive in world markets.

Bulgaria

The Bulgarian economy has in recent years been a byword for inefficiency, shortages and corruption. As much as 45 per cent of the country's industrial plant is reckoned to be obsolete.

Yet the 9 million Bulgarians have managed to live comparatively well. On measurements like telephones and cars, Bulgaria comes out well ahead of its neighbours. At 127 cars per thousand people, there are two and a half times as many private cars per person in Bulgaria as in the USSR. The *per capita* GDP in 1989 was almost US$6,000. As to telephones, Bulgaria is among the best served in the whole Comecon area with rather less than half the average in Western Europe.

Bulgaria's good times, such as they were, are at an end. The country has been more dependent on Comecon trade than has any other Eastern European nation; its foreign trade has made up one-quarter of the economy, and Comecon accounted for three-quarters of its foreign trade. Comecon's collapse has therefore been disastrous.

In 1990 Bulgaria's economic difficulties became so serious that it defaulted on payments on its large US$10bn foreign debt. That resulted in a freeze on Western credits to Bulgaria and a sharp fall in imports as well as exports. Industrial production fell 12 per cent for the whole of 1990 and 18 per cent in the last quarter alone, and by the end of the year inflation rose to over 60 per cent. There are fears that the end of 1991 will see a further 30 per cent drop in output and soaring unemployment.

The task of turning Bulgaria's economic collapse into an orderly transition to a market economy was taken on in

December 1990 by Dimiter Popov, a politically independent former judge and academic who became the head of a coalition government.

Popov introduced a tough, IMF-backed reform programme whose measures range from price liberalization to the slashing of State subsidies. In February 1991 he freed prices, and although some rose six-fold at least the move brought food back into the shops.

He also cut state subsidies, which have accounted for 35 per cent of the State budget, and set a target for reducing the State budget from 10 per cent of the GDP to 4 per cent within three years. Popov's programme included the raising of interest rates from 11 per cent to 15 per cent to attract savings and combat inflation, as well as privatization, land reform and reform of the banking system.

Bulgaria needs, and is receiving, financial assistance from the West in the shape of IMF stand-by credits to cover its balance of payments deficit and both development and humanitarian aid from the European Community. What Bulgaria wants most of all, say observers in Sofia, is for the West to stop lumping it together with Romania and treating the two countries as if they were Siamese twins.

Romania

Romania is potentially a rich country, endowed with a comparatively well-educated population of 23 million and considerable natural resources. But its economy is in serious trouble. The legacy of the Ceaucescu years is an industrial and agricultural base that has deteriorated almost beyond repair. Worse, the National Salvation Front government that took over when Nicolae Ceaucescu was overthrown and executed in December 1989 has failed to introduce a coherent reform programme.

Western analysts are widely in agreement that Romania will be the last of the Eastern European countries involved in the 1989 revolutions to make the transition to becoming a multi-party democracy with a free market economy. Its deep-seated problems are both economic and political.

EC Commission experts have described Romania's industrial infrastructure as 'among the most backward in Europe', and add: 'its workforce is particularly demoralized and badly trained.' Romania's statistics are not very reliable, but it is thought that during the first nine months of 1990 industrial output dropped 28 per cent, productivity was down 23 per cent and investment slumped by 45 per cent.

The country is so poor, say visiting economists, that for many people the goal is survival. They feel they cannot afford the short-term losses implicit in reform, even though they know there would probably be longer-term gains. For that reason, Romania's youthful and technocratic prime minister, Petre Roman, has been meeting considerable resistance to his attempts to introduce radical economic reforms.

Romania's reform programme has not been pushed forward by the country's president, former communist politburo member Ion Iliescu. His belief is that before introducing the more radical reforms favoured by Petre Roman, the country should first receive credits from abroad to finance them. 'The reforms will have a negative effect on living standards', President Iliescu has said. 'Liberalizing prices leads to higher prices. But external credits to finance these reforms are scarce. As a result it will be difficult for us to normalize the situation.'[6]

Human rights questions and the way the government seemed to condone violent demonstrations by miners against opposition parties in mid-1990 put a brake on Western and EC efforts to assist Romania. The National Salvation Front's communist roots mean there also remain lingering doubts in the West about Romania's commitment to democracy. In mid-1991 the US was still withholding the 'most favoured nation' trade status that it had previously granted to the Ceaucescu regime in the 1970s.

Romania has in fact made some progress towards economic reform. In November 1990 it introduced the first stage of a price liberalization programme, when the prices of non-essential goods were tripled. But even that modest step provoked public unrest.

Petre Roman has drawn up a plan to privatize 50 per cent of State assets by 1994 and to streamline Romania's State-run industries into free-standing companies. He also intends to modernize the tax system and introduce VAT, and above all he is aiming to introduce partial 'internal' convertibility of

Romania's currency, the leu, by 1992 with the aim of boosting foreign trade with the West.

The IMF has been working with Romania on a reform and economic austerity package. The leu has been substantially devalued and the country received a US$1bn IMF stand-by loan in April 1991. G-24 has also put together a US$800m credit to underpin the IMF effort. The EC, which had limited itself to humanitarian aid pending reassurances on human rights matters, is making a US$500m grant in urgent, non-refundable aid.

Yugoslavia

When the definitive history of Eastern Europe's reintegration into the wider European economy comes to be written, Yugoslavia may well go down as 'the one that got away'. The political crisis tearing Yugoslavia apart risks undoing a Westernization process that began in the mid-1960s.

Tito's prickly non-alignment had placed Yugoslavia firmly outside the Soviet bloc, and during the 1970s the effects of tourism and trade were bringing the country steadily closer to the West. Tito died in 1980, at the point that Yugoslavia signed a cooperation agreement with the EC. In the years since then, relations between Belgrade and Brussels have become warmer still.

When the revolutions of 1989 launched Eastern European countries on their various paths to democracy and free market economies, Yugoslavia seemed likely to be among the most successful. Two years on, ethnic pressures are fragmenting – or 'Balkanizing' – what was a post-World War I, man-made country back into its constituent parts.

So far as the economy is concerned, the result has been very negative. During 1990 Yugoslavia had earned the respect of Western governments for the determination and speed with which the federal government in Belgrade had implemented an economic reform and austerity plan. By 1991, its achievements had seeped away.

The programme introduced by federal premier Ante Markovic was wide-ranging and ambitious. It was an example of shock therapy at its toughest. It embraced currency convertibility, privatization, a federal-based fiscal policy and a tight monetary policy. Its most spectacular success was in the major problem area of inflation; Yugoslavia's raging hyper-inflation of 2,655 per cent in 1989 was tamed to 120 per cent in 1990, and at one magic moment during June of that year it had actually dropped to 0.2 per cent a month. By the end of 1990 it was 8 per cent a month.

Markovic also concentrated on currency convertibility, and tied the Yugoslav dinar firmly to the Deutschmark. The effect on Yugoslavia's exporters was brutal and that, coupled with stern wage restraint, pushed average living standards down by 18 per cent in 1990. But the measures also established the country's economy as a stable and reliable environment for foreign investors. Yugoslavia seemed all set for an economic take-off.

It has since been torn by strife between the rival republics, reviving memories of Yugoslavia's bloody 1941 civil war and raising fears of the country's dismemberment. Yugoslavia has a dozen ethnic groups with their own languages, three religions and two alphabets. The tensions between the republics make it hard to believe that Yugoslavia can slough off its internal difficulties and concentrate anew on making the transition to an efficient free enterprise system.

The deadlock between Yugoslavia's six republics over the 1991 federal budget also had the effect of blocking a US$1bn IMF stand-by credit to the country. The credit is destined to aid the restructuring of Yugoslavia's banking system, and would open the way to further a US$2.3bn in loans from other Western financial institutions.

The role of Western assistance

Eastern Europeans have their fate in their own hands as they strive to turn their economies around. It is not an easy task, because at first sight the switch to a market economy brings with it injustices and social hardship.

The choice with which Eastern Europe's new governments are faced is often between the full-employment conditions of State-run industries, however inflexible and loss-making they may be, and a free market that seems to offer nothing more than soaring unemployment and falling living standards.

Western governments have a role to play both in assisting financially and in showing Eastern Europe that there is light at the end of the tunnel. They are also, along with institutions like the World Bank and the IMF, the only source of money that can cover Eastern Europe's financing gap.

Western financial assistance is divided broadly between microeconomic and macroeconomic aid. The former is the detailed project finance being provided under national programmes and, above all, by the EC's PHARE programme. Between 1990 and the end of 1992, PHARE will have spent Ecu 2.25bn on investment and technical assistance in areas such as environmental control, agriculture, training and industrial restructuring.

Macroeconomic assistance is aimed at underpinning the Eastern Europeans' more fundamental economic policy reforms. It is financial aid that is often closely linked with the advice and conditions set out by the IMF and the World Bank, and consists of funds subscribed by the G-24 network of Western nations coordinated by the EC Commission. The G-24 mechanism is administered by a special unit inside the Commission's external relations directorate, and in addition to EC 'Eurocrats' there are also a number of officials who have been seconded from the governments of non-EC countries in G-24.

The first major macroeconomic measure to be mounted by G-24 was the US$1bn Polish Stabilization Fund which was agreed to in 1990 as an essential support of Poland's 'big bang' tactic of embracing currency convertibility, devaluation, price liberalization and a deflationary incomes policy in a single programme.

The G-24 nations have since subscribed US$1bn in balance of payments support for Czechoslovakia that will also help to underpin the partial convertibility of the koruna, and a similar US$500m G-24 loan has been made to Hungary. Bulgaria is to receive a US$800m macroeconomic assistance loan from G-24 and US$1bn will go to Romania.

These macroeconomic adjustment programmes have in general been very successful. There is, though, a trend that is giving rise to concern on both sides of the Atlantic. The

United States and the Western European nations are not working together as the single team that had been hoped for.

The Europeans complain that the US government has grown steadily less supportive of financial packages for Eastern Europe and appears to take the view that Eastern Europe 'is a European problem'. About half of G-24 financial assistance is subscribed by the 12 EC nations, and less than 7 per cent by the US. In some cases, Washington has offered derisory contributions when Brussels has passed round the G-24 hat, notably when raising funds for loans to Czechoslovakia and Hungary.

American interest in assisting the USSR seems much greater. The superpower relationship between Moscow and Washington is certainly a factor, as the concern of the US is that any collapse of the Soviet economy could destabilize not only the USSR itself but also many other parts of the world. America's role as the world's policeman therefore gives it a direct interest in the future of the USSR.

The European Community is also partly responsible for this 'division of labour'. Simple geography coupled with the EC membership aspirations of several Eastern European countries gives the Community the dominant role. The EC nations' political body language has made it clear to the US that they see Eastern Europe as an EC backyard where America should tread with sensitivity. But it is nevertheless important that the G-24 team spirit should not be lost.

Fine-tuning microeconomic assistance is in many ways trickier than organizing macroeconomic support. The main channel for microeconomic assistance is the EC's PHARE programme, launched at the same time as G-24 in July 1989. It was originally intended to funnel aid to Poland and Hungary (its French acronym stands for *Pologne, Hongrie: aide à la restructuration economique*, and also means 'a beacon of light'), but has since been expanded to include Czechoslovakia, Bulgaria, Romania and Yugoslavia.

PHARE is run by the EC Commission, and both the EC officials involved and the Eastern European recipients of PHARE funding have begun to draw interesting conclusions about the nature of economic assistance and the ways in which it can be tailored to the needs of individual countries.

Tom Garvey, the senior EC official who heads the PHARE team, emphasizes that the programme operates on two levels. In the first place it is designed to address immediate problems such as environmental pollution and food production. At the second level it aims to help Eastern Europe to set up the financial structures that are essential to a market economy.

'PHARE means advice on the reform of their banking systems, helping to design a new tax system and tax collection methods and the introduction of proper accountancy standards', says Garvey. It is also mounting a major effort to bring Eastern Europe's industrial standards into line with those of the EC.

As well as implementing EC assistance programmes, PHARE has the job of trying to prevent Western nations and institutions from tripping over one another in their efforts to help Eastern Europe. PHARE is meant to prevent wasteful duplication of assistance, while at the same time helping the EC's 12 member governments to mount complementary projects.

PHARE is responsible for seeing that EC efforts run parallel to the World Bank's development projects, and that the two dovetail as neatly as possible. It is also concerned with 'co-financing' operations in which the EC acts in partnership with other G-24 governments.

'We are not negotiators, but mechanics', explains Tom Garvey. 'We put into effect what has already been decided. One of our major problems is being lobbied by different factions from within the same Eastern European government. We're very keen that it should be *they* who decide what it is they want.'

For a small and rather rigid bureaucracy such as the EC Commission, PHARE has been an undoubted success. Most EC-level initiatives face the twin problems of inflexible EC officialdom and the demands of the member governments that they should be fully consulted at every step. The urgency of Eastern Europe's problems has helped PHARE to cut through both constraints.

The PHARE programme nevertheless has its critics. Not surprisingly, Eastern European governments have found the amounts of money involved to be inadequate when set against their needs. Milan Cernohuby, a senior Czechoslovak diplomat who deals with the EC Commission on a day-to-day basis, says: 'It's only a fragment of what we really need.' Czechoslovakia received Ecu 35m in PHARE spending in 1990, and Ecu 100m in 1991.

Polish criticisms of the way PHARE works are somewhat different. 'We can see a need for a more formal system of meetings, both in Brussels and in the Eastern European capitals, in order for there to be more of a dialogue', says Jan Truszczynski, who handles economic relations at Poland's embassy to the EC. 'We have already indicated to the EC Commission that we believe there should be more regular contacts.'

Ivan Szasz, a senior Hungarian diplomat in Brussels, considers that the size of PHARE spending is not the crucial factor. Hungary received Ecu 100m in 1990 and Ecu 137m in 1991, but is more concerned with inflows of private capital. 'The important thing', he says, 'is not so much the aggregated value of the loans and grants. What counts is the ability of a country to absorb assistance. We believe aid has to be combined with massive foreign investment and with other institutional help if Hungary is to be integrated with Western Europe. Aid on its own doesn't help countries; look at the Third World.'

Mikhailo Crnobrnja, Yugoslavia's ambassador to the EC, believes that in some ways the PHARE programme may be the victim of its own success, even though his own country has benefited from PHARE's extension. He comments: 'The widening of PHARE from just Poland and Hungary to include Czechoslovakia, Bulgaria, Romania and ourselves has watered down its effects. It was originally more coherent and efficient. PHARE's sense of direction and unity has been diluted. The way to counteract this is more resources, but objectively I can see this isn't likely to happen.'

Crnobrnja adds: 'There is a sense of disillusionment. Not because we think we've been led by the nose, but because things are truly very difficult.' He says the PHARE objectives can also be seen as 'slightly overblown. In 1990 it was rather oversold, and now in 1991 we can see that PHARE is not going to make a big difference in switching Eastern European countries to becoming market economies.'

What economic integration with the West would mean

Unanswered, and often unanswerable, questions abound. How can the Eastern Europeans' progress towards economic integration be measured, and should timetables be established to give a sense of urgency? Is the West adopting enough of a systematic approach, or is the problem too profoundly cultural for checklists of reform measures to be of any use?

André Leysen, the Belgian industrialist who gives Eastern Europe 25 years and the USSR 50 to make the transition, believes there are five criteria that must be met before a country can say it is on the way to becoming a market economy. And he says that of the five the first two must be fulfilled 'before it makes sense to spend a single dollar in Western financial assistance.' His criteria are:

- There must be an absolute public and governmental will to switch to a private enterprise system.

- There must be an adequate legal framework so that property rights are clearly established.

- An Eastern European government must have launched its own efforts to overhaul infrastructure and foster new industries.

- Private capital must have begun to invest in substantial amounts.

- There must be a transfusion of Western know-how and technology.

The picture that is emerging is of a far more complex process of economic transition than was at first expected. The sheer detail involved in drawing up draft legislation on such topics as competition rules, taxation, company law, employment conditions, industrial standards, investment services and social security, to name but a few, is daunting. The OECD has set up a Centre for Cooperation with European Economies in Transition to help with expert advice, and already the signs are that it is clearly going to be a long and difficult process.

To establish a free enterprise economy means that Eastern Europeans must dismantle many of the institutions and systems on which their society is based. They are finding that the layers of problems are like onion skins – not, as they had hoped, like orange peel.

Notes

1. *The Solvency of Eastern Europe*, by Daniel Cohen, CEPREMAP, Paris, January 1991.

2. *The Future of Relations between the EC and Eastern Europe*, Club de Bruxelles, 1990.

3. 'Thoughts on Marketizing State-managed Economies'. A paper presented by Paul W McCracken at the Hudson Institute to the Blue Ribbon Commission drawing up plans for Hungary's economic transition, January 1990.

4. *Stabilization, Liberalization and Devolution: Assessment of the Economic Situation and Reform Process in the Soviet Union*, Commission of the European Communities, December 1990.

5. 'The Houston Report: The Failure of Perestroika', by David M Kemme. In *Economic Insights*, the journal of the Institute for East-West Security Studies, New York, January-February 1991.

6. *Financial Times*, 20 May 1991.

4

Industry:

Could the Eastern Europeans be Tomorrow's 'Technology Tigers'?

Searching for the tell-tale signs of a high-tech future – Lessons from the Asian 'four tigers' – CoCom's unlamented demise – Why the technology gap may already be too wide – The key element will be low wage costs

Antony Steiner is a youthful, self-confident British manager who considers he has his head screwed on the right way. He is in no doubt about why his company is moving into Czechoslovakia. 'The lower end of the castings market in Britain and the rest of Western Europe has been taken by Taiwan. Our Czech operation gives us a chance to fight back, and it's also a strategic foothold in Central Europe.'

Steiner's company, Triplex Lloyd from England's engineering heartland of the West Midlands, has taken a 50 per cent stake in an ultra-modern investment casting plant on the outskirts of Prague. Thanks to very low wage costs and Czechoslovakia's heritage of skilled precision engineering, it believes it can strike hard at the competition from South-East Asia. There is a buoyant world market for the sophisticated steel castings the plant supplies, which go into turbine blades and the like, so the signs are that Triplex Lloyd has made a significant move.

Antony Steiner has moved his family to Prague and has taken on the job of running the new venture. He is no starry-eyed idealist and reckons that, for the time being, demand in Eastern Europe for his precision castings will be disappointing. 'There's no market in Czechoslovakia, it's going down the Swannee', he jokes grimly, 'but in five years' time we'll have an important strategic advantage.'

Five hundred kilometres to the south-east in Budapest, a much more rosy view of the immediate future is expressed by Peter Vadasz, an electronics whizz-kid who is a Hungarian version of Steve Jobs, the man who launched Apple Computers from his Silicon Valley garage. Vadasz started his computer company in 1983 with a capital of US$3,000, and today it has sales of almost US$40m a year. 'Asian and American high-tech companies are keen to use Hungary as a low-cost assembly area for the Western European market', he says. 'Companies like General Electric, Suzuki and United Technologies are already moving in and transferring their technology to Hungary.'

Vadasz's company, Microsystems, imports and assembles personal computers, fax machines and telecommunications equipment and writes software for its Hungarian customers. It is highly successful, and for Hungarians it has become a celebration of the free market system. A picture of Margaret Thatcher hangs on the wall in Vadasz's office – 'I met her once, and admire her very much' – and her spirit imbues the company's thinking.

'I'm very optimistic about Hungary's future in high-technology', says Peter Vadasz. 'We have the dynamic of foreign investment, particularly from America and Western Europe. Our closest competitor in this area is Czechoslovakia. They have the industrial culture, but they're three or four years behind.'

Searching for the tell-tale signs of a high-tech future

It is the burning question in Czechoslovakia, Hungary and Poland. Do the Central Europeans' high education levels and low wage costs hold out the promise of a South-East Asia-style high-technology lift-off, and can they hope to attract multinational corporations whose activities will by the early twenty-first century start to spawn local high-tech entrepreneurs? The answer lies as much with these countries' determination to keep their wages competitively low as with their ability to absorb new technology.

Poland, Hungary and Czechoslovakia would dearly love to see themselves as the 'three tigers' of Central Europe whose booming knowledge-based industries could put them on a par with the famous 'four tigers' of South-East Asia – Taiwan, Singapore, South Korea and Hong Kong.

At first, it seems a far-fetched idea. The region's faltering economies, its down-at-heel cities and the obsolete industrial products that Eastern European countries are able to sell only to one another do not inspire much confidence. There seem to be all too few signs that a technological revolution is in the offing.

Much the same could have been said 25 years ago of the Asian countries. They had few natural resources, and their aspirations to compete with Japan and the United States in both advanced and consumer electronics appeared laughable. Yet in a few short years they came from nowhere. Their highly competitive prices, technological wizardry and determined marketing methods have enabled them to wrest market share from long-established US, Japanese and European multinational corporations.

Central Europeans are asking 'Why not us too?' After all, these countries have a firmer educational and industrial base than did the Asians, they are on the doorstep of the European Community's wealthy Single Market and also have their own hungry and unsatisfied home markets to supply.

It is a view that some Western analysts are beginning to share. 'Skill-intensive goods, such as cars and electronic consumer goods, will play a significant role in East European exports', predicts the London-based Centre for Economic Policy Research (CEPR) in its study on 'The Impact of Eastern Europe'.

The CEPR report by an international team of economists foresees the arrival in Eastern Europe of a wave of multinational corporations who will be eager to transfer their technology and will also bring managerial skills. And it rejects the idea that the host countries of Eastern Europe would be denied the spin-off from these foreign companies' research and development efforts.

'The experience of Singapore is instructive', say the CEPR authors. 'It is now developing from a host to multinational production into a home base for multinationals with production elsewhere in South-East Asia. Given the high levels of education and skill in such countries as Czechoslovakia and Hungary it is entirely conceivable that they could become the hosts of "upstream" activities of multinationals.'

The scenario that the report puts forward is that growth in the countries of Eastern Europe – but not the USSR – could enable them to double their GDPs in ten years. In other words, they would be achieving the same growth rate as South Korea since the mid-1960s and West Germany in the 1950s. That sort of growth, the CEPR economists add, implies huge sales of Western capital goods to Eastern Europe as well as a strong flow of investment. They hazard a rough guess at a figure for the two of US$135bn a year.[1]

Western high-technology companies are certainly showing signs of interest in Central Europe, although not so much in the more backward and ill-educated Balkan countries like Romania and Bulgaria. Franz Nawratil, a senior executive at Hewlett-Packard, one of the leading American computer makers, says that business in Eastern Europe is expanding 'beyond our wildest dreams'.

Hewlett-Packard is an electronics multinational that sprang originally from Silicon Valley in California and still has deep roots there. It is the sort of technology-led company that Eastern Europe most needs. The 88 per cent sales growth that it enjoyed in Eastern Europe during 1990-91 could be just a beginning.

'Specific areas where Western companies can help Eastern ones', comments Nawratil, 'are in automating their plants and training their people to work in small service businesses like software, distribution and technical service.' He goes on: 'Many Eastern and Central Europeans have exceptional computer technology skills . . . The challenge for companies such as ours is to introduce those goods, services and educational skills that will build success from these inherent skills. There can be no crash-course, but rather a gradual building of the technology infrastructure.'[2]

Other computer giants, notably IBM which has maintained a presence in Hungary since before World War II, are becoming very active indeed. So too is Germany's Siemens, whose joint ventures include a deal to make digital controls for machine tools in partnership with Czechoslovakia's venerable electronics and electrical goods manufacturer, Tesla.

There are also a number of scientific pockets of excellence in areas outside electronics. Hungary, for example, is a major participant in the global pharmaceuticals industry and is also strong in pure research in biotechnology and life sciences.

The USSR should not be ruled out of the high-technology picture. It is still, after all, one of the world leaders in space exploration and technology, and has plans to switch much of its military research effort into civilian technologies. Its State Committee for Science and Technology has said it will be transferring roubles 5bn a year from the Soviet defence budget to civil industries. Soviet scientists claim they are already generating 100,000 'inventions' a year, though Western analysts say such statements should be taken with a large pinch of salt.

Lessons from the Asian 'four tigers'

If the Central Europeans care to do so, there are some useful 'dos' and 'don'ts' to be learned from the meteoric rise of the 'four tigers' of South-East Asia.

They have exported their way to prosperity, and along the way they have shed their old image of producing cheap, shoddy copies of Western goods. Now they are admired as technological competitors who can teach the West valuable lessons about quality and innovation.

Their common denominator has been an almost obsessive emphasis on education. University graduates have poured out of their newly-constructed colleges in steadily rising numbers. Taiwan, with a population of only 20 million, now has more graduate job-seekers every year than Britain. South

Korea has twice as many engineering students as Germany, yet is a quarter of its size.

In most other respects, the Asian tigers took different paths to success. Singapore wooed the multinationals, whereas Hong Kong encouraged its entrepreneurs to trade up from making gimcrack souvenirs and cheap garments to producing added-value goods like consumer electronics.

Taiwan has had a totally 'hands-off' approach that has encouraged foreign capital to flood in and float a myriad small companies that have to be dynamic to stay alive. South Korea, by contrast, has been 'dirigiste' and the government has directed cheap credit to fund the ten massive conglomerates – called *chaebols* – that now account for two-thirds of the country's GNP.

Where the four tigers have acted as one has been in their insistence on running open economies. They have all maintained liberal import regimes that attracted technology transfers and ensured that their own exports would not be discriminated against.

In the 1950s South Korea had briefly attempted to encourage its infant industries with an import-substitution policy that discouraged foreign goods. After several years of slow growth it abandoned that. For the past 25 years all the Asian tigers have had in common is their booming export industries and the speed with which they attract and adapt new technologies. Their economies have grown by 8-9 per cent a year and the volume of their exports by about 16 per cent a year.

For Eastern European governments who may be tempted to try to limit the industrial job losses caused by opening up to the free market, the Asians' experience should be both a warning and an encouragement. Attempts to limit imports will stifle growth and technological progress, while openness to imported technology quickly fosters export success. Eastern European governments that may be contemplating import controls to give their industries a breathing space should think again.

Co-Com's unlamented demise

So far, it has not been the Eastern Europeans who have limited the flow of new technology into their economies. It has been the West. The supply of Western high-tech products to Eastern Europe and the USSR has been severely monitored and restricted since the 1960s. This technological embargo was one of the West's chief weapons in the Cold War, and was based on the obvious need to deny militarily useful equipment to the countries of the Warsaw Pact.

The technology ban was enforced by a mechanism called the Coordinating Committee for Multilateral Export Controls – universally known as CoCom. It operated out of a basement in the United States Embassy in Paris and laid down strict limits on the equipment that could be sold to Warsaw Pact and other 'unfriendly' countries by the members of Nato and by Japan.

Now that the Cold War is no more, it can be seen that CoCom's restrictions had a devastating impact on the civilian economies of Eastern Europe, whatever the effect they may or may not have had on the Warsaw Pact's military capabilities. CoCom even proscribed the sale of goods such as IBM personal computers on the grounds that they might indirectly strengthen the Soviet war machine. The result is that Eastern Europe has missed out on much of the computer revolution of the 1980s and is still in the high-tech equivalent of the Stone Age.

There are estimated to be no more than half a million personal computers in the whole of Eastern Europe and about 400,000 in the USSR. The number of PCs in the United States is 35 million and is about the same in Western Europe. Put another way, there is one computer for every 250 people in Eastern Europe and for every 600 in the USSR, as against one between every six people in the West.

The two dominant computer producers in the Comecon area have been the USSR and East Germany. Neither has been in the forefront of computer technology, and the CoCom embargo has meant there was neither the spur of competition from the West nor a steady flow of technologically superior products to copy.

The Soviet industry has still to produce a PC with a hard disc and its chief models, the Iskra and the Agat, are old-fashioned and unreliable. The Agat is a clone of the Apple II that during the early 1980s was the predecessor of the Apple Macintosh range. Computers made by the GDR's Robotron Kombinat were little better as they suffered from interface problems that made them unlinkable with Western equipment. Following Germany's reunification, Robotron changed its name to Soemtron and embarked on a determined drive to upgrade both its products and its image.

It is hard to tell how much damage may have been done by CoCom's stranglehold on technology transfers, and how much by the former communist states' dislike of computerization and the greater access to information that it brings. The result of those two factors, combined with the rigidities of central planning, has been to severely handicap Eastern Europe and the USSR.

CoCom today is all but dead. Over the protests of the military, chiefly in the US, the list of proscribed products has been slashed from 120 to only 10. This 'core list' still denies Eastern Europeans access to a number of important technologies, but the signs are that it will not be policed with the same fanatical vigour as before.

The product categories are nevertheless worrying, because they suggest a Western determination to keep both the USSR and Eastern Europe firmly under control. They are: high-speed computers, advanced telecommunications equipment and information protection devices, advanced materials and machine tools, sensing systems, navigation and avionics equipment, and marine technology and propulsion systems.

It is now looking more and more as if the massive conventional forces of the Red Army and its former Warsaw Pact allies were never as powerful a threat as they seemed. Their technological backwardness has been an eye-opener, and leaves little doubt that most of the CoCom core list amounts to unnecessary overkill. The problem for the West will not be to limit the flow of technologies to Eastern Europe but rather to help these countries to absorb and harness them. It may already be too late.

Why the technology gap may already be too wide

Eastern Europe could find that it is too slow off the mark to catch up with the electronics revolution. The emphasis under the communist régimes on heavy industry and the overwhelming problems of switching from State-controlled manufacturing to private enterprise may eclipse the importance of recovering lost ground in information technology.

Not only may Eastern Europe's industrial structures prove to be too old-fashioned, but also there seems to be a cultural problem. Under communism, the State did not encourage the widespread dissemination of information to all and sundry, and the lack of well-developed channels of communication is now a striking feature of business and industry, and even government. It is poor soil in which to plant the seeds of the information revolution.

Even the best of Eastern European companies seem to be having difficulty adapting to the international marketplace. For instance, Hungary's biggest electronics company, Videoton, won a licence to assemble television sets for France's giant Thomson group, but although it achieved impressive productivity gains and cut its manufacturing time for a TV set to 4 hours from 24, other inefficiencies mean that its costs are still far too high and that it is losing US$120 on each television set it produces.

Similar problems have been dogging Ikarus, Hungary's famous bus maker. It is having to switch its sales away from its former Comecon trading partners, whose orders have dried up because they must now pay in hard currency, and is finding the world market a tough place. To compete internationally, Ikarus needs to greatly improve the quality of its buses, but the cost of doing so looks as if it will price them out of the world market.

In Poland, Prime Minister Jan Krzysztof Bielecki has been publicly bemoaning the failure of Polish industry to adapt to free market needs and conditions. After a tour of the huge Azoty chemical works in Silesia, Bielecki told a *New York Times* reporter that although it had a lot going for it, the company was still frozen in a socialist time-warp. 'This company has entered an international market and holds 5 per cent of world production [of a PVC component for pipes and tubes], yet it doesn't work at all on marketing.'

Czechoslovakia has similar stories to tell, and so does East Germany. Before World War II, when Czechoslovakia was the sixth greatest industrial power in the world, the Tesla brand name was uttered in the same breath as Philips or Siemens. Today, its digitally-controlled machine tools are of good quality, but are 15 years behind the times. Czech experts are not optimistic about the company's future.

In East Germany, the end of partition in autumn 1990 also promised the reunification of the celebrated Carl Zeiss company, which had been split into two. The merger scheme would have meant, however, that the much less efficient eastern operation in the original factory at Jena would have suffered appalling job losses. Having already cut its work-force from 70,000 people to 23,000, the East German Carl Zeiss was told it would eventually have less than 5,000 workers. It broke off the merger talks and decided to go it alone in the hope of stabilizing its payroll at 10,000.

The situation looks unpromising for a high-tech rebirth of Eastern European industry. 'In my view', says Milan Cernohuby, an industry expert in Czechoslovakia's diplomatic mission in Brussels, 'we will never become competitive in electronics. Under the previous régime much of the State's investment spending went into electronics, but to no avail. We are 15-20 years behind the industrialized world. Our only hope is cooperation agreements with major electronics companies.'

Cernohuby's assessment is widely shared in both Eastern and Western Europe. Christopher Wilkinson, an English EC official who heads the international economics affairs division of the European Commission's information technology and telecommunications directorate, says that in Eastern Europe he sees 'more parallels with South Wales and Strathclyde than with Korea or Thailand'. Wilkinson comments: 'Research activity in Central Europe is quite strong, but I don't see the situation there as anything like what's going on in South-East Asia. Those countries have been able to apply high levels of technology and low wage rates to a newly industrializing situation. In Central Europe the focus is on streamlining old industries.'

He adds: 'What I am saying is not entirely pessimistic. Industrial conversion, with the right mix of policies for freeing production and encouraging innovation, can work. But it is not easy to make great leaps forward in this area, as the Community itself has discovered of late.'

The idea that the Eastern Europeans may be able to 'jump a generation' by installing state-of-the-art technology that will transform both their service sectors and manufacturing industries is an attractive one. Christopher Wilkinson does not rule it out. 'It sounds a bit glib, but it is true that they'll be buying in new technology and using their high levels of education to apply it. They could jump a decade.'

The comparison with the Asian tigers is not always seen as the right approach. Hungary's Industry Minister, Peter Akos Bod, believes that the whole idea of emulating them risks being a red herring. 'I don't think the example of the newly industrialized countries in South-East Asia is a good one', says the Minister, who until being propelled into high office was an economist in a Budapest think-tank. 'I think Spain and Portugal are better examples.'

His point is that the poorer Mediterranean countries now being integrated into the EC economy are more akin to Eastern Europe than the Asians. Bod emphasizes that electronics is not the only yardstick for rapid economic development. He believes that Hungary stands a good chance of becoming a regional financial centre for Central Europe.

The signs are, though, that South-East Asia is very much the model that Central Europe should be aiming at. It is not just the glamorous high-technology aspect of the tigers' success but also their determination to peg wages and remain competitive, while at the same time being motivated enough to start small businesses by the thousand.

The key element will be low wage costs

Eastern Europe's highly competitive wage costs are the region's chief asset. As Hewlett-Packard's Franz Nawratil puts it: 'In the East, where talent is easily affordable – about US$660 a month for the best field engineer in Poland – and above all smart, with tremendous basic R&D skills, economics still favour human capital.'

If Western engineering and high-tech companies are to move into Eastern Europe in strength, it will be cheap labour costs that attract them most of all. Keeping wages down may turn out to be the most important of all the challenges facing the newly emerging market economies.

It will be hard for the political leaders of Eastern Europe to restrain the natural desire of their voters to improve living standards overnight. That aim was, after all, the driving force of the revolutions of 1989 that finally ousted communism.

But it is essential to do so. The people of Eastern Europe must understand that they cannot reap the benefits of free enterprise until they have started to make substantial profits. The 1990s will be a period when they have first to pay the bill for their past inefficiencies, be these in agriculture, in energy and the environment, or in industrial production.

Western observers are unconvinced that Eastern Europe's low labour costs will last for long. Tom Garvey, who heads the EC Commission's PHARE programme of technical and financial assistance to Eastern Europe and sees events from a privileged vantage point, is pessimistic. 'I think the variety of goods required to respond to the consumer's needs and demands may impair the Eastern Europeans' cheap labour advantage', he comments. 'In the next two or three years these countries will be constructing a whole new social security fabric, and that's going to be a serious charge on business in the future.'

Events have been bearing out his forecast. The developments that brought the new democratic governments of Eastern Europe into power were popular revolutions, and the political pressures on the new rulers to respond with higher living standards is intense. Coupled to this there is the legacy of socialist welfare arrangements.

Poland, Hungary and Czechoslovakia all have unemployment benefit systems that risk becoming cripplingly expensive. Housewives and school leavers in all three countries have been signing up to receive benefits that can be higher than the minimum wage.

Michal Boni, Poland's Labour Minister, says that over 40 per cent of his country's May 1991 total of 1.2 million people unemployed were school leavers and college graduates. As well as drawing benefit, many of them are working in Poland's black economy. As to the victims of factory closures and redundancies, they account for only 14 per cent of those getting the dole.

Scrapping the generous fringe benefits of socialism is also proving difficult. Women employees in Czechoslovakia are entitled to three years' maternity leave, for example. In Poland, 78 per cent of people have been taking early retirement under one special scheme or another. Breaking the paternalistic relationship between State and citizen is not proving easy. Only Hungary had by mid-1991 started to tackle that problem by creating Eastern Europe's first private unemployment insurance fund.[3]

Higher social security costs mean higher taxes, and higher taxes would probably mean higher wages. It is a spiral that Eastern Europeans must avoid if they are to capitalize on their high educational standards and their well-developed industrial culture. For many people it will seem that they are being denied the fruits of free enterprise and freedom. But the lesson to be learnt from the Asian tigers and from post-war Japan is that global competitiveness is within the reach of any nation.

Notes

1. *Monitoring European Integration – The Impact of Eastern Europe.* Annual report of the Centre for Economic Policy Research, London, October 1990.

2. 'Information Systems: Challenges and Opportunities for East Central Europe'. A paper by Franz Nawratil. Vice-President, Hewlett-Packard Co, to the Conference Board, London, May 1991.

3. *The Economist*, 4 May 1991.

5

Trade:

Comecon's Collapse – Putting Humpty Dumpty Together Again

The death of Comecon — Europe's East-West trade is re-launched — Why the trade barriers could be going up — Comecon reborn — The case for an Eastern European payments union — The Ecu could replace the transferable rouble (and the US dollar) — There must be no EC export bonanza in Eastern Europe

---

The line of stationary trucks waiting to cross the frontier into Poland stretches to the horizon and beyond. Their drivers stand gossiping in knots, and some of the older hands who have experience of the Stettin border post play cards or cook campfire meals. For several kilometres the tarpaulined goods vehicles stand nose-to-tail like patient elephants along the patched and uneven autobahn that leads out of eastern Germany. The contrast with the increasingly free-flowing traffic across the frontiers between European Community countries is inescapable.

Whether the hold-up is due to the inertia and officiousness of petty officials and customs men or is a deliberate instrument of Polish government policy is anybody's guess. Since 1990 Poland, along with the USSR and Hungary, has operated a system of import and export licensing.

As they struggle to become market economies, the Eastern Europeans are finding themselves faced with unaccustomed difficulties. During the 40 years in which their foreign trade was chiefly to one another within the socialist 'club' of Comecon, each Eastern European country's main concern was to avoid exporting more than it imported. Suddenly, the game is played the other way around.

Under the Comecon system a country that exported more goods than it imported was liable to end up the loser. Of course, that country would have its surplus in trade credited to it in the transferable roubles devised by the USSR in 1963. But these were never acceptable outside Comecon, and therefore were not genuinely convertible. The reality was that there was no actual economic benefit to any of the Eastern European countries to run a trade surplus in transferable roubles.

Now the Eastern European countries find themselves in the unfamiliar and unwelcome world of balance of payments crises and the increasingly difficult decisions on monetary and economic policy that stem directly from their foreign trade position. The need to make their industries globally competitive has become paramount. So too, in Eastern European eyes, has become the need to replace their dependence on the Soviet market with access to the EC Single Market.

The reorientation of Eastern European and Soviet trade towards the West will be a central issue of the 1990s. It is essential that a new East-West trading relationship should be created – without trade their economies will wither and die. But it cannot be achieved overnight. In the harsh new climate of the market economy, their ability to trade will depend on their competitiveness. Trade within Comecon was easy, if minimal; there was little or no competition, no commercial risk and no danger of losing one's customers. The future is much less certain.

During 1990 and 1991 the trade of the former Comecon partners indeed swung dramatically towards the West, but towards Western imports into Eastern Europe rather than exports westwards, though there have been a few notable exceptions.

The former Comecon countries, and particularly Poland, Czechoslovakia and Hungary which all aspire to EC membership, would like to see the European Community offer them privileged trade terms that will nurture their own infant industries and provide them with temporary shelter against competition from more technologically advanced and efficient producers in the West.

To some extent the EC wants to oblige. The aim of the association agreements with the three Central European countries is to set 'asymmetrical' trading conditions that will help their exports and handicap those of the EC countries. The Central Europeans have complained that these terms are not generous enough – there have been jibes that the asymmetry was in the Community's favour – but the real problem is that the former Comecon countries are fundamentally uncompetitive.

Until the efficiencies of free enterprise have begun to take effect, Eastern Europe's exporters will be well advised to continue trading, if they can, with their former Comecon partners. The most constructive approach that the EC and the West in general can take is to restrain Western companies, where possible, from turning the collapse of Comecon into an export bonanza for themselves.

EC policy-makers also seem to be moving towards the idea that the best solution to Eastern Europe's trade problems lies in resuscitating Comecon's trade flows. Sir Leon Brittan, Britain's senior EC Commissioner, has proposed a plan for giving Western financial aid to the USSR on condition that it spends it on imports from Eastern Europe. Other ideas centre around the launching of a payments union for the region, a financial mechanism that would overcome the hard currency shortage that is now stifling trade between the former Comecon partners.

The death of Comecon

In the wake of the events of 1989, the world has watched the

USSR's trading bloc fall apart with devastating speed. Comecon, or to give it its full name, the Council for Mutual Economic Assistance (CMEA), is dead, even though Moscow has been making desultory efforts to reanimate it under the new name of the Organization for International Economic Cooperation (OIEC).

Stalin saw the Comecon system as the means to create a planned socialist economy on a grand scale. Czechoslovakia would make the railway locomotives, Hungary the buses, East Germany the machine tools, and so on. Wasteful duplication would be eliminated, just as he believed it was being eliminated in the USSR and in the domestic economies of its new satellite states.

The collapse of Comecon has been as spectacular as Stalin's dream was grandiose. During 1990, trade between the European partners of Comecon (Vietnam, Cuba and Mongolia were also members) crashed by at least one-fifth and possibly as much as one-third.

Trade statistics inside Comecon are not straightforward. Because of the difficulties of calculating the value of goods when exchange rates have been works of political fiction, reliable figures are scarce. The United Nations Economic Commission for Europe estimates the fall-off in trade between the Eastern European countries at 18-21 per cent.[1]

The Institute for East-West Security Studies has said the collapse is so serious 'that it is jeopardizing prospects for stabilization and transition in the region'. It puts the 1990 trade contraction at 30 per cent, and expects it will have fallen another 30 per cent in 1991.

Other analyses are more dramatic still. Sergei Lykov, deputy head of the international department of Gosbank, the Soviet State Bank, told the *Financial Times* in April 1991 that, in the first quarter of the year, trade between the USSR and Central and Eastern Europe stood at only 10 per cent of the volume in the same three months of 1990.

Whatever the precise statistics of the collapse, the impact that it is having on the ex-Comecon economies is brutal. Poland, for instance, has found that no less than 200 factories are directly dependent on Soviet orders. Companies such as WSK Mielec, a leading Polish aircraft manufacturer which laid off a quarter of its 20,000 workforce in 1990, reported that by the spring of 1991 Soviet payments had so dried up that it was having difficulty paying its wages.

By early 1991 Poland's exports to the USSR were reported to be at a near standstill. It is far from being a purely Polish problem, however. Throughout Eastern Europe the engineering plants that have relied on business with the USSR for much of their livelihoods are being squeezed hard. Hungary's Ikarus has huge parking lots crammed full of unsold buses that were destined for the USSR. In all, half a million Hungarian jobs depend on exports there.

In 1989, 25 per cent of Hungary's foreign trade had been with the USSR; by early 1991 it was running at only 4 per cent. Long-term contracts between Hungarian suppliers and Soviet buyers for 1991 stood at US$1.5bn, but it was expected that Hungary's exports to the USSR for the year would reach less than one-third of that.

In East Germany, the collapse of Comecon and the monetary union that in July 1990 preceded the October reunification of the two Germanies is having a devastating effect on industry. The GDR had been the second largest of the Comecon trading partners after the USSR, and 40 per cent of its exports went there. Now, the combination of Soviet economic chaos and the uncompetitive effect on export prices of the switch to Deutschmarks is decimating payrolls.

During 1991 East German exports to the USSR will have fallen by two-thirds, wiping out a quarter of total exports. In the machine tool sector 50,000 jobs could be lost. The famous Rostock shipyards are also facing a grim future. The Warnow and Neptun yards have seen Soviet purchases of their freighters and factory fishing vessels dry up almost overnight. If they survive it will be with payrolls slashed by at least half.

Czechoslovakia also had about 40 per cent of its foreign trade with the USSR. During 1990 that fell abruptly to 25 per cent and is still sliding. The forecasts suggest that by the start of 1992 it will be little more than 10 per cent. Czechoslovakia's trade with the Comecon bloc as a whole is also sliding, and during 1990 it dropped from 60 per cent to 50 per cent.

The disappearance of so much Soviet business has had a knock-on effect on trade throughout Eastern Europe. Factories that have lost crucial Soviet contracts are no longer in a position to place orders with suppliers elsewhere in Eastern Europe. That is why trade between the Comecon partners plummeted by between one-fifth and one-third in 1990, at a time when world trade as a whole grew by 5 per cent.

This trade crisis was precipitated by the USSR's decision to insist on hard currency trade within Comecon as of 1 January 1991. When the then Soviet Premier Nikolai Ryzhkov announced this at a Comecon meeting in Sofia, Bulgaria, in January 1990 he said it was in response to demands from the USSR's trading partners. There is some truth in this, because the newly democratic Eastern European countries were baulking at the constraints of Comecon and its use of the so-called transferable rouble to calculate payments.

But Moscow's own motive for the switch to hard currency trading was that it believed it would profit handsomely. The USSR wanted first of all to stop selling its oil and gas to its Comecon partners at what amounted to subsidized prices, sometimes as low as US$7 a barrel. Its aim was to sell at world market prices and earn dollars. Moscow also hoped to benefit from the spread between immediate payment for its energy exports and the 180-day standard credit terms it could obtain from its Eastern European suppliers of manufactured goods.

Of course, the USSR shot itself in the foot. Its own falling oil output and the stagnation of world oil prices despite the Gulf War in early 1991 meant that the USSR failed to hit the jackpot. Instead, it has itself had to find hard currency at a time when its economic woes and the burden of servicing its large foreign debt have made foreign exchange extremely scarce.

The Comecon countries did not have to wait until 1991 to suffer the ill effects of the change. Many companies and trade banks began to demand hard currency payment during 1990 in anticipation of the switch. At the same time, the USSR's announcement that it would no longer engage in the various types of barter trade practised within Comecon also had an immediate and inhibiting effect on trade.

As for the USSR itself, the shock waves that followed Ryzhkov's announcement in Sofia were so damaging that its exports to other countries in Comecon fell by 18 per cent during 1990. The year marked the end of a long and uninterrupted run of foreign trade surpluses that had begun in the latter 1970s.

The impact on the least developed members of Comecon was also disastrous. Bulgaria's exports during 1990 plunged by 26 per cent and those of Romania by 46 per cent.

Europe's East-West trade is re-launched

Comecon's demise has been accompanied by almost as dramatic an improvement in the volume of trade between some of the Central European countries and the EC. There are high hopes in Warsaw, Budapest and Prague that before long a new and more healthy trading relationship with the Community will replace the artificial structure of Comecon.

Hungarian exports to the EC rose by one-third in 1990 and the Community supplanted Comecon as Hungary's principal trading partner. Throughout the 1980s the Hungarians had been making strenuous efforts to reduce their dependence on the Soviet market and strengthen links with the EC. By 1989 the country's EC trade had grown to 27 per cent of its total and in the following year overtook exports to the whole of Comecon, which had themselves dropped almost one-third.

Hungary's exports to the Community were running at about US$1bn a quarter in 1991, up 56 per cent on the year before. They now account for two-thirds of all Hungarian hard currency trade. Poland has also made a major effort to switch to hard currency trade with the West. During 1990 a large devaluation spurred its exports to rise 15 per cent overall, and those to the EC by 44 per cent. Polish hard currency exports soared from US$500m in 1989 to US$11.5bn in 1990. As for Czechoslovakia, it increased its westward exports by 14 per cent that year, but its imports from the West rose 15 per cent.[2]

The question that haunts the Hungarians and the Poles over their new-found EC export success is 'Can it last?' The signs are that at its present rhythm it cannot. A number of factors are liable to slow the Central Europeans' new trade relationship with the West, and they could yet turn it from a dream into a nightmare.

To begin with, the former Comecon members are likely to suck in more imported goods than they can export. They will be obliged to import Western equipment on a massive scale to modernize their industries, and they are also likely to attract consumer goods as they open up to trade with the West.

'There will be a strong increase in Eastern European exports to the Community', comments EC Commission official Antonino Pitrone, who is an Eastern European trade expert. 'But I also have a feeling the EC's traditional trade deficit with Eastern Europe will turn into a surplus. Look at the Eastern Europeans' hunger for Western goods.'

They will need to boost their hard currency earnings sharply in order to pay for these imports and to service their growing foreign debts. In the medium term, they risk being swamped by imported goods. Poland, for instance, achieved a US$3bn surplus in its balance of payments in 1990, but this is expected to have turned into a US$5bn deficit by the end of 1991.

Trade analysts fear that the Eastern Europeans' lack of competitiveness will be an enormous handicap. They point out that during the 1980s the shares of Eastern European trade in the rich markets of the OECD industrialized nations decreased in all cases except that of Hungary.[3]

Why the trade barriers could be going up

To stem the tide of imports, the Eastern Europeans are already finding themselves tempted to introduce trade barriers. Some of the newly democratic governments of Central Europe feel that the liberal import policies they have introduced could handicap their domestic economic reform programmes unless tempered with some form of import controls. 'We are naked', says Peter Palecka, Director General for Multilateral Trade Policy at Czechoslovakia's Foreign Trade Ministry.

By mid-1991 the Czechoslovak federal government was casting around for ways to introduce 'temporary protection' for its industries. Its complaint is that it has dismantled almost all of its tariffs and import licences, yet has received little compensatory advantages from the European Community. 'We're still puzzling over the precise workings of the GSP', comments Palecka on the EC's decision in October 1990 to extend to the whole of Eastern Europe the easier trade terms of its Generalized System of Preferences.

The protectionist mood is to be found elsewhere. In April 1991, Andrzej Zawislak, Poland's Industry Minister, called for import tariffs to protect Polish industries. 'No country has ever had as liberal an import policy as we have at the moment, and something has to be done', he said.

The West, meanwhile, does not necessarily urge the total abandonment of trade protection by the former Comecon countries. Pablo Benavides, who heads the Brussels Commission's Eastern Europe directorate, recalls an offer by one of the three Central European countries to adapt its tariff levels to those of the Community. 'It was a suicidal idea. Happily, we talked them out of it.'

Much the same advice was given to the USSR by the International Monetary Fund. In its report on the Soviet economy it warned the USSR against trying to move suddenly to free trade and advised a set of temporary import tariffs of up to 30 per cent.[4]

For the Eastern Europeans and the USSR to maintain some degree of trade protection from their Western competitors presents no real problem. The important thing to avoid will be protectionism by the former Comecon trade partners against one another. A spiral of trade barriers and competitive currency devaluations, aimed at giving their exporters an edge, could deal a serious blow to trade in the region.

Comecon reborn

Soviet proposals to replace Comecon with a new body named the Organization for International Economic Cooperation (OIEC) have been greeted with reserve by most Eastern

European governments. Moscow's refusal in 1990 to heed requests by Poland and Czechoslovakia, echoed by others, that Comecon's switch to hard currency trading should be phased in over three to five years has not endeared the USSR to its former partners.

For wider political reasons that are easily understandable, the Eastern European countries like to feel they have shut the door on Comecon. Laszlo Csaba, a leading Hungarian trade expert, summed up the feeling when he told companies in Hungary that the best advice he could give them regarding the Soviet market was: 'Forget it as quickly as possible.'[5]

It was, however, the wrong advice. Comecon must be reborn, if not as an institution then as a functioning trade network. Determined steps have to be taken to prevent trade from drying up any further among the Eastern European countries and between them and the USSR.

In spite of all the euphoria about the increases in East-West trade, it may be a long time before the European Community trades with Eastern Europe on a really substantial basis. At present only 6 per cent of EC trade is with the Eastern Europeans, while the much smaller Scandinavian countries grouped with Switzerland and Austria in the European Free Trade Association (EFTA) account for 25 per cent of the Community's trade.

The Eastern European countries cannot expect their increased exports to take up all the slack from their lost business in the USSR. Hungary's greatly increased exports to the West in 1990 compensated for only one-third of the drop in its Comecon trade. At the other end of the spectrum, a country like Bulgaria could take decades to find new markets to replace those of Comecon, which have been taking nearly 70 per cent of its exports.

A new trade mechanism is needed that can help to re-establish Comecon's trade patterns. Some Eastern European governments, notably the three Central European ones, have been discussing the setting up of a free trade zone. That would certainly discourage protectionist tendencies and would also provide a framework for economic cooperation. The more important first step, however, is to establish a payments system.

The success of any new post-Comecon trade structure depends on its having a reliable system for settling trade payments between the Eastern European countries without their needing to use hard currencies like dollars and Deutschmarks.

The Eastern European countries are well aware of this and have themselves been discussing new clearing systems that would overcome the difficulties of not having fully convertible currencies of their own. 'It would be absurd and impractical to ignore intra-Eastern European trade', comments Janos Martonyi, Secretary of State at Hungary's Ministry of International Economic Relations. He notes that Hungary and the USSR intend to set up a bilateral payments system that would probably involve settlement of trade debts on a monthly basis.

The case for an Eastern European payments union

A number of bilateral clearing arrangements are likely between the former Comecon partners. It would make much more sense, though, for a multilateral payments system to be set up that would cover all trade in the region. It could be operated under the aegis of the proposed OIEC successor to Comecon, but it would probably make more sense for it to be funded by the Group of 24 industrialized nations and operated by the European Commission in its role as the G-24 coordinator.

The model for an Eastern European Payments Union (EEPU) is widely held to be the clearing system that was introduced in 1950 in Western Europe as part of the Marshall Plan. Called the European Payments Union (EPU), it played a crucial part in the regeneration of trade in post-war Europe at a time when European currencies were unconvertible and there was a severe shortage of dollars.

The EPU was set up with US$350m provided by the United States, and that comparatively small amount of money was the kernel of a system that enabled billions of dollars-worth of trade to flow between the nations of Europe. Until the advent of the EPU, traders in post-war Europe had found themselves trapped by the absence of a reliable basis of credit on which to make cross-frontier deals. Exports were usually done on a barter basis or as part of ponderous bilateral government-to-government agreements.

The impact of the EPU on Europe's stagnating trade flows was immediate. The 15 Western European nations involved were able to settle their trade payments on a monthly basis, and their industries found themselves free to buy and sell in the knowledge that exchange controls would not prevent invoices from being paid.

The mechanism adopted by the EPU was for each participating nation to be given a monthly credit quota that reflected its size and its foreign trade activity with the other countries in the union. When settlements day came round each month, those countries that had a deficit in their trade inside the union were able to draw on their credit quota, but had also to pay for a proportion of the money owing in gold or dollars drawn from their own convertible reserves.

It was not the seed money that was important but the agreement of the EPU's members to grant one another credit to cover trade. The purpose of the US$350m float was to cover the time lags between settlements by the countries in the union. The sums of money involved in the settlements system soon blossomed into much greater amounts.

The surge in exports and imports across Europe that followed the EPU's introduction led to rapid economic growth. As the economies of the Western European nations strengthened, so too did their currencies. In 1957 the European Community was launched by its six original members – France, Germany, Italy, Belgium, the Netherlands and Luxembourg – and by 1958, when most European currencies had become convertible again, the EPU could be disbanded.

Trade economists believe a broadly similar payments union could have a very positive effect on the economies of Eastern Europe. Jozef van Brabant, a member of the United Nations Secretariat in New York, is a leading advocate of a new payments union. He calculates that such a settlements system could be set up with a fairly small float, depending on which countries would be grouped in it, and would quickly pay handsome dividends in increased trade.

Van Brabant's preference would be for a Central European Payments Union (CEPU) which would link Poland, Hungary and Czechoslovakia, and possibly the USSR. He is doubtful about the advantages of including the USSR if its pledges to undertake economic reform remain unfulfilled. Because the Central Europeans' trade with one another is broadly in balance the float would be only US$5-6m, says van Brabant. If the union were to be a wider Eastern European one that included the USSR it would require a capital fund of at least US$2.5bn.

Hungarian economist Attila Szilassy believes that the need for a payments union is urgent. 'One of the biggest dangers to East-Central European recovery', he warns, 'is the introduction of the dollar clearing of Soviet trade. This threatens to slow down the reform process by creating balance of payments difficulties.'

Szilassy continues: 'Trade among the East-Central European states is at an extremely low level and dependence on the USSR is high. Trade is hindered by the lack of hard convertible currencies and credit facilities. In the short term the establishment of a CEPU could help to fill up the financial gap created by higher Soviet oil and energy prices.'

Szilassy's estimate is that a CEPU would need a capital fund of about US$3bn over its first three years of operation, and he says that it should be linked with a free trade zone. 'The small countries under balance of payment pressure will be strongly tempted to adopt protectionist policies. This is why the concept of a Central European Free Trade Area (CEFTA) is so important.'[6]

He proposes a CEPU-CEFTA structure that would be loosely attached to the European Community. It would be a halfway house for Eastern Europe on the way to being part of the European Economic Area. For some countries it would be a halfway house on their way to attaining EC membership.

The conviction that a payments union would mark a stage in Eastern Europe's transition to being fully part of the European economy is shared by a number of analysts. Peter Bofinger of the Stuttgart-based Landeszentralbank sees a payments union as a 'useful intermediate stage for the East

European economies in their transition to the full liberalization of their international transactions'.

Bofinger sees an Eastern European payments union as leading the way towards the eventual integration of Eastern Europe into a wider European monetary framework. It would encourage the Eastern European countries to move towards full currency convertibility.[7]

Richard Portes, a Professor of Economics at London University who also runs the Centre for Economic Policy Research, notes that a payments union would not worsen the convertibility problems facing Eastern Europe, but would not necessarily solve them. 'One could envisage a looser, informal payments union without credit facilities, in which trade surpluses would actually be transferable', he comments. But he stresses that to implement and sustain convertibility the Eastern Europeans would need a currency stabilization fund that the West would have to back with 'ample financial resources'.[8]

The Ecu could replace the transferable rouble (and the US dollar)

The question of convertibility is crucial to the Eastern Europeans' economic well-being. Until their currencies can be freely exchanged against those of Western nations then their foreign trade will be stifled and their economies will stagnate. It is a classic chicken-and-egg problem, of course, for only a buoyant economy will sustain a stable and freely convertible currency.

The term 'convertibility' is used rather loosely by governments, especially when they are seeking to disguise their currency's lack of genuine convertibility. In Eastern Europe, there are many shades of unconvertibility.

Although Poland and Yugoslavia have made determined progress towards currency convertibility, most of the Eastern European nations, including the USSR, have not. Even the Polish and Yugoslav moves are only partial. Poland's 'big bang' of economic reforms in January 1990 introduced 'internal convertibility' which gives legitimate traders, as opposed to speculators, access to foreign exchange provided that in return they surrender their foreign exchange earnings by changing them into zlotys.

Poland's semi-convertibility means that it maintains a ban on capital transactions in and out of the zloty. A similar approach was taken by Yugoslavia, which in December 1989 introduced wide-ranging currency reforms that included convertibility not only for traders but also in a limited way for private individuals. The following year Yugoslavia suffered a massive capital outflow, and to staunch what was threatening to become a haemorrhage it reimposed a measure of exchange control. The country's political problems make a return to full convertibility unlikely.

Czechoslovakia introduced 'internal convertibility' in January 1991. It operates a system of foreign exchange licensing to cover its foreign trade with the West, but has no convertibility system that could support its trade with its former Comecon partners or with countries in the Third World that might be interested in taking some of the industrial products no longer being bought by the USSR.

Hungary, despite the advanced state of some of its economic reforms, had by mid-1991 no formal system for introducing currency convertibility, nor apparently any plans for introducing one. Private citizens are allowed to buy small amounts of foreign exchange every year but there is no sign that the forint will shortly become freely convertible.

Romania and Bulgaria seem very far away from convertibility, and in the USSR the stalemate is unbroken between those economic advisers who tell political leaders to take the plunge into rouble convertibility and those who warn that to do so could precipitate economic collapse.

Free convertibility of these countries' currencies, either with one another or with the hard currencies of the West, is not just around the corner. There is therefore a compellingly strong case for a payments union that would help to overcome the problem by promoting trade, and that could eventually resolve it by pushing its members towards convertibility.

What would such a payments union look like? There seems widespread agreement among European economists that an

Eastern European Payments Union should be based on the Ecu, the EC's accounting unit and embryo single currency. The European Currency Unit, to give it its full name, is a stable and reliable unit that all trade transactions can be measured against, and it is also a powerful political symbol.

'All claims in the union should be denominated in Ecu and exchanged at agreed rates against the Ecu', says Jozef van Brabant of the UN secretariat. The Ecu Banking Association, which groups the European banks that are most active in using the Ecu, agrees. It has proposed that 'a sort of transferable Ecu could be used as a substitute for the transferable rouble. A group of West European banks could participate in the realization of this project by creating a "clearing" for the transferable Ecu'.

The Ecu bankers have also looked closely at the structure for a new payments union. 'It could be based on a grid of fixed parities between the reference currency of the system', which they believe should be the transferable Ecu, 'and the currencies of the participating countries. The setting up of this grid will probably create problems, the complexity of which must not be underestimated, since the prices in these countries have hitherto been heavily administrated and artificial.'[9]

A project for an EC-based payments system for Eastern Europe is being actively promoted by Istituto Bancario San Paolo di Torino, backed by Deutsche Bank and Credit Lyonnais. The European Commission was in mid-1991 still studying the idea, which it is being asked to support financially, and officials from Gosbank, the Soviet State Bank, have been taking part in talks with the three sponsoring banks.

The system would be based on the existing Basle-based Ecu clearing system that was launched in 1986, groups 45 banks and handles Ecus 30bn in transactions every day. The aim would be to launch an Eastern European version by the spring or perhaps the summer of 1992.

Encouraging the use of the Ecu to refloat Eastern Europe's sinking trade would be an important EC contribution. It would also be a highly significant political act. The introduction of an Ecu-based payments union would mean that the European Community was seeking to establish its own

'Euro-currency' as a substitute for the universally accepted US dollar.

The chief drawback would be, of course, that the Ecu is not money. It has only ever been issued in the form of commemorative coins that are in fact worth the gold or silver they are minted in. But that does not mean the Ecu would not serve very well as a *numeraire* for trade credits and payments.

The much more serious obstacle in the way of an Eastern European payments union has been the stubborn resistance of the Eastern European governments themselves. And although some of them may be slowly coming round to the idea as their foreign trade evaporates, much of the initial Western enthusiasm for the idea has died away.

'The trouble is, no one wants it', explains Mario Nuti, an adviser to the EC Commission. He points out that OECD experts in Paris have said it would be 'lethal' to the Eastern European economies if such a payments union were to remove the incentive to achieve currency convertibility. And European Community policy-makers, he adds, are increasingly reluctant to back a payments union 'because it looks like a blank cheque'.

The creation of a payments union was originally urged at government level by the UN's Economic Commission for Europe, which envisaged an important new job for itself as the administrator. Just as the Bank for International Settlements, the 'central bankers' club' in Basle, had run the EPU in the 1950s, the UN ECE was aiming to play a special role in the 1990s. The idea was quickly taken up by the EC Commission and in April 1990 was proposed to the Eastern Europeans by Frans Andriessen, the EC's External Relations Commissioner.

'It was rubbished by them', recalls Michael Leigh, a senior member of Andriessen's personal staff. 'They thought it was a "poor man's solution" to their problems.' Paul Rayment, the UN ECE's chief economist, remembers slightly different reasons for the Eastern European governments' negative reactions. 'They thought it was a crypto attempt to keep Comecon on its feet.'

Almost any EC policy proposal that does not appear to lead straight towards their goal of Community membership risks being rejected by the three Central European governments as a 'sidetrack' or a 'waiting room'. That became the fate of the payments union.

Throughout the summer of 1990 the three governments sent out muddled signals on the issue that convinced Western governments there was little point in proceeding. In June 1990 Hungary rejected as 'untimely' a Polish suggestion for a payments union that would also include Czechoslovakia. Yet Czechoslovakia's finance minister Vaclav Klaus is generally credited with having 'killed' the EC proposal, while Hungary is often seen as the most supportive of a payments union.

There are a few whispers in the wind that Eastern Europe's leaders may be reconsidering the idea, but nothing more than that. In May 1991 Bulgaria's foreign economic relations minister, Atanas Paparizov, called for a payments union as a way of reviving trade, but this was immediately opposed by a number of ministerial colleagues. Peter Akos Bod, Hungary's industry minister, made it clear in the same month that Budapest is not warming to the idea. 'We don't need a new currency or a payments union', he commented, 'we need funds and we need investment.'

Jozef van Brabant, the tireless promoter of a payments union, has no illusions. 'Eastern Europe is against it, the IMF is also resolutely opposed to it, and the EC Commission is divided internally between those officials who still support the idea and those who do not. The chances of an Eastern European payments union are zero.'

There must be no EC export bonanza in Eastern Europe

If the European Community is unable to make things better, through the creation of a payments union, it can at least stop making matters worse. The EC countries' use of export credits is all set to drive Eastern European suppliers out of business. Germany's sales to the USSR, for instance, climbed from US$4.3bn in 1987 to almost $7bn in 1990.

Almost one-third of the financial assistance being granted to Eastern Europe under G-24 programmes is in the form of export credits. Western companies are preparing to mount a sustained export drive in the untapped markets of the former Comecon countries. It is an export bonanza that could do irreparable harm.

The situation is very tricky. The new technology that these Western exporters can introduce to Soviet and Eastern European industries is essential to their modernization. At the same time, the West must be careful not to swamp local suppliers and thus suppress regional trade and local jobs. The risk is that the export credits being made available in support of Western exporters could take business away from Eastern European manufacturers who are struggling to survive.

Two American experts have put forward an ingenious scheme that could counter the ill effects of export credit from the West. Daniel Bond, chief economist at the US Export-Import Bank, which is America's official export credit agency, and Anthony Solomon, a former President of the New York Federal Reserve, suggest that the Western nations should subsidize an export reinsurance scheme that would back Eastern European exports to the USSR.

Bond and Solomon believe that Western companies are now bidding for much of the US$20bn in yearly sales that Eastern European suppliers have traditionally placed in the USSR, and they estimate that Western export credits will ensure that about US$4bn of that is switched to Western companies.

To counteract the unfair advantage of the G-24 nations' export credits, they propose that Eastern European govern-ments should be encouraged to offer credit guarantees. These in turn would be guaranteed by Western governments in case Soviet customers failed to repay the bank loans. The plan's authors say that no immediate outlay would be needed, but that about US$400m should be available to cover possible Soviet defaults.

The need to kick-start a resumption of trade between the USSR and its Eastern European trading partners prompted the idea being advanced by EC Commissioner Sir Leon Brittan. 'If Europe, and the West more generally, is to give assistance to the USSR, why not tie that assistance to the revival of trade between the USSR and the countries of

Eastern and Central Europe?' asked Sir Leon when unveiling his plan in June 1991. This suggestion that financial assistance to the USSR should be spent with Eastern European suppliers has also been put forward quite independently by Poland's prime minister, Jan Krysztof Bielecki.

The lesson to be learned from Eastern Europe's worsening trade crisis is that Western governments cannot just let market forces rip. Eastern Europe could easily be engulfed in a wave of consumer goods and Western industrial equipment that will drown its few entrepreneurs and plunge it into savage balance of payments difficulties.

Yet nor should the West molly-coddle Eastern Europe's industries. If they are given special protection, say by Western export restraint, the inefficient may survive and the incentive to modernize outdated products and processes would be taken away. The likelihood is, though, that the collapse of Comecon's trade flows will weed out the worst of the 'museum pieces' of Eastern European industry. The hard part will be to prevent companies with potential from going under too.

The best that Western governments can do for Eastern Europe is to revive the idea of a payments union, and underpin it with schemes such as the export reinsurance idea and the tying of aid to the USSR by its Eastern European imports.

Eastern European governments that have been reluctant to take part in a payments union should be told that it is a condition of future G-24 and EC aid. The West can be sympathetic to the former Soviet satellites' desire not to return to the 'bloc' from which they have only recently escaped, but the G-24 governments must also be firm. If insisting on the need for a payments union amounts to coercing the Eastern Europeans, it is nevertheless a case of being cruel to be kind.

Notes

1. *Economic Survey of Europe in 1990-91*, by the UN Economic Commission for Europe, April 1991.

2. Ibid.

3. *Assistance to Reforms in Eastern Europe*, by Attila Szilassy, Netherlands Institute for International Relations, February 1991.

4. *The Economy of the USSR.* A study by the IMF, the World Bank, OECD and the European Bank for Reconstruction and Development, December 1990.

5. *Financial Times*, 2 May 1991

6. Szilassy, *op. cit.*

7. 'The Role of Monetary Policy in the Process of Economic Reform in Eastern Europe' and 'A Multilateral Payments Union for Eastern Europe?' Centre for Economic Policy Research Discussion Papers Nos 457 and 458, Peter Bofinger, August 1990.

8. 'The Transition to Convertibility for Eastern Europe and the USSR'. CEPR Discussion Paper No 500, Richard Portes, January 1991.

9. 'Reforms in Eastern Europe and the role of the Ecu'. A report by the Macro-financial Study Group of the Ecu Banking Association, chaired by Alfred Steinherr of the European Investment Bank, Luxembourg, June 1990.

6

Investment:

Getting Capital to Flow Eastwards

The outlook for foreign investment — Disincentives to investment - Where investors are most active — The uncertain future of privatization — Joint ventures: the chief investment vehicle - 'Financial' investments — Increasing the flow of investment — What still needs to be done

---

A new 'club' of influential and distinguished power brokers has lately joined the ranks of the Club of Rome and the Club of Paris. In late April 1991, behind discreetly closed doors, the Club of Moscow was formed. Its aim is to assist in the overhauling of the Soviet economy and to boost Western investment.

The Club of Moscow is not a household name, and does not intend to become one. The world's press paid little heed to its inaugural meeting in Brussels, even though the gathering was addressed by Jacques Delors, the EC Commission's President, and by the then Soviet Prime Minister, Valentin Pavlov.

The Club's members are the heads of major corporations in Western Europe and their opposite numbers at the top of the USSR's industrial Nomenklatura. Western companies involved include such blue-chip names as Shell, Fiat, British Aerospace, Elf-Aquitaine, Smithkline Beecham, Gaz de France, Olivetti, BSN-Gervais Danone and Thomson, to name but a handful. By 1992 the Club intends to close its membership at 50 European industrialists and 50 Soviet leaders.

The Club of Moscow claims to have already chalked up an important success. It points to the USSR's decision in July 1991 to permit the full repatriation of profits by foreign investors as a resounding victory. The Club had used its influential network of members to pound home the message that without that freedom there would never be significant Western investment.

The Soviet authorities took the point. Suspicion and reluctance have in the past been the hallmarks of Soviet officialdom's attitude to foreign investment. But, like the whole of Eastern Europe, they now recognize that Western capital and technology will be vital to their efforts to modernize and regenerate their economies.

It remains to be seen whether the coup attempt of August 1991 and its aftermath of political turmoil will have frightened investors away or, on the contrary, will have allayed their fears by accelerating economic reform.

If not the lifeblood of the new Eastern European market economies, foreign investment will certainly be an essential plasma. Transfusions of Western capital and know-how will be needed to help keep the Eastern European economies alive until their new market mechanisms can begin to function satisfactorily.

If investment funds start to move eastwards once more, Europe might hope to return to the golden years of the late nineteenth century when the combination of Western European capital and Eastern European markets appeared to offer boundless opportunities. Before the Russian Revolution, the largest manufacturing plant operated by Siemens was not in Berlin but in St Petersburg. French private investment played such a dominant role in developing activities such as oil, textiles, railways, mines, minerals, metals and chemicals that Russia was once labelled 'France's Far West'.[1]

Inducing capital to flow to the East will not be easy. The region's huge market of 425 million largely unsatisfied consumers does not in itself exert enough magnetism to counteract the pull of either developed economies or the investment-hungry markets of South-East Asia. And private investment is an area where governments and institutions like the European Commission can do little, other than to help improve the business conditions and economic infrastructures of the host countries.

The former European members of Comecon have so far attracted pitifully little foreign investment. Only 0.5 per cent of all foreign direct investment worldwide has gone to them, calculates Norman Scott, who heads the trade division of the UN Economic Commission for Europe. To a large extent this tiny share of international investment funds reflects the ideological refusal of the former Soviet bloc countries to allow projects that might have 'contaminated' socialism. It also reflects, unfortunately, the deep-seated nature of Eastern Europe's economic difficulties.

By mid-1991 the total amount of investment committed by Western investors to the USSR, Poland, Czechoslovakia, Hungary, Romania and Bulgaria was estimated at US$7-8bn. The figure had risen quite encouragingly from US$5.3bn in October 1990, although UN officials in Geneva stress that as the investment trend strengthens it also becomes more difficult to distinguish between those projects where funds have been earmarked and those where they have actually been spent.[2]

The average size of foreign investment projects in Eastern Europe is small. Although headline figures of tens of millions of dollars have become commonplace in the automobile sector, smaller-scale joint ventures in services and light manufacturing activities bring the average down to US$1.4m per project.

The outlook for foreign investment

The outlook is no more than moderately encouraging. The first rush of interest by Western companies and banks has subsided into a much more cautious rhythm. Political uncertainties and a growing awareness of the scale of the economic problems facing the region have dampened enthusiasm among many would-be investors.

Hungary is far and away the most favoured destination for private investment by Western companies. The Hungarians have received half of all the foreign investments being made in the former Comecon countries. By mid-1991 it was estimated that US$2bn had been committed – most of it to the 8,000 joint ventures that have sprung up, and some to the activities of the 2,000 Western companies that have begun to operate in Hungary.

Some of the companies doing business in Hungary are household names, such as Nestlé, Electrolux, Sara Lee and Ikea. The dynamic effect on the Hungarian economy may eventually be considerable. The Hungarians maintain that already as much as 25 per cent of their export earnings are being contributed by joint venture companies.

For other Eastern European countries, though, the flow of Western investment has been much less encouraging. Poland had received only US$350m by mid-1991, Czechoslovakia some US$500m, Romania US$150m and Bulgaria virtually nothing following its decision in March 1990 to default on its US$10bn foreign debt.

The USSR remains the largest single recipient of foreign investment, with about US$3.5bn in early 1991. On a *per capita* basis that is much less impressive, of course, and foreign investment in the USSR has been growing at a much slower rate than in Eastern Europe as a whole. Doubts about the collapsing economy and the commitment of the Soviet government to economic reform have had a discouraging effect. Much the same can be said of Yugoslavia, where the comparatively healthy total of US$1.2bn in foreign investment at the end of 1990 has since been frozen by the deteriorating political situation.

These amounts are, however, a fraction of the investment spending that the Eastern European countries need and can reasonably aspire to. Foreign investment in a healthy and developing industrial economy such as Spain contributes some 1.5 per cent of the Gross Domestic Product. If, for example, Poland were to achieve that, it would receive over US$3bn a year in Western investment.

The hard and fast figures under discussion by Western companies add up to considerably less than that. When 128 major corporations with annual sales or assets of US$1bn or more were asked their investment intentions in Eastern Europe, two-thirds answered that they are planning to invest and 42 per cent were already investing there. But the total amount destined to be invested by them was no more than US$3.3bn over five years, which came down to an average of less than US$15m yearly per investor.

The authors of the report, management consultants DRT International, found grounds for optimism. They believe that much more foreign investment is in the pipeline than these figures appear to suggest. 'The results of our survey lead us to believe', they commented, 'that corporate investment commitments of anything from US$20bn to 50bn may well be on the drawing boards, earmarked for Eastern Europe.'[3]

The survey revealed a sharp contrast in attitudes between Japanese corporations and European and North American ones. The Japanese account for about US$1bn, or one-third of the likely investment spending, but intend to place that in large-scale, long-term projects rather than the smaller and more immediate projects favoured by Western investors.

The intentions of Japanese investors are scrutinized carefully in Europe's boardrooms, because Japan's industrial giants are seen as bell-wethers of economic growth. So far, Japanese business has treated Eastern Europe with extreme caution. Only US$20m in private investment had been put into the whole of Eastern Europe by the Japanese in mid-1991, and a survey by Japan's Association of Corporate Executives found that only 26 Japanese companies had plans to invest 'substantially'. The uncertain economic prospects of Eastern Europe are a major factor, and so too is the USSR's continuing refusal to discuss a settlement over the disputed Kuril Islands chain in the Pacific.

Leaving aside Eastern Germany, where Western German investment is expected to triple during 1991 to reach DM 10bn, it is clear that there is to be no Klondike-style Gold Rush of Western investors in Eastern Europe. Quite apart from the uncertainties and shortcomings of the emerging market economies, there remains considerable doubt about the sort of investments Western capital may have in mind.

Are investors looking, for instance, for low-wage assembly plants from which to serve world markets? Or are they looking for more sophisticated manufacturing operations that could serve the whole Eastern European market? Do they view their investments in relation to the Eastern Europeans' modest purchasing power, or in relation to their own global market share? Do they envisage their investments as part of a pan-European economy and, if so, how soon do they expect to get full access to EC markets?

Disincentives to investment

The disincentives confronting Western investors are legion. There are the problems of unconvertible or only partially convertible currencies. There is continuing uncertainty in many Eastern European countries over property ownership. Banking and financial services are rudimentary. Company and commercial law is often non-existent.

In addition to that there are the more obvious problems of possible political instability in infant democracies, the economic shocks that stem from adjusting to a market system, and the heavy burdens of foreign debt and neglected infrastructures.

EC Commission officials believe that Western investors are influenced by what they term 'circles of political instability'. Pierre Buigues, a development expert at the EC Commission, draws a set of concentric rings to demonstrate the position. At the centre are the three Central European countries – Poland, Hungary and Czechoslovakia – where investors believe the risks of political instability are comparatively low. The next ring represents Bulgaria and Romania, where the likelihood of political upset is that much greater. The outer ring, representing the maximum threat of political uncertainty, is of course inhabited by the USSR and Yugoslavia.

Disincentives to investment in Eastern Europe go much deeper than political risk. They also reflect the cultural differences that still mark the former socialist countries' approach to industry and employment. Eastern Europeans are not finding it easy to convert to the flexibilities demanded by a market economy.

In a report to EC governments and the European Parliament, the EC Commission summed up the more serious problems. These included poor levels of industrial competitiveness, obsolete capital equipment, inadequate and old-fashioned infrastructures ranging from transport to energy and financial services to telecommunications, overmanning and structural for most basic necessities.

The study left little room for doubt that foreign investment holds the key to the economic rebirth of Eastern Europe. 'The success of the economic reforms', it stressed, 'depends largely on support being provided by the industrialized countries, notably by businesses in those countries that are capable of improving through cooperation the technological content, performance and structures of the economies making this transition.' It also made it plain that the vital first step towards attracting these investors is for the host countries to improve their basic infrastructures.

The report cited as further disincentives to foreign investment the scale of countertrade and barter when exporting goods from one Eastern European country to another, and the difficulties of obtaining supplies of both raw materials and high-quality semi-manufactures. Above all, it identified the lack of transparency in Eastern and Central Europe that makes it hard for investors to identify specific difficulties. 'There is a serious problem of transparency as regards the real industrial situation which is deterring foreign investors.'[4]

Illustrations of what the Commission's experts had in mind are not hard to find. From banks to chemical companies, Western European managers involved in joint ventures have often been appalled to find how backward are their new business partners.

When Belgian glassmaker Glaverbel bought an initial 40 per cent stake in Czechoslovakia's Sklo-Union in November 1990, it discovered an astonishing level of overmanning. The Czech glass company's 9,500 employees amounted to 50 per cent more than the workforces in all Glaverbel's 27 plants in Europe, North America and Morocco. In Hungary, where General Electric of the US snapped up the highly-prized Tungsram lighting company, it has emerged that GE intends to gradually slice the 15,000-strong payroll by one-third.

Some major companies admit to being thoroughly discouraged by the high manning levels in State-owned industries.
John Mitchell, head of Eastern European operations of the major
British chemicals group ICI, has explained why ICI has not been
eager to switch from exporting some US$300m-worth of goods a
year to the region to investing there instead.

'They've got far too many people', says Mitchell of ICI's
decision not to buy any of the several Eastern European
chemical companies it has looked at. 'The management is awful.
The motivation is to maintain the perks. There may be pollution
under the ground, and the safety and health in the plant is
substandard. In many cases, they would have to pay us for it to
be profitable.'

The poor state of the Eastern European countries' industrial
and business fabric is a major drawback. The most serious
disincentive is the lack of infrastructure in services such as
transport, telecommunications and banking.

Telecommunications is perhaps the greatest barrier of them
all. If Western investors cannot link their new operations in
Eastern Europe to their activities elsewhere, they are liable to
decide against starting up at all. The gap between Eastern
European telecommunications and those of the developed
world will not easily be bridged.

The OECD in Paris says that there are on average about 12
telephones per 100 people in the six Eastern European countries, as against 40 per 100 in the EC. That puts Eastern Europe
20-30 years behind Western Europe and on a par with many
Third World countries. Just to halve the telecoms gap between
Eastern and Western Europe will cost somewhere between
US$60 and 80bn over ten years.

Western telecommunications companies are vying with one
another to do business with Eastern Europe, and World Bank
and G-24 finance is being made available to fund the modernization drive. Investment in telecommunications infrastructure
totalled US$12.6bn in Eastern Europe in 1990, and is expected to
average US$20bn annually in the years ahead.

Where investors are most active

For all these drawbacks, Western capital *is* beginning to

establish patterns of interest. By no means is all investment in response to Eastern Europe's begging bowls. In a number of key industrial sectors, Western manufacturers are competing fiercely to secure a toe-hold in markets that they judge will before long be thriving and lucrative.

Far out in the lead is the motor industry. Automobile manufacturers foresee boom years in a region where car ownership has been very depressed, while Eastern European governments see the motor industry as the dynamo of their countries' future industrial growth.

Western computer-makers and other electronics specialists have been hanging back because of the region's lack of a sound high-technology infrastructure, but the world's major automobile companies have felt themselves under no such constraint. During 1990, ten companies announced plans that will involve some US$25bn being invested in Eastern Europe. The impact on a host of satellite industries and service sectors is likely to be dramatic.

During the 1980s, car production throughout Eastern Europe became frozen at 2.3 – 2.4 million units a year, leaving car ownership far below Western European levels. In the EC and the United States there are 500 vehicles per 1,000 people, while in Eastern Europe car ownership ranged from a high of 216 cars per 1,000 people in Eastern Germany to a low of 43 per thousand in Romania.

To close the gap would require an extra 23 million cars overnight, and replacement needs thereafter would probably mean there is an annual demand for 5 million cars – rather more than twice as many as are currently being produced.

The company with the longest track record in Eastern Europe is Fiat. The Italian company's first deals with the USSR were in 1922, and the Polski Fiat in fact goes back to before World War II and so pre-dates communism there. Fiat is planning to turn its decades of experience in the region to advantage with an ambitious strategy that stretches from the USSR to Yugoslavia.

In theory, the centrepiece of Fiat's strategy is a US$7bn joint venture project to produce an extra 900,000 cars a year in the USSR. A giant automobile plant – comparable to the one that Fiat built in the late 1960s at Togliattigrad on the banks of the Volga River – is to be built on the Kama River at Yelabuga, about

1,000 kilometres east of Moscow. It is due to be completed by 1996, when it will almost double the USSR's present output of 1.3 – 1.4 million cars a year.

In practice, Fiat's operations in the USSR are developing somewhat differently. The Soviet economic crisis has thrown a spanner in the works of the Yelabuga project. It was put on hold in May 1991, and in the meantime Fiat is expected to take a 30 per cent stake in the Togliattigrad-based Volskij Automobilnij Zavod. It manufactures the Lada and is the biggest Soviet car maker, accounting for 750,000 vehicles a year. Under the new deal, the first phase of the Yelabuga project is being transferred to VAZ's Togliattigrad plant.

The scale of Fiat's Soviet ambitions is impressive, even if the company's plans are not progressing smoothly. But Umberto Agnelli, Fiat Auto's chairman, is cautious about whether it will have a strong dynamic effect on industry elsewhere in the USSR. 'It looks big', he says, 'but in reality it is a financial enclave within Soviet territory which doesn't yet have much of an impact on the economy as a whole.'

In Poland, Fiat is working with both of the established Polish automobile manufacturers – FSM and FSO – and has proposed a US\$2bn investment plan under which it would work with them to completely restructure the Polish motor industry over the next 15 years. In the meantime, Fiat has defeated Daihatsu of Japan to win a contract under which it is providing Warsaw-based FSO with the know-how to produce 120,000 Fiat Tipos a year.

FSM's Bielsko Biala plant in Silesia is to produce 160,000 newly designed Fiat Micros a year, rising eventually to over 200,000. Fiat has emphasized that lower Polish wage costs in fact make the Fiat Micro deal viable at production levels that would not be acceptable in Western Europe.

A question-mark hangs over Fiat's Yugoslav activities, as it must over those of other foreign investors. Before the deterioration of the Yugoslav crisis, Fiat had envisaged the country as an important element in its Eastern European strategy. Its plans call for increasing to a majority shareholding the 18.5 per cent stake it took in 1968 in Zavodi Crvena Zastava (ZCZ), the dominant Yugoslav motor manufacturer which has 70-80 per cent of the domestic market.

Fiat has already begun assembling its Fiat Uno model in Yugoslavia, and has been contemplating transforming its activities there into fully integrated manufacturing operations that would make Italy and other EC markets.

Volkswagen is aiming to become a major player in the Eastern European automobile industry. VW claims it is just ahead of Fiat as Europe's No 1 volume car producer, and has struck a US$6.5bn deal with Czechoslovakia's State-owned Skoda that will eventually raise VW's initial minority stake of about one-third of the equity to a controlling 70 per cent of the Czech motor manufacturer. The deal was won against formidable opposition from Renault and Volvo, and VW has said that it intends to introduce a far-reaching expansion and restructuring pro-gramme that will be similar to its revitalization of Spain's SEAT during the latter 1980s.

VW has embarked on two major investments totalling DM 5bn in Eastern Germany, as well as a more modest joint venture in Yugoslavia. It is to build a 250,000 cars a year integrated manufacturing plant at Mosel, near Zwickau, on the site of an old Trabant factory, and it is modernizing an engine plant at Chemnitz, formerly Karl Marx Stadt and the birthplace of VW chief executive Carl Hahn.

Dr Hahn is in no doubt about the fillip that the unsatisfied markets of Eastern Europe could give to the major European car producers. 'The opening of Eastern Europe', he says, 'is certainly bringing new potential to industrial activity in the Western world. These countries have an almost unlimited demand for modernization and restructuring. Added to that, the introduction of free market economies will in itself mean higher productivity.'

The investments being made by other motor manufacturers have been less ambitious, but nevertheless represent a signifi-cant surge of interest throughout the automobile sector. Stut-tgart-based Daimler-Benz is investing DM 1bn in Eastern Germany, and other European 'quality' car producers are also looking carefully at possible greenfield projects in Central Europe.

Of the US-owned producers, General Motors has announced that it will invest US$150m in Czechoslovakia's Bratislavske Automobilove Zavody (BAZ) in a project to make 250,000 car transmissions a year for export to GM plants in Western Europe. The company, which is the world's largest car manufacturer, is also to assemble 20-25,000 Opel Kadetts and Vectras in Bratislava, beginning in 1992.

In the longer term, GM plans to establish new assembly plants in Eastern Europe that will raise its total European vehicle assembly by a further 25 per cent, to total more than 2 million units, by the mid-1990s. GM has a joint venture with Raba, Hungary's leading producer of engines for buses, in which the Hungarian plant will make 200,000 engines yearly by mid-1992 and assemble a limited number of Opel Kadetts. In Eastern Germany GM is to produce 10,000 cars yearly in a DM 1bn project at Eisenach, and may eventually raise that to 150,000 units a year.

Ford is investing US$80m in a wholly-owned Hungarian plant for the production of ignition coils and electronic petrol pumps. The company clearly has more ambitious long-term plans there, for it has negotiated a 100 per cent tax exemption over ten years, on the understanding that it will be reinvesting most of its profits.

Elsewhere, Japan's Suzuki has undertaken a complicated joint venture involving 62 Hungarian companies, and with the backing of World Bank funds will build a US$230m plant to produce 60,000 Suzuki Swift models a year by 1997. Also in Hungary, South Korea's Hyundai is investing in a plant there to supply automotive parts throughout Eastern Europe.

No other industry presents the same coherent investment picture. The common denominator among potential investors in most other sectors is caution. This is especially true in the information technology sector, where involvement in manufacturing will require a substantial commitment of technological know-how as well as funds. IBM is sniffing around at the possibility of establishing a dealer network in the USSR; Hewlett-Packard is hanging back until Soviet internal affairs become more stable; Siemens indicates that it will serve Eastern Europe from its hugely expanded Eastern German operations, where an investment of DM 1bn will double its labour force to 30,000 people.

High-tech companies such as these are most in demand, of course. The Soviet government has been actively soliciting US

'...mmunism' is dismantled in Prague, 1989   *Photo L Hajsky – Ceteka*

...gary's brief foretaste of freedom: Stalin's statue in Budapest is broken up during the ...sing of 1956   *Photo Popperfoto*

Days of the Iron Curtain: Frontier guard on the Czechoslovak/Austrian bor
1968... *Photo Popperfoto*

... the barriers are rolled back between Austria and Czechoslovakia, Decen
1989 *Photo Ceteka*

ut turn: Soviet tanks enter Prague, August 1968 . . .   *Photo Popperfoto*

d withdraw from the Czechoslovak town of Frenstat, February 1990   *Photo Kurz-Schuh*
rast/Gamma

Greenpeace protests against unsafe Czechoslovak nuclear plant in Bohunice   *Ph*
Schuh – Contrast/Gamma

School children wearing protective masks in the polluted Czechoslovak cit
Mezihori   *Photo V Cech – Gamma*

strial pollution in Estonia   *Photo F Mayer — Magnum*

ution road: A horse drawn cart passes a rubber dyeing factory in Copsa Mica,
nania   *Photo P Dejong — Associated Press*

Romanian refugees make camp at Tourville-La-Riviere, France *Photo G Saussier*
Gamma

Demonstrators against the construction of the Gabcikova – Nagymaros power plant
the Danube form a human chain *Photo Matusz/Interfoto MTI*

ow shopping: A Polish farmer ponders
test in agricultural machinery   *Photo*
eerle – Gamma

o   Picking   in   present-day
d   *Photo F Lochan – Gamma*

Towards a high-tech future: Sigma M5000
computer   assembly   line   in   Vilnius,
Lithuania   *Photo A Uloziavitchus – Gamma*

'All of you at the same time?'

Wałesa (*right*) and Delors (*left*) raise their glasses to the future, Brussels, M
1991   *Photo EC*

Havel (*right*) and Dubček (*left*) celebrate Civic Forum's success, December 1989
I Berry – Magnum

industrial cooperation in the sensitive business of re-converting over 400 military equipment producers to civilian activities. Its 'tanks into tractors' policy has led to the creation of a special investment fund that it is hoped will channel up to US$1bn into converting the Soviet defence industry to making civilian high-tech products. Typical of this strategy is the agreement between Boston investment specialist Batterymarch and the Soviet State Commission on Military-Industrial Production. The idea is that companies in the US, Europe and Japan are to be directed towards opportunities in sectors that include civilian airframe and optics, metallurgy, medical systems and communications.

In areas such as energy, transportation and aviation new partnerships are beginning to emerge in the USSR, although often the Western partners clearly feel constrained by the limitations that continue to be imposed on these relationships. There seems, for instance, little likelihood that Soviet energy resources could be turned over to the free market in such a way as to allow the 'Seven Sisters' of the international oil business access to the sector. The sensitivities that oil provokes were amply illustrated when the republic of Azerbaijan ignored Moscow's wishes and attempted to block a deep drilling project awarded to Macdermott International of the US. The move was prompted by fears of foreign 'exploitation'.

Many US business leaders are anxious to accelerate the pace of industrial cooperation with the USSR. When US Commerce Secretary Robert Mosbacher led a high-powered team of 15 company chairmen to Moscow in 1990, John Murphy of Dresser Industries explained why the visit was significant. 'With full backing at last from the US government, we now have a chance to do good business in the USSR after being badly beaten for years by Europeans who had the government support we lacked', he commented.

During the visit it emerged that Transisco, a US company that had hitherto concentrated on energy transportation in the USSR, was linking up with Soviet aircraft producers Sukhoi, and that Pratt & Whitney together with Israeli suppliers would be cooperating to re-engine Tupolev and Illyushin aircraft.

The area of investment that has the most political importance is consumer goods. For years the lack of fashionable clothing, electronic gadgets and consumer durables emphasized the differences between the Communist and Western cultures. Now some of these goods are beginning to be made in the East.

In the USSR, France's leading cosmetics group l'Oreal has launched a joint-venture manufacturing operation, and RJR Nabisco is planning to open a cigarette-making plant in Leningrad and a biscuits factory in Kashira. Colgate-Palmolive has been negotiating to start production in the USSR, as have Eastman Kodak, 3M and Johnson & Johnson.

In Czechoslovakia, the giant Bata footwear company has reopened after a 42-year absence. In Hungary, the new media barons include such names as Murdoch, Maxwell, and Germany's giant Bertlesmann publishing empire.

The uncertain future of privatization

The privatization policies being pursued by Eastern European governments are a crucially important part of the foreign investment picture. It will be the interest shown by Western companies in investing in traditional heavy industries such as petrochemicals and engineering that will decide the speed and effectiveness of the Eastern Europeans' transition to being market economies.

The different national policies over privatization are examined in Chapter 3. In each country, vital questions have still to be answered about the future course of the privatization programmes being carried out. There are considerable differences between the Polish, Hungarian and Czechoslovak governments over how quickly privatization should be carried out, and how best the people can be given a fair share of the proceeds of sales to foreign investors.

The argument in favour of speed is chiefly that these countries have no time to lose in streamlining their creaking socialist economies if they are to satisfy rising expectations, and thus guarantee their vulnerable new democracies. The argument against scrambling to privatize as fast as possible is that by proceeding more calmly one avoids holding a clear-out sale that commands only bargain prices.

Hungary has been moving the fastest in its drive to sell off formerly State-owned enterprises. The Hungarian government's State Property Agency has made determined efforts to accelerate privatization, and in October 1990 it issued guidelines on 'How to buy a company in 100 days'. The Hungarians have selected 20 businesses, including hotels and department stores, whose sale to foreign investors is seen as a priority. The government has also stated that it is 'open to offers' for all and any of the 10,000 concerns on the State's privatization list.

Poland has adopted a rather more restrained policy. It has a structured privatization programme in which some 40 'flagship' industrial enterprises are being sold off by the end of 1991. Foreign investors have been assured that in practice there will be no limit to the proportion of a company they may buy.

Czechoslovakia is also taking a cautious approach. Government ministers have said they are in 'no hurry' to privatize the country's industries. The sprawling small business sector of State-owned restaurants, shops and services is being sold off to individuals, but privatization of large-scale concerns is being conducted at a more considered pace.

The other two privatization programmes of note are those of Eastern Germany and Romania. Following German reunification, the former has become something of a family matter, for of the 400 companies that by early 1991 had been sold off by East Germany's Treuhand for a total of DM 2.5bn, almost all were bought by West German companies. Indeed, non-German bidders have complained that a secret 'Germans only' policy is being operated there to prevent outsiders from gaining a toehold.

Romania's privatization programme attempts to retain limited State ownership of key enterprises, and is ambiguous about the degree of foreign ownership that will be permitted.

The eventual speed and style of privatization in Central Europe is still unclear. Because of the sheer size of the State-owned sectors, privatization programmes during 1990 and 1991 have been making little impression in the overall problem. The 20 major Hungarian enterprises selected for immediate privatization represented only 1 per cent of State property in that country, while in Poland it has been calculated that on present showing the privatization programmes will take until the end of the twenty-first century to complete.

As the Eastern European countries wrestle with the problems of how best to distribute the proceeds of privatization to the people, potential foreign investors watch with undisguised interest. Issuing share coupons to the populace may sound like a good idea, but is a considerable disincentive to foreign investment. 'If a company has 10,000 shareholders, nobody owns it', notes Sir William Ryrie, executive vice-president of the World Bank's commercial arm, the International Finance Corporation.[5]

The solution that Ryrie and a growing number of experts favour is creating mutual funds or unit trusts that would concentrate domestic ownership and make it easier for foreign interests to deal with. The snag, from a political perspective, is that for the people of Eastern Europe it makes privatization look more like a sleight of hand conjuring trick than a division of the proceeds from becoming a market economy.

Joint ventures: the chief investment vehicle

For the foreseeable future, joint ventures will remain the chief vehicle for foreign investment in Eastern Europe. Partnerships between local interests and Western investors have soared. By mid-1991 over 17,000 joint ventures had been registered in Eastern Europe and the USSR.

Unfortunately, not too much significance should be attached to the gross number of joint ventures. In the USSR only about one-third are actively trading. In all too many cases new joint venture companies have been launched to provide tax or hard currency dodges for domestic entrepreneurs. In Hungary, for instance, 10 per cent of joint ventures are reckoned to be bogus.

Joint ventures vary enormously in their size and character. By no means all of them are small or dubious. The sort that the Soviet government most wishes to encourage is exemplified by the huge US$200m aluminium joint venture that is taking shape in Siberia at Sajanogordsk, on the USSR's borders with China and Mongolia. The Soviets have gone into partnership with a US-Italian group made up of Reynolds Metals, the No 2 US aluminium producer, Fata of Italy, which is supplying technology, and Istituto Bancario San Paolo di Torino.

'Financial' investments

Financial – as distinct from industrial – investment is also increasing, although the lack of banking and financial services makes the business climate in these formerly socialist countries less attractive.

Hungary, which has been the most 'capitalist' of the Eastern European countries since the mid-1980s, had over 30 commercial banks in early 1991. Yet the President of the Budapest stock exchange, Lajos Bokros, went on record with a warning to would-be financial investors. 'In Hungary, portfolio investment has less chance than direct investment', he said. 'It's a miscalculation for foreign investors just to come here with money.'

Western banks and financial institutions have nevertheless begun to take an interest, chiefly in Central Europe and most of all in Hungary. Much of it is aimed at financing trade and investment. Euroventures, the venture capital fund that is owned by leading companies grouped in the European Round Table, such as Asea Brown Boveri, Bosch, Fiat, Olivetti and Petrofina, has launched a US$15m fund aimed at helping traditional Hungarian companies to introduce new production technologies.

Other financing sources include the US$50m Austro-Hungary Fund launched by Merrill Lynch, the leading Wall Street stockbroking and securities firm, the Hungarian Investment Company launched in the City of London by investment managers John Govett, and the First Hungary Fund, sponsored by Bear Sterns of New York and the International Finance Corporation.

The big question is how long it will be before Eastern Europe can boast anything approaching a 'financial centre'. The availability of sophisticated financial services is of crucial importance to inward investors, while the existence of efficient financial markets will be essential to the development of market economies. For the present, though, the list of Western banks with operations in Eastern and Central Europe is still a short one.

Heading the list in the USSR is a consortium formed to provide credits for joint ventures, made up of Banca Commerciale Italiana, Bayerische Vereinsbank, the Austrian Creditanstalt and France's Credit Lyonnais. In Hungary, Istituto

Bancario San Paolo di Torino is engaged in fully-fledged commercial banking, and Citicorp is offering securities trading and investment banking services. French banks have shown growing interest in Eastern Europe, and France's Societe Generale owns 75 per cent of a Czechoslovak joint venture called Societe Generale Komercni Bank which aims to service corporate investors in the country.

Increasing the flow of investment

One of the most visible parts of the drive to promote private investment in Eastern and Central Europe is the European Bank for Reconstruction and Development, generally known by its French acronym BERD. Launched in the spring of 1991 to a fanfare of publicity, the BERD has at very least succeeded in capturing the European public's imagination.

It is far from being the only vehicle for promoting investment, and it remains to be seen how prominent a part it will play in the West's efforts to help develop the market economies of Eastern Europe. So far, the BERD's own political problems have provoked many of the headlines in its clippings book.

The new bank, headed by Jacques Attali, a former close aide of France's President Francois Mitterrand, has had some difficulty in establishing a positive relationship with a number of the relevant officials in Washington. Of the 40 governments backing the BERD, the US was notable for withholding its ratification of the project until the very last moment.

The London-based BERD has attracted a team of top-level economists and financial specialists from Eastern Europe, the USSR, Western Europe and North America. By early 1991 - several months before it officially came into being – the BERD was hard at work evaluating some 200 possible investment projects. It announced its first investment in June 1991, which was a US$50m loan over 15 years to a Polish bank based in Poznan to finance energy efficiency projects.

How soon the BERD will start to make its mark on the economic situation in Eastern Europe is still unclear. Some experts believe that at the earliest it will be 1993 or 1994 before the first fruits of the BERD's efforts will be seen. Jacques Attali is concerned that if the BERD is tempted into financing risky short-term projects it may endanger its own credit rating on the international capital markets. His concern also reflects suspicions that the BERD's initial capital of Ecu 10bn will quickly prove too modest.

The BERD does not intend to restrict itself to being only an investment fund. Attali's prospecting trips to Eastern European countries have indicated that BERD experts are being offered to governments there as advisers on their privatization programmes. If the BERD develops an economic and legal advisory role, it will emerge as a force to be reckoned with in Eastern Europe.

As a high profile newcomer, the BERD has grabbed many headlines. But it is far from being the only player in the investment field. Its efforts will be just part of the array of programmes and instruments being operated by the European Commission, the European Investment Bank, the World Bank and the International Monetary Fund.

The EC Commission has the job of refereeing the game and of playing in it too. Following the July 1989 decision that the Commission should coordinate the efforts of G-24, Brussels has become the focal point for government-level investment efforts.

Most of the PHARE and G-24 projects are directed at non-investment areas, but some are specifically targeted at public investment needs. In telecommunications, for instance, the EC member states have launched a special assistance programme to help upgrade the very poor telecoms networks that are such a major disincentive to foreign investment. Worth Ecu 500m in 1990, Ecu 820m in 1991 and Ecu 980m in 1992, the telecoms investment action is being handled in the medium term under the G-24 aegis, and in the longer term is due to become a BERD responsibility.

High-tech activities such as telecommunications are not the only area where EC funding is helping to restructure Eastern European industry. European Coal and Steel Community (ECSC) loans worth up to Ecu 200m have been earmarked for investment in the modernization of the Polish, Czechoslovak and Romanian steel industries.

The EC Commission has also begun to turn its attention to improving the financial climate in which Community-based investors must operate if they begin manufacturing operations in Eastern Europe. The argument is that many potential investors will only set up in Eastern Europe if they can be sure of exporting goods from low-wage operations there to world markets.

The EC Commission has therefore proposed to member governments that an EC export reinsurance scheme should be set up. Major EC contracts with a lifespan of two years and over would be underwritten by the pool, which would in effect strengthen cooperation between national export credit guarantee agencies in the Community. The pool is due to cover trade between EC countries and Bulgaria, Czechoslovakia, Hungary, Poland, Romania and Yugoslavia.

What still needs to be done

To many observers familar with the way that EC policy-making tends to march at the speed of the slowest member state, the Community's response to the challenge of channelling investment spending eastwards has been surprisingly swift. But there remain areas where both EC-level and G-24 actions could clearly be improved or given sharper focus.

The view of both the development economists and industrial policy experts in the Commission is that the Community's primary role in encouraging investment is to help to lay the groundwork in terms of road and rail communications, more efficient use of energy, the introduction of electronics-based streamlining, common business and technical standards and the nurturing of an entrepreneurial culture.

The cultural point is important. OECD small-business expert Sergio Arzeni has stated in a report to the OECD's Centre for Cooperation with European Economies in Transition (CCEET) that in Eastern Europe 'the dominant culture is still anti-SMEs (small and medium-sized enterprises)'. Arzeni has called for an ambitious effort to foster entrepreneurship in these countries.

The drawback, with the entirely laudable emphasis from both the EC Commission and OECD on overhauling Eastern Europe from the ground up, is that it requires a time-frame that looks politically vulnerable.

Time is short if the Eastern European economies are to be turned around before popular dissatisfaction becomes a serious problem. Democratization and the embracing of the market economy have raised expectations high, even though the more realistic analysis was always that the switch away from socialism would in the short run depress living standards quite substantially. If the EC and other Western nations wish to guarantee Eastern Europe's new-found democracy, steps must be taken to offset the unemployment and depressed incomes that must result from the greater efficiencies of the marketplace.

The best way to relieve the political tensions that will arise in Eastern Europe is to increase the flow of new investment in the region. So far, much of the investment interest by major Western corporations has been window-shopping.

Notes

1. Jean-Baptiste Duroselle, *Europe – A History of its Peoples*, Librairie Academique Perrin, France, 1990.

2. 'Foreign Direct Investment, Joint Ventures in Particular, Among the Pentagonal Countries,' by Norman Scott, Director, Trade Division, United Nations Economic Commission for Europe, 14-16 October 1990, and the July 1991 issue of the UN ECE newsletter *East-West Joint Ventures*.

3. *Corporate Investment Plans for Eastern Europe*, DRT International, Brussels, September 1990.

4. 'Industrial Cooperation with Central and Eastern Europe – Ways to Strengthen Cooperation'. Communication from the EC Commission to the Council and the European Parliament, SEC (90) 1213 final, 13 July 1990.

5. Sir William Ryrie, *Financial Times*, 4 February 1991.

7

Immigration:

The Spectre of Mass Migration from the East

Forecast of millions moving westwards — Will the West welcome immigrants? — Europe's immigration nightmare — A liberal regime is also a brain-drain — Why free movement between East and West is essential — Towards an EC immigration policy

---

A full moon illuminated the landscape with chilling clarity. The ground that stretched across to where the frontier lay was bathed in sharp white moonlight that would betray the slightest movement. The starry southern European night sky was bright enough to read a newspaper by.

Eugen Szekely and his two companions huddled in the shadows cast by a row of vines. Tormented by indecision, they debated in whispers what to do next. The guide who had charged them each ten months' salary to bring them across the hills to within a few hundred metres of the border had gone, and ahead lay the unexpectedly moonlit plain of the high-security frontier zone. They cursed themselves for not checking the lunar calendar.

It was 3 am on the morning of Saturday, 16 September 1989. First light would be in less than two hours. With their hearts in their mouths they picked their way across soggy ground that sucked noisily at their feet. With a sense of relief they reached a field of maize standing seven feet tall, but hurriedly abandoned it on finding that the dried leaves and stalks made enough racket to waken the dead.

The border itself proved to be no more than a wide band of carefully raked earth, and a tripwire that glinted wickedly in the moonlight. Beyond it a river ran swiftly between deep banks. With a prayer that the raked earth was intended solely to record footprints and not to conceal landmines, the three young men crossed from Ceaucescu's Romania into Yugoslavia.

In a wood on the outskirts of the little Serbian town of Bella Crkva they changed their sodden clothing for western-style jeans and tee-shirts that would attract less attention. They had several hours to while away until their rendezvous with the car that would take them 400 kilometres across Yugoslavia to the Austrian border.

Eugen Szekely and his two friends were in many ways typical of the political refugees who were prepared to risk jail sentences to flee from Ceaucescu's Romania. Szekely, a 25-year-old electronics engineer, had nursed dreams of escaping from the oppressive Ceaucescu régime since boyhood. A year earlier he had tried to flee, but had been forced to give up the attempt and had returned home disconsolately to Timisoara.

As he dozed fitfully in the car that bore him across northern Yugoslavia, Szekely thought of the system he was quitting and the new life he would make for himself and his wife Raluca in Belgium, which he had somewhat arbitrarily selected as the country in which he would settle. His stubborn refusal to follow both his father and mother into the ranks of the Communist Party had made him a marked man, whose pitiful monthly salary of lei 3,000, or US$20, was unlikely to improve. In Belgium, he reflected, he would be master of his own destiny.

Szekely's attempt to cross into Austria ended in arrest and imprisonment. Eventually, though, he talked his way out of a refugee camp near Belgrade and into Hungary. By late October he was on his way to Budapest. Belgium still beckoned as strongly as before, and on the night of 30 October he stole quietly past the frontier posts at the main crossing into Austria. He reached Brussels two days later.

Like so many Eastern European immigrants before him, Eugen Szekely soon found that his welcome was less than rapturous. 'You see all that stuff on television here about supporting freedom and democracy in Eastern Europe', he observes sourly, 'but it doesn't mean a lot.'

With the fall of Nicolae Ceaucescu in December 1989, the Belgian immigration authorities decided that Szekely was not a political refugee but rather an economic immigrant, and consigned him to a bureaucratic limbo. He has a job in a Belgian electronics company that pays a technician's wage, even if his employers are happy to make use of his more advanced abilities, and he and his wife can be deported from Belgium with three days' notice.

The Szekelys are thinking about trying for Canada or Australia, where prospects for an electronics engineer look better and where Raluca may be able to resume her career as a dentist. Both feel a sense of betrayal, because they had for so long looked to Western Europe as a symbol of freedom and hope.

Eugen and Raluca Szekely are among the first of what may be millions of emigrants from Eastern Europe who could come flooding westwards in search of a better way of life. Now that the borders are open, young people and those with marketable skills may well choose to exchange the rigours of life in Eastern Europe or the Soviet Union for what they hope will be the comforts of the West. It is a prospect that raises crucial questions about the future policies of Western European nations towards these emigrants.

Forecast of millions moving westwards

'I have no doubt that millions of Soviet citizens will go to seek jobs in the West, when it becomes possible', comments Vladimir Chemiatenkov, who was the Soviet ambassador to the EC from 1989 to 1991. Thanks to the new law relaxing Soviet restrictions on emigration, he says, 'emigration will become very substantial, because people work very hard in the USSR yet are paid miserable wages. There is a very widespread view that life is better in the West.'

Ambassador Chemiatenkov believes that once the flood-gates are opened by the Soviet authorities, 2-3 million Soviet citizens would seek to emigrate to the West. 'There is a tradition of mobility among the Soviet people', he points out. 'One and a half million people move every year to northern and eastern parts of the USSR, attracted by wage differentials. A major factor will be that they have no property to lose by emigrating westwards.'

Trying to forecast how many people in the USSR and elsewhere will abandon everything and move westwards in the next few years is little more than a numbers game. There have been 'scare' predictions, one by no less an authority than the Interior Ministry of the USSR, of an exodus of over 7 million people from that country. And already the volume of emigrants from the East has risen sharply. During the 1970s and 1980s no more than 100,000 people moved to the West every year. In the 12 months after autumn 1989 the figure rose to 1.3 million.[1]

Vladimir Scherbakow, who headed the Soviet delegation to a major conference organized in Vienna by the Council of Europe in January 1991, took a rather more moderate view. He told the Conference on the Movement of Persons that Soviet emigration might be between 1.5 and 2 million people a year 'for the next couple of years'. He added that surveys in the USSR currently show that between 5 and 6 million people 'are not satisfied with their present work or with their social conditions'.

As to Eastern Europe, the number of emigrants who may try their luck in the West is also anyone's guess. Estimates tend to be extrapolations of unemployment figures that are themselves forecasts. Even so, falling living standards and ethnic tensions could mean that the transition of Eastern European countries towards becoming market economies will be marked by the departure of millions of able-bodied people.

Several key factors will determine the scale of the emigration problem.

- The degree of unrest in the USSR and in Eastern Europe. If the economic and political crisis of the USSR leads to its disintegration, and that in turn triggers strife and perhaps even civil wars between ethnic groups, tens of millions of people could be uprooted. Refugees from civil unrest in the USSR and Eastern Europe will have some prospect of being received by the EC as 'asylum seekers'.

- The willingness of Western Europe to accept immigrants. The public mood towards immigrants from the East will influence the level of entry conditions. Immigration will increase competition for jobs and housing, although it can also have positive side-effects. By swelling the labour supply it can help to generate economic growth and greater prosperity.

- The ability of Western European countries to create jobs that will provide employment for immigrants. A major training effort would probably be needed to equip Eastern Europeans with the skills needed to compete in the Western jobs market.

- The willingness of Eastern European countries to accept Soviet immigrants. In the event of a mass migration from the USSR, its neighbours in Eastern Europe would become transit routes for those heading West. They would also be the final destination of some refugees, particularly those who fail to gain admission to Western Europe. The Eastern Europeans' policies will be of key importance.

- The degree to which Eastern Europeans and the USSR will permit unchecked emigration. If the newly democratic governments of Eastern Europe are to remain true to their ideals of freedom and individual liberty, they will not impede emigration. But they risk opening up a brain-drain that could damage their efforts to restructure and streamline themselves into market economies. Their best brains are likely to be among the first wave of emigrants.

Will the west welcome immigrants?

It was no accident that Vienna played host to the Council of Europe's Conference on the Movement of Persons. Austria has received 2 million people from Eastern Europe over the post-war years, of whom about one-third settled there permanently. Austrians fear that the melting of the Iron Curtain will see their country engulfed in a sea of immigrants. In 1990, as Eastern European countries relaxed their border controls, Austria introduced visas for Poles, Bulgarians and Romanians and posted extra military units to patrol the frontier with Hungary.

The welcome that awaits Eastern Europeans is uncertain. The Vienna conference yielded no more than a bland final communiqué. The representatives at Vienna of the 35 governments that are signatories to the European Conference on Security and Cooperation (CSCE) could agree only on a text that spoke of controlling migration by keeping would-be emigrants inside their country of origin and discouraging illegal immigration through the misuse of tourist visas.

The communiqué no doubt came as a disappointment to any Eastern European governments that had been hoping the West would welcome their return to democracy by opening wide the borders. The enthusiasm in the West that greeted the fall of the Berlin Wall in November 1989 has since been tempered by more hard-headed attitudes.

Even in Western Germany, the welcome extended to fellow Germans from the East is becoming muted. Trades union representatives in Western Germany have begun to complain about 'cheap labour' from the former GDR and the pressure on accommodation is increasing fast, particularly in what were border areas.

Germany is likely to bear the brunt of immigration from Eastern Europe, and the Bonn government has so far shown itself to be more liberal and progressive in its attitudes than have most other Western European countries. The federal government will nevertheless have to contend with popular attitudes that are often less positive.

In early April 1991, when Germany, Italy, France, Belgium, Luxembourg and the Netherlands lifted their visa requirements for Poles, there were ugly scenes at the German-Polish border. At Frankfurt-on-Oder, some 250 German neo-Nazi youths stoned buses and cars as they crossed from Poland into Germany. Similar incidents have occurred at other border crossing points and there have been violent assaults on Polish visitors to Eastern Germany.

During 1990 as many as 20 million Poles visited Eastern Germany and, above all, Berlin. The disruptive effects of their shopping expeditions and their forays into unauthorized petty commerce to help finance these have provoked considerable resentment among Berliners. Dieter Heckelmann, the head of Berlin's interior department, went on the record in the Spring of 1991 to say that the city could not be expected to tolerate the 'illegal trade, crime and filth' that was being brought in by Polish visitors.

Resentment is being shown by German workers who are suffering as a result of competition from the newcomers. In the building industry, the German Construction Workers Union has called on the Bonn government to stamp out the illegal hiring of low-paid Polish workers.

The impression given by these tensions is unfortunate, for Germany is perhaps the most liberal of all Western European countries as regards Eastern European workers. Bonn has been showing the way to other nations with a range of measures designed to give job seekers from Eastern Europe a chance to acquire skills and experience without settling permanently.

Special 'guest worker arrangements' have been agreed that allow Eastern European workers (unaccompanied by their families) to be employed in Germany for 18 months. The first of these pacts were with Poland and Hungary, and later they were extended to Czechoslovakia and the USSR. The agreements provide, however, for only very small numbers of workers: in the case of Poland 1,000, and for Hungary 500.

Eastern European companies have been granted permission to bring their own employees to Germany when working on a contract there. This applies mainly to the building and construction sector, and the ceiling for such workers is 70,000 people at any time.

Germany has introduced special work permits for Eastern Europeans who live on the border and cross into Germany every day. This system was launched in September 1990 to enable Czechoslovak workers to find jobs in the border zone, and is being extended to cover the German-Polish border.

It is doubtful that the federal government in Bonn will be prepared to relax entry conditions much further. Germany's constitution guarantees entry to all people of German origin, and during the 18 months to the end of 1990 more than 700,000 ethnic Germans from Eastern Europe, the USSR and, of course, Eastern Germany arrived to settle in Western Germany.

Germany is already host to 1.6 million Turks and 600,000 Yugoslavs, and the influx is placing severe strains on the housing and labour markets. Elsewhere in Europe the number of immigrants is already a major problem. France has an immigrant population of 6 million people, and public opinion is set against any substantial increases. In all, there are about 15 million registered immigrants in Western Continental Europe, and experts reckon that illegal immigration brings the true total to nearer 22 million, equivalent to the population of Scandinavia or the Benelux countries.

Europe's immigration nightmare

The prospect of millions of Soviet and Eastern European refugees hammering at the doors of Western Europe is a daunting one, particularly so because it brings into sharp focus the wider immigration problem that most Western European governments prefer to ignore – that posed by North Africa and the Eastern Mediterranean.

The next 30 years will see the populations of the countries along the southern and eastern Mediterranean increase from their present 300 million to about half a billion. To maintain employment at its present inadequate levels these countries will need yearly economic growth rates of 6-9 per cent, rather than their present rates of 3-4 per cent. The likelihood of achieving this seems remote.

The result will be political instability on an alarming scale, and that will no doubt trigger a massive effort by the Western European nations to help develop the economies that they have so far generally overlooked. Inevitably, though, the size of the illegal immigrant population in Western Europe will also increase substantially.

This background picture of Western Europe besieged by North African and Middle Eastern 'boat people' is a crucial element in the situation facing emigrants from Eastern Europe. Western European governments dare not be liberal towards Eastern European refugees for fear of setting uncomfortable precedents. Italy, which has a liberal track record regarding immigration, acted promptly to repatriate Albanian refugees who had fled across the Adriatic in the spring of 1991.

But the pressure from the East will not abate because of that. Soviet Jews have been leaving the USSR at the rate of 1,000 a day, with Israel their prime destination. By 1995 the total number of Jews to have quit the USSR could be 2 million. The Israeli government has warned that it will not be able to accept unlimited numbers.

The emigration of ethnic Germans is also expected to continue. There remain some 1.3 million Germans in Poland and Romania who could yet decide to move to Germany, and there are major ethnic minorities scattered around Eastern Europe and the USSR who could be dislodged by civil unrest.

An estimated 60 million citizens of the USSR close to one-fifth of the country's population, live in republics in which they are an ethnic minority. In Eastern Europe, the arbitrary re-drawing of national boundaries after World War I, with the break-up of Austria-Hungary and the collapse of Tsarist Russia and the Ottoman empire, meant that about a quarter of the region's population became minorities forced to live under foreign rule.

There are 2 million Hungarians living today in Romania, chiefly in the flashpoint area of Transylvania. Other Hungarian communities include 700,000 people in the Slovak republic within Czechoslovakia, 170,000 in the USSR's Ukraine, and 400,000 in the Yugoslav republic of Serbia.

There is, meanwhile, a small community of 10,000 Romanians living in Hungary, and there are 600,000 Romanians in the Soviet republic of Moldavia.

Within the USSR, of course, the ethnic tensions are greater still. There are currently 600,000 refugees within the USSR who have been displaced by strife in Armenia and Azerbaijan.

Unrest and violence will not be the only forces pushing people to migrate. Economic pressures will also intensify. The Strasbourg-based Council of Europe has forecast a sharp increase in the number of economically-driven refugees in Eastern Europe and the USSR.

In a report submitted to the Vienna Conference on the Movement of Persons the Council warned that joblessness could rise to 40 million in the USSR and 5 million in Poland. Average unemployment in Eastern Europe could be 10 per cent, rising to 50 per cent for young people. 'In countries whose borders have long been closed', says the report, 'the young are disillusioned and the temptation to go elsewhere is strong.'

The unknown factor in any future mass migrations will be the attitudes of Central and Eastern European governments. They will be the first stop for Soviet and other refugees on the route westwards.

Hungary's President Arpad Goncz – like Czechoslovakia's Vaclav Havel, a writer by background – has made it clear that Hungary intends to follow a very liberal policy on immigration. During a trip to Brussels in April 1991 he emphasized that Hungary has never closed its own frontiers to refugees, and would not do so even if faced with an onslaught of Soviet immigrants. 'I think that the risks of a mass migration from the USSR have been greatly exaggerated', said President Goncz. 'I don't think we should expect to see more than 1 per cent of the Soviet population leaving their motherland. At the worst, that means that 2 million people would emigrate.' If such a migration were to take place, Hungary would be ready. 'Poor people are used to sticking together', he added.

A liberal régime is also a brain-drain

The challenge that faces the nations of Western Europe is how to construct a more open immigration régime that will not have the negative effect of siphoning off the most talented and highly qualified people in Eastern Europe.

If Western Europe's immigration rules become qualification-based, as is the case with countries like the United States,

Canada and Australia, then the risk is that only the best and the brightest from Eastern Europe would be accepted. If the managerial and professional classes are drawn away, the West will be dealing a severe blow to Eastern Europe's chances of economic recovery. A more liberal immigration policy could easily be counter-productive.

Opinion in Western Europe seems evenly divided over the best course of action on immigration. Catherine Lalumière, the Council of Europe's secretary-general, advocates a much more open approach. She had only stern words for the EC when she addressed the Vienna conference. 'The anti-immigrant reflex is widespread in several Western countries', she said. 'This "every man for himself" temptation has clearly come to the fore within the European Community.'

The view from the Berlaymont is somewhat different. Adrian Fortescue, a senior official in the EC Commission's Secretariat-General, warns that a much more liberal approach would not necessarily improve matters.

'The big question', says Fortescue, 'is whether the Community, in order to appear positive, will do the worst of all possible things and adopt a qualifications-based immigration policy that would cream off all the best scientists.' That sort of Western European brain-drain, he warns, could sap Eastern Europe's precious manpower resources.

Eastern European countries have already begun to experience the effects of an EC brain-drain. Polish experts have noted that the total of almost 60,000 well-educated emigrants who left Poland between 1983 and 1987 was almost the same as the average annual number of university graduates in the country: in other words, a substantial proportion of students at Polish universities try to find work elsewhere. Emigration levels are particularly high among Polish engineers and scientists.[2]

Why free movement between East and West is essential

An EC immigration régime that risks aggravating the brain-drain problem must be avoided at all costs. But the

Community must nevertheless operate an open system that encourages short-term visits to the West.

If the newly democratized countries of Central and Eastern Europe are to be integrated into a pan-European economy, and eventually into the European Community itself, they cannot be fenced out. On a purely practical level, Eastern Europeans need work experience in the West to help them to acquire the skills needed in a market economy.

Part of the European Community's assistance effort is aimed at encouraging short-term visits. Its TEMPUS programme – the acronym stands for Trans-European Mobility Programme for University Students – funds student exchanges. The scheme began modestly enough in 1990 with Ecu 25m being spent on bringing several thousand students from Eastern European universities to spend all or part of an academic year in the West, and has since begun to gather momentum. By 1993 its budget will have risen to Ecu 100m.

It is the sort of approach that Eastern European governments appreciate. Jan Kulakowski, Poland's ambassador to the Community, remarks: 'We don't want to encourage massive emigration. But we can envisage a system that would encourage Poles to visit the Community, be trained there, become imbued with the entrepreneurial spirit and then return to Poland.'

The EC Commission's Adrian Fortescue believes that the Community's answer to the immigration problem will be a system in which exchanges and visits play an important part. 'Community countries', he comments, 'are likely to say, "Come and visit, but don't come and stay". That, after all, is more or less what we say to visitors from other Western European countries that are part of EFTA, and to people from, say, the United States and Australia; and it is what they say to us.'

Constructing a workable EC immigration policy will probably be a good deal more complicated than that. Immigration is one of the most sensitive and jealously guarded national competences of the EC's member governments. Although a set of Community-level immigration rules is clearly called for, there seems little consensus on what they should look like.

Towards an EC immigration policy

The hurdles to be overcome before the EC can operate a common immigration policy are legion. Legally, the subject is a minefield. Immigration is not covered in the EC's Treaty of Rome, although freedom of movement and employment within the Community is promised to EC citizens by the Single Market. The situation of non-EC citizens is a matter for a debate that has not yet taken place. But clearly the 1992 deadline will put pressure on the EC member states to agree on criteria for admission of non-EC passport holders into what will be a single labour market.

The need to bring immigration into the Rome Treaty was touched on when EC heads of government met at the Rome summit in December 1990. It was listed as one of the issues that needs to be tidied up if the EC is to progress towards its goal of political union. But a treaty revision that made immigration more of a Community competence would not resolve the many inconsistencies that are the hallmark of member states' national immigration policies.

Different EC countries have very different approaches to social security and employment rules. They also have different health and housing systems. These differences are the factors that determine a country's level of illegal immigration. In France or Spain, for instance, unregistered immigrant workers find it much easier to find a job and lodgings than, say, in Germany or Britain. The result is, often enough, their systematic exploitation by unscrupulous 'sweat shop' employers.

Before ironing out the differences in their social security structures, however, the EC member states first need to agree their approach to immigration in general and Eastern European immigrants in particular. There is a wide range of opinion in EC countries about the line to be taken.

Some believe that the purpose of a Community-wide approach would be to discourage immigration. France's Nobel prize-winning economist Maurice Allais is among those hardliners who argue that all EC economic assistance to Eastern Europe and the USSR should be made conditional on a total standstill of emigration westwards.[3]

A tough approach can also be found in Britain. Kenneth Baker, the UK's Home Secretary, was uncompromising when he addressed the Vienna conference on migration in early 1991. 'The uncertainty about the prospects of a future increase in immigration from Eastern Europe', he said, 'as well as continuing trends of increasing migration from other regions, underline for us the importance of maintaining effective frontier checks to control the movement of non-Community nationals within the Community, as well as from outside the Community.'

Germany, meanwhile, is anxious to share the burden of Eastern European immigration with its EC partners. It has borne the brunt so far, and Interior Minister Wolfgang Schauble has called for EC-level rules to be agreed concerning refugees, and for a burden-sharing scheme to be instituted under which member states would together shoulder the problem of absorbing refugees from the East. In the European Parliament, Detlev Samland, a German Socialist MEP, has demanded that EC foreign ministers should agree on a system of national quotas for immigrants.

The Community is edging closer to the idea that some sort of cooperation is inevitable. But what sort is unclear. In 1989 the Italian government raised the question of immigration policy at the EC's Strasbourg summit and called for an inventory of the national policies operated by 'the Twelve'. But the EC Commission is meeting considerable resistance from member states. It is plain that many are unwilling to abandon their national rules unless it is in exchange for equally tough EC ones.

Notes

1. Bimal Ghosh, Senior Consultant to the Geneva-based International Organization for Migration, December 1990.

2. *Financial Times*, 12 February 1991.

3. Maurice Allais, 'La Construction Europeene et les Pays de l'est dans le contexte d'aujourd'hui'. To the Third European Construction Symposium, London, 3 April 1991.

8

Agriculture:

The East Could Become the Granary of Europe

The crisis in agriculture: mediaeval and wasteful – One day the granary of Europe? – But first, greater efficiency – What the European Community is doing to help – The importance of access to EC markets – Can access be reconciled with CAP reform?

'The baby food factory I was visiting in Rostov-on-Don was far bigger than anything we have anywhere in the world', recalls Paul Corddry, who runs the giant Heinz group's European operations. 'The scale that plant is built on was breathtaking, but that's about all. Long conveyor belts rolled past, carrying every now and then a solitary jar of baby food.'

Undeterred, Corddry and his fellow executives at Heinz have their own ambitious plans for the USSR and Eastern Europe. They can see the day coming when the fertile agriculture of the region and its peoples' unsatisfied demand for processed food products will create boundless opportunities for Heinz.

'When we look at the big picture', Paul Corddry adds, 'we find the upside outweighs the downside. Eastern Europe is definitely somewhere we'll be doing more and more business.' Heinz already has a major baby foods business in the People's Republic of China, and getting into Eastern Europe holds few fears for the US$6bn a year group. 'All we really need to know', says Corddry, 'is that we can get our money out. Once we have that guarantee, we feel happy to leave it where it is. Then we plough our profits back into local investment.'

If all goes according to plan, in the next few years Heinz will be making its mark in Poland, Czechoslovakia and Hungary, as well as in the USSR. Its burgeoning activities in these countries could well be the shape of things to come, for more and more Western food companies are likely to find irresistible the combination of cheap raw materials and a largely untapped market.

It is vitally important that other companies should follow Heinz's lead, for the economic benefits to Eastern Europe would be substantial. An efficient farm sector together with an internationally competitive foods industry could be the lifebelt that will keep the economies of Eastern Europe afloat while they make the difficult transition to the free market.

The opportunities are boundless. From the fertile black *chernozem* soil of the Ukraine to the rich alluvial plains of Central Europe, the region has the potential not just to feed itself but to help nourish a hungry world. Farming in Eastern Europe and the USSR can offer a prosperous livelihood to tens of millions of people. First, though, years of neglect, restrictive practice and technical backwardness have to be overcome.

If the Eastern European countries can launch a determined agricultural exports drive, they will have developed an important means of earning foreign exchange. A major boost to their exports of food products and bulk commodities could give these countries a vital economic breathing space while they restructure their industries.

The benefits of revitalizing Eastern European agriculture will be much more than purely economic. It would lead to a sounder and more durable relationship between the two Europes. A healthy interdependence would be created if Western Europe were to come to rely much more on food from Eastern Europe. The 'begging bowl' image that Eastern Europe now has would vanish. Eastern Europe is unlikely to bridge quickly the industrial and technological gap that separates it from the West, but it can hold its head high and regain its self-respect if it becomes the granary of Europe.

The big question-mark is not so much over the willingness of Eastern Europeans to improve their agricultural sectors but over the readiness of the European Community to accept a surge of farm exports. For the EC is profoundly schizophrenic in its attitude. It is pouring money and technical expertise into Eastern Europe to help raise farmers' yields, and at the same time it guards its own markets against cheaper produce from the East. Worse, it uses its own export subsidies to deny Eastern Europe's farmers entry to world markets, for the EC easily undercuts even the most competitive food producers.

It remains to be seen whether the radical reform of the EC's Common Agricultural Policy (CAP) being proposed by Farm Commissioner Ray MacSharry will work for or against the interests of Eastern Europe. The EC's 17 million farmers and many of the Community's member governments can be expected to protest loudly against any moves to discriminate in favour of Eastern European farmers. On the other hand, the sacred cow of the CAP may at last be on the point of being slaughtered; the time is ripe for Eastern Europe to urge its cheaper food imports on EC consumers.

The access the Community eventually grants to Eastern Europe's farm exports will be of critical importance. It will help to determine such basic economic conditions as foreign currency earnings, international creditworthiness and employment levels. In short, a restrictive agricultural imports policy could wreck the EC's overall strategy of re-launching the economies of Eastern Europe.

Before Eastern European farmers can become a serious threat to EC farmers, however, they will need to take some very long strides towards greater efficiency. Both the collective farms and the peasant smallholders have achieved wretchedly low levels of output.

The crisis in agriculture: mediaeval and wasteful

The Central and Eastern European countries and the USSR all have huge farming populations, by Western standards, and yet they often cannot feed themselves. Mediaeval farming methods, a lack of machinery and agrichemicals, incoherent investment policies and short-sighted pricing that has favoured the consumer at the expense of the producer are the chief characteristics of Eastern European agriculture.

The sheer size of the farming workforces of these countries is astonishing. In the USSR, one-fifth of the working population is engaged in agriculture, in Poland it is 25 per cent, in Hungary and Bulgaria 20 per cent, and in Romania almost 30 per cent. Even in highly industrialized Czechoslovakia the figure is 12 per cent, or three times the EC's average farm population of 4 per cent.

The size of these farm sectors is matched only by their inefficiency. Yields can be 25-40 per cent below EC levels, and wastage that results from poor transportation and inadequate storage can widen the gap still further. Even with determined modernization backed by the EC through its PHARE assistance programme, Eastern Europe's agriculture will not turnaround overnight. EC experts tend to think it will take 5-10 years for farm productivity in Eastern Europe to reach EC levels.[1]

How structural the problems are of Eastern European agriculture is still unclear. Optimists point out that the freeing of price controls on food in most Eastern European countries has had a dramatic effect on production. Farmers responded at once to the financial incentive of realistic prices. In Poland, Hungary and Czechoslovakia, where farm production had been on a downward path, the trend has been reversed. By mid-1991 all three were self-sufficient in basics like milk and grain and, in some products, were achieving small surpluses.

The pessimists fear that there are nevertheless many profoundly structural inefficiencies to be overcome. Brian Gardner, a leading European agricultural policy analyst, reckons that it will take until the turn of the century before Eastern Europe overcomes its problems and becomes completely self-sufficient. Throughout the 1980s, the region suffered from declining farm output.

At a time when Western nations have been trying to cope with the problems created by their agricultural over-production, Eastern Europe was forced to spend more on food imports. Gross farm output in Eastern Europe as a whole fell 1 per cent in 1990, and is expected to have dropped even further during 1991. The good news, as it were, is that the region's agricultural imports during 1990-92 will drop by some 15 per cent because of mounting economic difficulties.[2]

Although the malaise in agriculture strikes all the Eastern European countries in varying degrees, its root causes vary widely. The policies to cure these problems will therefore need to be individually tailored.

The USSR

The USSR provides the most graphic example of agricultural inefficiency. One-third of Soviet investment has gone into agriculture over the past 25 years, and still the country is unable to feed itself. The rolling wheatlands of Russia and the Ukraine so beloved of Soviet film makers are an illusion. They are so poorly farmed that each year the USSR must buy in an extra 30 million tonnes of cereals, chiefly from North America, to supplement its own harvest.

Much of the blame belongs with the fossilized Gos-agroprom State bureaucracy that has controlled every facet of activity in the collective farms. It was dismantled in 1989 as part of President Gorbachev's 'New Realism' drive to encourage farm reform, but its legacy will remain for years.

Inadequate inputs of fertilizer and herbicide, low mechanization, poor food processing technology and poor infrastructure condemn Soviet farming to remain very uncompetitive for the foreseeable future. Yields are often 40 per cent below EC levels, and the lack of roads and storage silos means that crops often rot in the fields. The wastage rate for wheat is about 20 per cent, compared to 2 per cent in the United States, and is about double that for fruits, green vegetables and potatoes.

The International Wheat Council has estimated that improvements in the management, harvesting, storage and handling of the Soviet grain crop 'could increase domestic availability of grain by 20-30 per cent'. That in turn would mean that the USSR could halve its cereals imports. Grain and sugar account for about half of the USSR's massive US$20bn a year food import bill.

Getting Soviet cereals production on to a rising trend will be essential. The Soviet population is due to increase during the 1990s from 291 million to 315 million by the year 2000. To feed this growing population and provide enough animal feedstuff to raise meat production, the USSR needs an annual grain supply of between 230 and 255 million tonnes. That would achieve Gorbachev's aim of bringing food consumption in the country to within 30 per cent of Western levels.

The Soviet farm sector still has a long way to go. While most Western countries have been chalking up steady increases of 3 per cent a year in their grain outputs, the USSR's output has stagnated. In some years during the 1980s it actually fell. In 1990 it produced 218 million tonnes of grain, even though the forecasts had been of a bumper crop of over 300 million tonnes.

There have been improvements in some parts of the Soviet farm sector, however, and these have often been in areas where peasant smallholdings have been playing an increasingly dominant role. Ever since Nikita Kruschev decided in the 1950s to allow the limited production of food by private individuals, the smallholders have proved themselves to be more productive and cheaper than the lumbering collectives.

Meat and dairy food consumption in the USSR has doubled since the mid-1950s, although it still stands at only half of northern European levels. Private smallholders provide 30 per cent of all meat and milk in the USSR, 35 per cent of the fruit, 40 per cent of eggs, 60 per cent of potatoes and 70 per cent of all other vegetables. And they do so with only 3 per cent of the country's agricultural land.

Giving the smallholders a free rein and encouraging them to take over a bigger share of the farm sector would clearly pay dividends. But before that can happen the grip of the agricultural bureaucracy must be neutralized, for the Moscow bureaucrats still have a stranglehold on the peasant sector. For example, it is said to be impossible to farm privately without breaking the law. Animal fodder has to be stolen or purchased illegally from the collective farms because the State monopoly on grain distribution has led to the complete disappearance of the country's feed, grain and bread markets.

Vladimir Tikhonov, a Soviet academician, has neatly summed up the situation: 'Until the State breaks the agricultural monopoly, the USSR will remain poor. The USSR gets one rouble in return for every 5 roubles 29 kopeks it invests in agriculture.'[3]

Soviet analysts are beginning to take a hard look at ways in which private farming can be encouraged, and are concluding that it needs a very comprehensive reform programme. Alexandr Nikitin, a journalist who specializes in the subject for the Moscow magazine *Literary Gazette*, believes that land redistribution measures, such as those contained in the Land Act passed by the Russian parliament, will not free small farmers from the grip of the State's agricultural bureaucrats.

What is needed most, according to Nikitin, is a ready availability of productivity-boosting equipment for smallholders, and a system of loans that could bring them within their reach. The sort of equipment he has in mind includes mini-tractors, hay balers, oil and cream separators, butter churns, mini-slaughterhouses, smokeries and sausage-making plants. All of it is equipment that could be produced in the USSR, either using domestic technology or perhaps under foreign licenses.

The major difficulty is that farming is deeply embedded in a command economy that has become riddled with inconsistencies. André Leysen, the prominent Belgian industrialist who heads Agfa-Gevaert, likes to point to the 'tomato ladies' of Tiflis, in Georgia, to show how confused the USSR's agricultural economy has become. He explains: 'Every morning the old ladies board the Aeroflot flight to Moscow, laden with bags of tomatoes that they sell in the open markets there. Normally, people have to wait months to get seats on that flight. But the little old ladies have no difficulty at all. Every evening they return home with their wallets bulging, and no doubt some of the loot is distributed to Aeroflot's employees.' Leysen continues: 'Sounds crazy? Well, it's no more than you would expect in an economy where tomatoes cost 25 roubles a kilo, and the return air-fare to Moscow is priced at 22 roubles.'

Poland

Poland is the largest agricultural producer of all the Central and Eastern European countries, but it is also extremely inefficient. Poland resisted collectivization, so 80 per cent of its farms are privately owned. They are also small and poorly managed. Yields in Poland are substantially less than in other parts of Eastern Europe: in cereals, for instance, Polish farmers produce one-third less per hectare than is the average in Hungary, Czechoslovakia and Eastern Germany.

There are 4.6 million farmers in all, of whom 4.1 million are independent smallholders working farms whose average size is 6.7 hectares, or less than 20 acres. When food prices were fixed, these subsidized peasant farmers could just about scratch a living, but now that food prices are being progressively liberalized they are being squeezed hard. Poland's smallholders are finding that competition from cheaper producers abroad is hotting up, so much so that eggs from Holland and Germany are increasingly commonplace.

Much needs to be done to restructure and modernize Polish agriculture. The smallness of Polish farms, together with the chronic shortage of machinery and agri-chemical inputs, means that the country's food output can be sharply affected by weather conditions at harvest time. That in turn has compounded Poland's dependence on imported food supplies, and cereals in particular.

There is light at the end of the tunnel, however. EC Commission experts believe that the freeing of prices that had been fixed at ridiculously low levels is beginning to pay off, so that not only are Polish farm yields rising but also food consumption is falling. Whether this structural improvement will take effect fast enough to head off discontent among the farmers remains to be seen. There is growing unrest among the many smallholders who find themselves trapped between falling incomes and rising costs. The Rural Solidarity organization may yet provide a focus of discontent.

Hungary

Hungarian agriculture is a success story, by Eastern European standards. Its fertile plainlands are a rich resource that by and large has not been neglected. In contrast to neighbouring countries, comparatively advanced farm machinery is a common sight on Hungarian farms.

More than one-fifth of the country's labour force is still employed in agriculture, although overmanning is such that a third of Hungary's farm workers are reckoned to be 'under-employed'. Farm output accounts for between 16 and 20 per cent of the economy, depending on which statistics one accepts, and makes a crucial contribution to the foreign trade figures. Farm produce and processed foodstuffs account for 23 per cent of Hungary's total exports and 30 per cent of its hard currency earnings.

Hungarian agriculture is nevertheless not as efficient as it should be. A joint World Bank-International Monetary Fund report in the mid-1980s revealed that yields in many of Hungary's 1,300 cooperatives were well below satisfactory levels.

Hungary's major problem at present is that the powerful Smallholders' Party is pressing for land reform policies that would break up the country's very economical large-scale farm units. In the short term, at any rate, fragmentation of Hungary's farms back into their pre-World War II sizes would be very inefficient.

So far as agricultural modernization is concerned, Hungary's chief priorities are the development of a stronger biotechnology sector and of its food processing industry.

Czechoslovakia

Although the most heavily industrialized of all the Central European countries, Czechoslovakia has pursued an active policy of modernizing its farm sector. Its farm population has fallen and its food output has risen. In 1960, 24 per cent of the country's population was on the land; now it is 12 per cent.

From the early 1970s, Czechoslovakia pursued a policy of achieving rapid growth in agricultural output, and its cereals production is generally stable today at about 10 million tonnes a year. The main policy emphasis has been on achieving self-sufficiency.

Romania

Almost one-third of Romania's working population is still on the land, yet the country remains unable to feed itself. In 1990 the EC despatched emergency supplies of meat, grain and animal feed to tide the Romanian population over the food shortages it was suffering as the result of drought.

Hunger is nothing new to Romania. The 'systematization' policy pursued under the régime of Nicolae Ceaucescu, which involved the destruction of rural villages, had a disastrous impact on food production. It was aggravated by Ceaucescu's further policy of exporting food to help pay off Romania's external debt.

Before World War II, Romania's fertile soil ensured not only that the country could feed itself but also that it was a major food exporter. The collectivization of Romanian agriculture produced a disastrous drop in farm productivity. During 1990, however, one-third of all farm land in Romania was returned to private individuals, and land reform is now continuing that process.

Bulgaria

While EC observers believe that Romania will again be able to feed itself before very long, they are less sanguine about Bulgaria's prospects. Bulgaria has some notable strengths, particularly in viticulture – so much so that it is the fourth largest exporter of wine in the world. But its agriculture is dominated by 300 giant and hugely inefficient agro-companies, each employing an average of 3,000 people.

Only 12 per cent of cultivated land in Bulgaria is privately owned, but this small private sector supplies half of all Bulgaria's meat and eggs and a quarter of its milk. Thanks to the collectivized sector, Bulgaria's overall output is much less impressive. Employing 20 per cent of the country's workforce, agriculture accounts for only 12.5 per cent of the economy.

One day the granary of Europe?

The role model is the People's Republic of China. If Eastern Europe and the USSR can achieve the sort of farm productivity improvements that have seen China's total agricultural output during the 1980s grow by more than 50 per cent, their economies will receive a substantial boost.

European conditions are very different, of course. Nevertheless, a major increase in output is within the reach of Eastern European and Soviet farmers. In the first place, private ownership and modern farming techniques should have a powerful impact on efficiency. Second, these countries may well be able to take advantage of the farming revolution being brought about by biotechnology.

Gene-spliced strains of wheat and barley now being developed promise average yield increases of 15-20 per cent. At the same time, genetic research is introducing new techniques that will revolutionize both meat and milk production. If biotechnology begins to reach into the backward farm sectors of Eastern Europe it could produce dramatic results.

Even without genetic manipulation, the outlook for Eastern Europe's farm sector is widely expected to be positive. Economists who contributed to a study by the London-based Centre for Economic Policy Research have forecast that Eastern Europe's grain production could increase by about one-third during the 1990s. 'We estimate possible increases in grain of about 30 per cent overall', they wrote. 'This amounts to about 89m tonnes, or about 5 per cent of world output of grains.'[4]

But first, greater efficiency . . . .

Eastern Europe's agriculture has one major advantage in its drive to become self-sufficient, and eventually a major exporter. Ironically, it is the legacy of Stalinism. Other than in Poland, where it never took hold, collectivization has resulted in huge farms. The average Eastern European farm covers 1,500 hectares, well over 3,200 acres and more than ten times the size of what in the European Community is considered a substantial holding. The economies of scale that could be gained are considerable.

Eastern Europe has the means to become efficient, provided that the large-scale farm units are left more or less as they are. Land reform is a burning issue throughout Eastern Europe, and the pressure is for governments to break up the big farms and distribute land as widely as possible. The collective farms were created by the confiscation of private property, and the demands for land to be returned to the rightful owners are persistent. That would, however, involve the fragmentation of farms into less efficient units.

The shake-up of land reform also risks being very unsettling. Eastern Germany made a blanket commitment to return all confiscated land, and the resulting legal confusion has seriously slowed down the whole privatization process. Furthermore, by no means all farm workers in Eastern Europe favour land reform. In March 1991, an angry demonstration of 15,000 collective farm workers marched through Prague to protest against the break-up of Czechoslovakia's collective farms.

In Bulgaria, where the setting up of agricultural cooperatives in fact pre-dated World War II, the communists did not nationalize the collectives when they came to power. The Bulgarian government is now reluctant to allow full private property rights for land as this could involve breaking up the cooperatives.

Before Eastern Europe's farmers can become a force to be reckoned with in world agriculture, they must first adjust to the rigours of the international market economy. Overmanning and generous subsidization has left them uncompetitive and vulnerable to foreign competition. In Eastern Germany, where farms are large and comparatively efficient, the agricultural workforce of 860,000 was cut by 200,000 people in the nine months to April 1991. At the same time, East German consumers were angered to find that they were paying about DM 210 for a shopping basket of food that in Western Germany cost DM 180.

What the European Community is doing to help

EC policy makers have begun to recognize that a prosperous agricultural sector will be essential to the economic rebirth of Eastern Europe. The new democracies will not thrive if the voters are hungry, and their farm exports are among the few means they have of buying in consumer goods and new industrial technologies from the West.

Agriculture has therefore been a top priority of the EC's PHARE action programme since it was launched in 1989. At first PHARE was designed to assist Poland and Hungary, and assistance to Czechoslovakia, Romania and Bulgaria followed soon after. In 1990, the first year of PHARE financial help, some Ecu 300m in technical assistance and food aid was given to Poland and Hungary, and Romania and Bulgaria received Ecu 80m between them.

The focus of PHARE's technical assistance is the development of their food processing and packaging industries as well as help in modernizing their methods of crop protection and animal husbandry. 'PHARE is very important as a means of developing the farm sector', comments John Maddison, an Eastern European expert in the EC Commission's Agricultural Directorate. 'It is making available inputs like pesticides and fertilizers and it is also helping with supplies of agricultural machinery for smallholdings, not to mention supplies of animal feedstuffs.'

In Poland, the EC has also mounted an imaginative scheme for ensuring that its food aid will help the farmer as well as the consumer. In January 1990, Farm Commissioner MacSharry visited Poland to launch a counterpart fund scheme in which Ecu 125m of surplus EC wheat, barley and beef was sold to Polish consumers, and the proceeds were parcelled into 4,000 small loans to help Polish farmers to buy farm machinery and fertilizers. The counterpart fund is administered by the Poles themselves and is now self-sustaining. A further Ecu 30m is available under a PHARE credit line for further schemes of this type.

Other types of PHARE help now being given in Eastern and Central Europe include rural development projects such as the installation of telephone, water and gas supplies. Training is another area where more and more assistance is coming from Western countries, often through their own national programmes.

One technique that has attracted much attention is for Western aid donors to finance farm trade between Eastern European countries, because the food shortages of some could be made good by the farm surpluses of others. An example of how this could work was provided in late 1989, when money from Japan and Switzerland paid for food to be shipped from Hungary to Poland.

'It's a very attractive idea, in principle', says John Maddison. 'The trouble is that it's not as straightforward as it looks. The Japanese and Swiss paid for 18,000 tonnes of Hungarian wheat to be sent to Poland, but it was all organized in a rather cumbersome way through the United Nations FAO agency, and it all went a bit wrong. By the time it was all set up, the Hungarians' wheat surplus had been exhausted and the Poles were anyway moving into self-sufficiency.'

Difficult and cumbersome it may be, but the signs are that Eastern Europe will need such schemes during the coming years. New mechanisms will be needed to maintain traditional food trading patterns that are being disrupted by economic crisis, by the collapse of Comecon and by the introduction of market forces.

The USSR has been the principal buyer of Eastern Europe's farm exports, but is showing signs of turning elsewhere. For instance, Hungary is now smarting over the loss of Soviet chicken contracts that have been a mainstay of its poultry industry. The USSR has found that it can buy chicken legs from the United States, where consumers prefer chicken breast, much more cheaply.

The importance of access to EC markets

The European Community finds itself on the horns of a dilemma. It wants to help Eastern Europe to develop a healthy farm sector, yet at the same time it does not want to aggravate its own agricultural problems. The best way to help Eastern European farmers is to grant access to EC markets for their exports, but each tonne of food imported from the East will add another tonne to the mountains of surplus food the EC is paying its own farmers to stockpile.

In different parts of the European Commission, officials are now pursuing what look to be irreconcilable goals. Those engaged on the PHARE programme are striving to improve the productivity of Eastern Europe's farmers. Down the corridor, though, are colleagues whose job it is to devise import régimes that limit the inflow of agricultural produce. Elsewhere in the Commission yet another group of officials nowadays has the job of trying to convince EC farmers to reduce their productivity.

'It's a conundrum', admits John Maddison, and says that if only the issue of Eastern European farmers' market access could wait a year or two, a satisfactory arrangement might more easily be worked out. But, with the Community in the throes of reforming its Common Agricultural Policy (CAP), there is little sympathy for the problems of farmers outside the EC.

The fur has been flying throughout 1990 and 1991 over the EC Commission's proposals to bring farm subsidies back under control. In spite of the reforms introduced in the mid-1980s, the free-spending CAP is once more accelerating away out of control. Brussels is proposing a fairly modest plan to trim 15 per cent off CAP spending by 1996, and has unleashed a political furore. Europe's farmers and their political representatives are in no mood to make concessions to their competitors in Eastern Europe.

Nevertheless, the Eastern European countries are desperate for a quick boost to their farm exports to the Community. Hungary and Poland would like to see an immediate increase from one-quarter to one-third of agriculture's share in their total export trade with the EC. Whether they will achieve that sort of ambitious target remains to be seen.

Eastern Europe already enjoys a surplus on its trade with the EC in food and agricultural commodities. For 1989, the region's farm trade surplus was Ecu 662m. Poland is a big exporter of game and fruit, especially red berry varieties, and chalked up a surplus with the EC of Ecu 134m in that year. In 1987 its surplus had been as high as Ecu 400m. Hungary had a farm trade surplus with the EC of Ecu 50m in 1989 and Bulgaria, Romania and Czechoslovakia all managed agricultural surpluses of varying sizes.

How much of the EC market should be opened to Eastern Europe, and in what products? Discussion over the degree of access to the EC that might be granted has centred, for the Central European countries, on the association agreements that are due to run for ten years from the start of 1993, and which may see their transition to full EC membership.

Poland and Hungary have already gained some improvement in access. The opening of the PHARE programme brought with it the immediate dismantling of the EC's quota restrictions on their imports, including many food products. Both countries were also brought into the Community's Generalized System of Preferences, which grants privileged tariff reductions for goods from poorer countries. EC officials estimate that the effect of this will have been to increase Eastern European agricultural exports to the EC by a further Ecus 150-200m a year.

But the negotiations over the farm aspects of the association agreements proved difficult from the start. EC Commission negotiators found themselves given very little room by the member states to manoeuvre. Access for beef soon established itself as a major issue, especially where the Hungarians were concerned.

Market access was not the only point at issue. Officials revealed that Hungary's negotiators were apparently aiming at targets that were 'totally unrealistic', such as EC membership by 1995, and furthermore wanted to align Hungary's prices on those of the CAP in order to avoid any transitional period. Polish negotiators, meanwhile, were suggesting that once their association agreement took effect CAP-style subsidies should be paid, with the EC footing the bill.

Needless to say, these hopeful suggestions were nipped in the bud. But the EC Commission team quickly realized that hopes of a successful outcome to the association agreement talks were being jeopardized by the Community's reluctance to make concessions on agriculture. In mid-April 1991 it sought a more flexible negotiating mandate from the EC member governments, and this was granted with the proviso that easier access would be reciprocated.

Can access be reconciled with CAP reform?

Agricultural politics in the EC is a tough business. The Common Agricultural Policy is defended by vociferous die-hards who still exert an extraordinary degree of influence. Yet the Community will have been ill-advised if it fails to bundle together CAP reform and the enlargement of Eastern Europe's market access and tackle them in parallel negotiations. Granting increased market opportunities to Eastern European farmers will not become easier after CAP subsidies have been reduced. More likely, it will be a lot harder.

The future of Eastern Europe's agriculture raises much more deep-seated questions than the Community's attitude on market access. It could be the catalyst for a radical change in public attitudes to the whole issue of farm support and food 'security'. Throughout the post-war years EC farmers have successfully argued for subsidies so that Europe can be sure it is able to feed itself. Plentiful and cheap food from Eastern Europe would soon show that up as an outdated doctrine.

Once consumers in the Community realize that their food bills could be slashed dramatically by buying from elsewhere in Europe, the nature of the CAP reform debate may change abruptly. The pressure for scrapping the CAP's restrictions on Eastern European imports could become insistent.

Consumers may come to realize that the CAP's direct cost of some US$40bn in 1991 is just the tip of the iceberg. If national subsidies and the cost to consumers of artificially high prices are added, the present yearly bill for farm support in the European Community rises to about US$135bn.[5]

Too great a share of the CAP's proceeds already goes to big land owners and wealthy storage contractors, and much of what is left is pocketed by part-timers. By the year 2000 it is estimated that half of the 7 million farmers in the EC will have a second job. In Eastern Europe and the USSR, meanwhile, there are roughly ten times as many farmers with no alternative livelihood.

The EC's farmers might be better advised to avoid any debate that shines the spotlight of public attention on the Common Agricultural Policy. Set against the dramatic problems facing Eastern Europe it looks more than ever like a gravy train for the undeserving.

Notes

1. 'The Community Agrifood Industry in the Single Market. A Club de Bruxelles study by Jacqueline Smith, Brussels, 1990.

2. 'Winners and Losers in the New Europe.' A paper presented by Brian Gardner, Director, European Policy Analysis, to the Agrifood East-West conference, Budapest, 29 November 1990.

3. 'Alternative Agriculture', by Yuri Karagach. In the March 1991 issue of *Business in the USSR*.

4. *Monitoring European Integration – The Impact of Eastern Europe*, published by CEPR in October 1990.

5. *The Economist*, 23 March 1991.

9

Energy:

The Key to a New East-West Partnership

Eastern Europe's energy gap — The outlook need not be grim — The shape of energy cooperation — Connecting up the power lines — Nuclear energy: the joker in the pack — The USSR after Chernobyl — Safety problems in Eastern Europe — Energy in crisis

---

The lights may soon be going out all over Eastern Europe. The 'brown-outs' that several countries have been experiencing will turn into prolonged black-outs. Business activity that at first was mildly discouraged by power shortages will before long be stifled. The brave attempts of Eastern Europeans to establish a market economy will splutter slowly to a halt, quite literally for lack of fuel.

This gloomy scenario is not inevitable. If Eastern Europe can shore up its energy position, with the EC's help, then the fledgling Eastern European market economies will stand a fighting chance. But to do so requires the building of a pan-European energy structure linking the USSR, the EC and Eastern Europe. In its plan for a 'European Energy Charter', the European Commission has begun to outline what this three-cornered energy relationship might look like.

It could amount to a virtuous circle. The idea is that Western European investment and know-how would release the fabulous energy wealth of the USSR and meet the energy needs both of Eastern Europe and the European Community. For the ailing Soviet economy, such a partnership looks like being its only chance.

The charter would seek to replace the energy relationship that formerly existed between the USSR and its satellites in Comecon. For 40 years the USSR subsidized the energy needs of Eastern Europe by trading its oil and gas on attractively cheap barter terms for their manufactured goods. In terms of the CMEA partners' centrally planned and interlinked economies, this cheap energy policy made sound sense. But with the collapse of Comecon and the Soviet announcement in 1990 that it would be selling its energy for hard currency, the Eastern Europeans found themselves left high and dry.

Subsidized energy was at the same time Comecon's greatest attraction and its greatest disadvantage. It has bred in the Eastern European countries an extravagance they can ill afford. Their inadequate energy infrastructures require huge investments in power stations and pipelines, and a determined campaign to become energy efficient.

Cheap energy has made Eastern Europeans wasteful. They consume far more energy per head than do Western Europeans, and to much less effect. Eastern Germany consumes 40 per cent more energy per person than West Germany. In the USSR itself, energy inefficiency has reached such a peak that the Soviets use two and a half times more energy, in relation to the size of the economy, than the average OECD country.

The Eastern European countries are well aware of their predicament, and have hurriedly launched energy conservation programmes. If, for instance, Poland, Bulgaria and Romania can meet the energy-saving targets they have set themselves, which range from 0.7 to 2.8 per cent a year, they will be able to save 650-700m TOE (tons of oil equivalent) by the year 2000.[1]

But they are shooting at a moving target, because a variety of other factors such as industrialization and stricter environmental controls will at the same time be boosting their energy consumption. Eastern European countries' energy use is forecast to rise between 25 and 50 per cent over the next 25 years, depending on the economic growth rates achieved.

Getting Eastern Europe's consumers used to the idea of paying realistic energy prices will not be easy, and for governments now wrestling with the difficulties of wide-ranging price reforms the temptation is to leave energy until later. In Eastern Germany, where unification is now providing the rest of Eastern Europe with a useful laboratory experiment showing the stresses and pitfalls of switching overnight from a command economy to a market one, it has emerged that electricity prices would have to triple before State subsidies of DM 11bn a year can be eliminated.

Eastern Europe's energy gap

Nuclear energy holds out the hope that Eastern Europe's energy gap can be narrowed. The nuclear situation is examined at greater length later in this chapter. But even if safety concerns do not slow the growth of nuclear power, only 5 per cent of Eastern Europe's primary energy is likely to be nuclear-generated by the end of this century.

The USSR

The more immediate problem is the USSR's inability to continue meeting Eastern Europe's hydrocarbon energy needs, whatever the price. The inefficiencies that characterize the Soviet economy as a whole are particularly serious in the oil and gas sector, and production is dropping at an alarming rate.

Soviet oil output has been falling since 1988, and shows no signs of recovering. From a level of 624m tonnes of crude oil in that year it dropped to 607m tonnes in 1989 and 570m tonnes in 1990. The shortfall in output has been at the expense of the USSR's exports, and Eastern Europe has borne the brunt of the shortfall.

In 1990 Soviet oil exports had dropped to 2.4m barrels a day from 4m in 1988, and unless the fall in Soviet output can be reversed its oil exports will be 'stabilized' at 1m barrels a day. The situation is so serious that the Soviet parliament has been told that on present showing the world's greatest energy producer may need to import oil at the rate of 146m barrels a year by 1993 or 1994.

Today, the USSR is no longer immune to energy starvation. Its coal output is declining and the targeted rate of growth for gas production is slowing, to the extent that domestic energy shortages inside the country are becoming economically disruptive. At the same time, its electricity generation system is under strain, and the construction of new power stations is being delayed.

It is particularly unfortunate for the USSR that energy production should fall just when it is most wanted. The revenues that are being lost are desperately needed to fund the country's economic reforms. It is, however, a case of chickens coming home to roost, for the Soviet energy sector has long been a byword for its outmoded technology and inadequate investment.

Only 15 per cent of Soviet oil production and refining equipment meets Western standards, say the country's own experts. Dr Eugene Khartukov, head of the Moscow-based World Energy Analysis and Forecasting Group, has stated for the record that 'almost 60 per cent of the oil production equipment in use is already obsolete. For the oil refining industry the figure is 75 per cent'.[2] According to Vladimir Kuramin, deputy chairman of the Bureau for the Fuel and Energy Complex, Soviet refineries recover only 60-65 per cent of a barrel of oil, compared with 85-90 per cent in the West.

The inefficiencies of the Soviets are staggering to Western eyes, both for economic and environmental reasons. Officials from the European Commission's Energy Directorate reported back the scale of wastages with unconcealed horror. In an October 1990 internal study of the prospects for EC-Soviet energy cooperation, they wrote that 'losses of 30-40 per cent in production and transport of natural gas were reported to us, without any apparent concern, even though methane is known to be one of the gases responsible for the Greenhouse effect'.[3] In all, some 16bn cubic metres of natural gas is flared away every year in the USSR, an amount equivalent to one-third of Britain's annual consumption of gas.

The Soviet government's response to the crisis has been to pour more money into the energy sector. Its subsidies have been running at around roubles 7bn a year for some time, and in early 1991 President Gorbachev decided to pump roubles

25bn of emergency investment into oil during the course of the year. Priority is being given to reopening oil wells that have been abandoned because of poor maintenance or lack of equipment.

One of the reasons for the worsening production crisis is that, in the centrally planned Soviet economy, three-quarters of the oil equipment industry is located in riot-torn Azerbaijan. Because of the ethnic conflict that has been paralyzing the Azerbaijan Republic, Soviet equipment manufacturers are able to meet only 25 per cent of the oil industry's needs. The Soviet government will therefore have to spend foreign exchange to buy much of the equipment it needs. The signs are that the extra spending will be able to halt the drop in output, but will not significantly raise production.

What is needed in the USSR is a determined oil efficiency campaign. Each 1 per cent cut in the country's domestic consumption of oil would increase its export earnings by US$750m-1bn depending on world prices, the International Monetary Fund has noted. At present, though, the signs are that instead energy consumption is on the increase. During the 1990s, Soviet electricity demand is due to rise between 21 and 33 per cent.

Because of the shortfall in Soviet energy deliveries, and the inefficiencies that were encouraged by the cheap energy relationship inside Comecon, Eastern European countries today face a bleak energy picture.

Bulgaria

The Bulgarian authorities have reported to the European Commission that one-third of the country's electricity needs are not being met. Bulgaria appealed to the EC during the winter of 1990-91 for emergency assistance of 150,000 tonnes per month of heavy fuel oil, amounting to an energy aid of Ecu 150m.

Bulgaria is anxious to diversify its oil and gas supplies away from the USSR, and has started by negotiating energy supply deals with Libya, Algeria and Nigeria in lieu of Bulgaria's outstanding loans to them totalling US$500m.

Czechoslovakia

The need to find hard currency to settle both Soviet and other oil import costs has dealt a blow to Czechoslovakia's economy. In 1990 it contributed substantially to the country's balance of payments deficit of nearly US$400m, and for 1991 there are fears that it will boost the payments gap to around US$2.5bn.

Some 60 per cent of Czechoslovakia's primary energy comes from domestic coal. The rest has been chiefly imported from the USSR, with roughly two-thirds of these energy imports in crude oil and oil products and the remaining one-third in natural gas.

The shortfall in Soviet oil supplies has been less damaging to Czechoslovakia than the new pricing requirements. Under a deal struck in late 1990, the USSR pledged to supply 13m tonnes of oil in 1991, only 3.5m tonnes short of their original pre-Gulf crisis commitment. Czechoslovakia is turning to other major oil suppliers, and the balance of its 1991 needs has come from Venezuela.

Czechoslovakia has not turned its back on the USSR, but has begun to by-pass the Soviet government. It has negotiated an unusual and highly significant deal directly with the Tyumen oilfield in Siberia. Under a barter arrangement with Tyumen, it will pay for 500,000 tonnes of oil with machinery, trucks, medicines and clothing.

The EC has granted US$500m in emergency aid to Czechoslovakia to help cover its increased oil import costs. In January 1991 the IMF approved a US$1.7bn stand-by loan that is intended to help Czechoslovakia to adapt to higher energy prices and to introduce its economic reforms.

Hungary

Hungary is particularly vulnerable to the growing insecurity of energy supplies from the USSR, who last year unilaterally sliced its oil exports to Hungary from a promised 6.5m tonnes to 4.6m tonnes. The Hungarians also rely on the USSR for much of the natural gas that represents 19 per cent of the country's energy consumption. Soviet gas shipments have also been cut back, and any further reductions could lead to serious industrial shutdowns in Hungary.

Hungary already benefits from Ecu 150m in emergency energy assistance aimed at helping it to overcome its difficulties of the winter of 1990-91. Its Prime Minister Jozsef Antall has further suggested to the EC that it should set up a special Compensation Fund to assist Eastern European countries as they adjust to higher energy prices that have to be settled in hard currencies. Otherwise, he has warned, there is a risk that Hungary might not be able to meet the economic performance targets that have been set by the International Monetary Fund as loan conditions.

Hungary currently imports about half of its energy needs, but that proportion is due to rise appreciably. Hungary's domestic oil industry accounts for 11 per cent of the country's total energy consumption, but its output is in decline. Extra oil imports of 1m tonnes a year will be needed by 1995.

Although forced to cast around for alternative suppliers to the USSR, Hungary would nevertheless prefer to buy its oil there where possible, because the costs of pipeline transportation are low. An additional technical reason for wishing to maintain the Soviet energy relationship is that Hungarian refineries are geared to match the characteristics of Soviet crude.

Poland

Domestically produced coal is overwhelmingly Poland's major energy source, but environmental pressures are pushing the Polish government to develop alternatives. The World Bank has lent Poland US$250m to help develop the country's natural gas industry, as Poland has estimated reserves of over 1bn cubic metres.

Oil represents only 13 per cent of Poland's energy consumption, but for that it is heavily dependent on the USSR, which has traditionally accounted for 95 per cent of Poland's oil imports. The Polish government is understandably anxious to diversify away from the USSR. In September 1990 Poland started buying Norwegian crude, and is also turning to Iran.

Romania

Like neighbouring Bulgaria, Romania has informed the EC that demand for electricity is currently outstripping supply by about one-third. Romania's energy problems, however, owe much more to structural inefficiencies than to dependence on outside suppliers.

Romania is second only to Poland in the degree of its energy self-sufficiency. The country produces about 89 per cent of its electricity, 53 per cent of its own oil, 82 per cent of its gas, 61 per cent of all the hard coal used and 97 per cent of soft coal. It has built up a major petrochemicals sector, so much so that petrochemicals and fuels today represent almost 20 per cent of Romania's industrial output.

While 47 per cent of Romania's oil needs still have to be imported, the country's policy has been progressively to reduce the USSR's share of that. Soviet oil shrunk from 38 per cent of Romanian oil imports in 1986 to 17 per cent in 1989, and by 1991 was estimated to account for no more than 15 per cent.

Yugoslavia

Yugoslavia shares many of the fundamental energy problems that afflict Eastern European countries. The country suffers from an over-consumption of energy and a lack of alternative energy sources. Its difficulties are compounded by the run-down of its domestic oil industry, whose proven reserves of 44 mmt can sustain present levels of production for only another 10 years.

Domestic oil currently accounts for some 25 per cent of Yugoslavia's oil consumption, and a major exploration programme is being conducted in the hope of sustaining that level. Oil import costs currently account for 17 per cent of Yugoslavia's total annual import bill, and the country can ill afford to see that proportion rise further.

Because Yugoslavia was not a member of Comecon, the USSR's switch to demanding payments for oil in hard currency has not had a substantial impact. Although the USSR supplies 55 per cent of all its oil imports, the new pricing policy added only US$28m to an oil bill that rose by about US$1bn in 1991.

Yugoslavia has nevertheless been keen to reduce its dependence on increasingly unreliable Soviet oil supplies. Unfortunately, it has jumped from the frying pan into the fire, having selected Iraq as a favoured alternative. Before the Gulf War, Iraqi crude represented 30 per cent of Yugoslavia's oil imports. To make matters worse, Yugoslavia has outstanding loans to Iraq of US$3bn.

Although the federal government in Belgrade has been seeking to diversify away from the USSR as an energy supplier, some of the country's unruly republics have had other ideas. The republic of Serbia has struck a Siberian barter deal similar to that reached by Czechoslovakia. Under the agreement the Serbs are trading consumer goods for crude oil to be supplied directly by Meganeftegas in the Tyumen region.

Meanwhile, the breakdown of the energy relationship between the USSR and its former Comecon partners also has a positive side for Yugoslavia. If the country's political crisis permits, it stands to benefit handsomely from transporting oil supplies to Hungary and Czechoslovakia through the Adria pipeline. It also has an increasingly lucrative business selling refined gasoline to Hungary and Poland.

The outlook need not be grim

The energy outlook for Eastern European countries is not necessarily as sombre as it looks. Although the Eastern and Central European countries are generally faced with a grim future so far as their own energy resources are concerned, there is almost limitless scope for the USSR's energy riches to be harnessed into a new pan-European energy partnership. Such a partnership would generate both wealth for the Soviet people and energy security for Eastern Europe and, indeed, for the countries of the European Community.

The scale of the USSR's energy potential is such that it could also alter today's global energy market. According to an international team of economists assembled by the London-based Centre for Economic Policy Research (CEPR), if the USSR was efficient it could, together with Eastern Europe, generate nearly half as much as the OPEC countries' total production.

In their report, the CEPR authors say: 'The precise timing of Soviet net export increases is uncertain, but it will certainly have a huge impact on world energy markets. World oil prices could tumble, perhaps by as much as one-fifth, squeezing high-cost producers like the UK, Mexico and Texas and reducing OPEC's market power.' The report adds that this cheaper energy would, of course, stimulate the Western economies.[4]

The complementary nature of the USSR's resources and Europe's needs is clear enough. The USSR has 38 per cent of all known gas reserves in the world, and Europe sees gas as the energy source of the future. Taking projections in Eastern Europe as a whole, three-quarters of all electricity generation and one-half of the energy needed for industrial and domestic use is to be supplied by gas. In Western Europe, where gas at present meets 16 per cent of all energy needs, demand for gas is expected to increase by 50 per cent over the next ten years.

Just how Western and Eastern Europeans will be able to harness Soviet energy resources to their own needs is far from clear. But the USSR's energy resources are so vast that it seems unlikely that they will remain untapped.

As well as its reserves of natural gas, the USSR has 7 per cent of the world's recoverable oil and 16 per cent of all coal reserves. In addition to being the world's biggest oil and gas producer it is also the third biggest producer of coal, hydro-electric power and nuclear energy.

Soviet energy reserves are, in short, fabulous. 'Today in western Siberia we have found about 40 per cent of the total potential oil, and 43 per cent of the gas', Dr Vladimir Spielman, deputy director of the Western Siberian Geology Institute, recently told the *Financial Times*. 'Only 9 per cent of the potential oil has actually been produced, and 3 per cent of the gas.' He added that there are at present 489 identified oil and gas fields in the USSR, of which only 123 are in production.[5]

Not surprisingly, Western oil companies are eager to get involved in the development of these riches. A number are already in the vanguard. In Kazakhstan, Chevron is negotiating a joint production agreement in the major Tengiz field beside the Caspian Sea, and Shell has a more modest joint venture at Nefteyugansk in Siberia's Tyumen region. In 1990 ConoCo and Elf-Aquitaine both signed declarations of intent with Soviet joint venture partners. BP, Shell, Elf and Agip all now have permanent Moscow offices and are seemingly poised ready to make major investment projects, while Agip is moving downstream and planning a chain of filling stations in the Moscow area.

The shape of energy cooperation

With Western energy companies beginning to flock to the USSR, what sort of East-West cooperation can be envisaged? A skeleton plan for a new three-way partnership is set out in the 'European Energy Charter' now being proposed to the European Community's member governments by EC Energy Commissioner Antonio Cardoso e Cunha.

The Commission's Charter has built on a plan originally put forward by Dutch prime minister Ruud Lubbers to his fellow heads of government at the EC summit in Dublin in June 1990. The Dublin meeting of the European Council backed the idea, and when it next met, in Rome in early December, it instructed the European Commission to draw up a detailed blueprint for pan-European energy cooperation.

The Charter aims at promoting broad energy links with the USSR and Eastern Europe in a number of areas, and puts nuclear safety and environmental protection at the head of the list. In all, it lays down eight specific areas for cooperation.

- Upgrading exploration and distribution systems, and the modernization of refineries.

- Upgrading of Soviet and Eastern European nuclear safety and security norms.

- Renovation of power stations, the interconnection of grids and streamlining of transit rights for high-tension electricity.

- Increasing natural gas production and transportation via high-pressure grids.

- Increasing renewable energy production.

- Development of 'clean' coal technology.

- Technology transfer.

- Energy efficiency.

Senior EC officials like Constantinos Maniatopoulos, Director General of the Commission's Energy Directorate, believe the Charter is an essential basis for foreign investment. 'If the Energy Charter is accepted by all concerned', says Maniatopoulos, 'we might one day have a situation where Western investors felt able to help build Eastern Europe's new energy infrastructures. It's important that they should, because the energy situation is absolutely crucial to the economic outlook of the these countries, and to their chances of improving their living standards.'

At present, the disparity between the amounts of foreign capital so far invested and the global figures for energy investment needs is sobering. In early 1991 the UN's Economic Commission for Europe reported that energy-related foreign investment in the USSR, Poland and Hungary had reached US$309m. At the same time, the Geneva-based United Nations organization put the energy investment requirements of the USSR and Eastern Europe over the next 20 years at a breathtaking US$1,200 bn.

Meanwhile, more immediate difficulties crowd in as the Eastern European countries struggle to maintain energy supplies to their industries, businesses and domestic consumers. The EC Commission has belatedly included energy in its PHARE programme of economic assistance, and has also brought emergency fuel aid into the G-24 effort.

The amounts of EC financial assistance under discussion are still very small. Some Ecu 50m is being suggested for technical assistance to the USSR in 1991, with an emphasis on nuclear safety, and in the PHARE context Poland and Hungary are each likely to receive Ecu 5m in energy aid for that year.

Constantinos Maniatopoulos is certain, however, that the European Community is not in any position to make good Eastern Europe's widening energy deficit. He points out: 'We don't have surplus capacity in energy. Our gas is imported, just like our oil he points out. After 1995, major new investments in electricity generating capacity will be needed in the Community. I don't see any possibility of massive energy transfers to Eastern Europe.'

Maniatopoulos goes on to explain: 'We can't plug their energy gap, and it's not just a question of foreign exchange and volumes of oil. It's more a problem of the way Eastern Europe's energy output is falling and a question, too, of nuclear safety requirements. What is needed is the long-term restructuring of Eastern European energy infrastructures. It will be very radical, very expensive and will require major sacrifices by Eastern Europe on the environmental front.'

The overall idea of pan-European cooperation based on a more positive EC-USSR energy relationship is now unchallenged, believes Christian Waeterloos, an energy policy specialist at the European Commission. Contacts between Moscow and Brussels have been intensifying since the autumn of 1989, when Soviet experts opened talks with the Commission on topics ranging from technical assistance across to nuclear safety and technology transfer.

Two broad categories of cooperation are being developed. The first consists of the ongoing efforts being made to tackle problems such as nuclear safety, environment controls, the retro-fitting of scrubbers to power station chimneys, and technology transfers. To help finance work on these issues the USSR wants to earmark Ecu 250m of the Ecu 400m in technical assistance that was approved at the EC's Rome summit in December 1990.

Among the cooperation ideas being advanced there is the 'twinning' of Soviet and European cities to encourage the local-level transfer from the West of technology and environmental protection techniques. The Soviets are also keen on developing cooperation on coal technology between their Kusbas region and the Ruhr basin in Germany.

Other cooperation projects now being mooted include an overhaul of Soviet refineries, where Western technological efficiency could quickly improve output by 10 per cent, and the transfer to the USSR of advanced new technologies such as combined cycle gas steam turbines and fluidized bed combustion.

The second category concerns the long-term investments in Soviet oil and gas that will be essential to any new pan-European energy strategy. The Soviet authorities have presented three long-term and very large-scale projects for which they are seeking both financial investment and technical assistance.

The first is the development of the giant Stockmanovskoye gas field in the ice-bound wastes of the Barents Sea. It is four times bigger than the Troll gas field, which is the largest in the North Sea. But the investment needed to produce some 20-40bn cubic metres of gas yearly and transport it by pipeline to Leningrad or Finland stands at about US$10bn.

The second mega-project is the development of the onshore gas field of the Yamal peninsula in north-western Siberia. To do that and build a 2,200 kilometre pipeline will entail an investment of at least US$15-18bn. Western experts like Peter Claus, Secretary-General of Eurogas, which groups the main EC gas producers, believe the total cost could be three or four times that figure.

The third Soviet proposal is for the exploitation of the Karatchaganak deposit of natural gas liquids in the Orenburg area north of the Caspian Sea. Western technology is needed to boost production there to 20-25bn tonnes a year, using high-pressure injection techniques.

How these projects would be structured is, for the time being, anybody's guess. The process of discussing such massive investments with Western corporations and their governments is a lengthy one, and is complicated by the Soviet authorities' own lack of a stable political and administrative hierarchy. There is a widespread complaint in the European Commission and elsewhere that progress is being slowed because Soviet officialdom does not clearly designate high-level decison makers. It took a visit by Jacques Delors to Moscow in June 1991 for matters to improve.

The Brussels Commission also complains that there is no sign of a Soviet energy strategy. Although a Bureau of the

Council of Ministers on Fuel and Energy Matters has been set up, energy continues to fall within the competences of at least eight different ministries in Moscow.

Slowly, though, clear-cut proposals are beginning to emerge from inside the Soviet government. One suggestion that has been greeted with cautious approval by the EC Commission, is that the USSR should swap long-term natural gas contracts against electricity imports from Community member states. 'This would appear possible', comments an internal Commission report, adding that obviously it would depend on the conditions.

The Soviets are also looking for Western European companies to become joint venture partners in an ambitious power station programme. The Soviet authorities are laying plans to build a new power plant that will generate 11.5 Gigawatts of electricity a year, and they also intend to modernize plants currently generating 22.5 Gigawatts. The total cost of this programme is due to reach about Ecu 30bn over 15 years, and the proposal is that half of that amount would be invested by non-Soviet partners.

Connecting up the power lines

The interconnection of gas pipelines and electricity grids is emerging as a major theme in energy planning. The Eastern European countries are particularly anxious that new natural gas transit systems should be developed as they want access to Norwegian and Algerian gas as an alternative to that of the USSR.

Czechoslovakia is lead manager in a study being carried out by Kellog International into the feasibility of a new grid for interconnecting the oil, gas and electricity systems of the five former Hapsburg empire countries now grouped in the *Pentagonale* – Hungary, Italy, Austria, Czechoslovakia and Yugoslavia.

Hungary is also looking at linking up with the European Gas Pipeline and importing 2-4bn cubic metres of gas through it, but construction of the link could take up to five years. At the same time, Hungary has said it will join the Western

European electricity grid, but to do so it must first switch to Western frequencies.

The difficulties of interconnecting systems that have been built to different standards are illustrated by the problems now facing Germany. Unification offers no magic solution. Western Germany is anxious to help cover Eastern Germany's energy deficit by switching supplies there, but interconnection difficulties will delay this until the winter of 1992-93 at the earliest.

At that time, deliveries of 2bn cubic metres a year of natural gas will begin to contribute towards the Eastern Germans' annual gas consumption of 14bn cubic metres, most of which has long been supplied by the USSR. The East German electricity grid, meanwhile, is also unable to receive West Germany's surplus electricity until technical incompatibilities have been overcome.

EC Commission officials are cautious about the amounts of electricity that Community countries will be able to transfer to Eastern Europe. Constantinos Maniatopoulos emphasizes that interconnection is no solution to Eastern Europe's problems. 'Even if the Community had the electricity to spare, there's no means of transferring it.' And he points out that major losses of power are involved when electricity is transported over long distances.

His colleague Christian Waeterloos is less downbeat. He notes that it will take three years or more before the Eastern European and European Community grids are linked. By the mid-1990s, he says, it is likely that a strong East-West grid pattern will have emerged in Europe.

Nuclear energy: the joker in the pack

If imported energy from Western Europe is not the answer to Eastern Europe's problems, what of nuclear energy? Does it hold out the promise of plentiful domestically-produced electricity that could close the Eastern Europeans' energy gap? Or does it, rather, raise the spectre of Chernobyl-style nuclear accidents that could devastate not only large parts of Eastern Europe but of neighbouring Western Europe too?

Many of the nuclear reactors built in Eastern Europe are Soviet designed, and a number of nuclear power station projects have been either shelved or abandoned because of design flaws. The European Commission has reported that there are serious safety problems at 21 nuclear reactors in Eastern Europe and the USSR.

Eastern Europe is nevertheless still looking to nuclear power as its fastest growing energy source. The 1990s are due to see an 80 per cent increase in the volume of nuclear power that is generated, raising the nuclear sector's share of primary energy in Eastern Europe from 3.1 per cent today to almost 5 per cent by the year 2000.

The USSR after Chernobyl

In the aftermath of the Chernobyl disaster, the USSR's nuclear programme slowed abruptly. The USSR currently gets 35 Gigawatts, or nearly 10 per cent of all its electricity, from nuclear power. Reactors with a further capacity of 20 Gigawatts were to have been started on between 1987 and 1989, but were abandoned. Residents of the Crimea persuaded Moscow to cancel a nuclear power plant that was to have been built on the Kerch Peninsula because it is an area of considerable seismic activity.

Other seismic-related closures or construction halts have been ordered in Azerbaijan, Georgia and Armenia. But the USSR is nevertheless pressing ahead with ambitious plans to boost its output of nuclear-generated electricity. Provided that its nuclear safety problems can be resolved, the USSR is due to increase the nuclear sector's electricity output from 23.6m to 61m kWh by the end of the 1990s.

Safety problems in Eastern Europe

Bulgaria is causing neighbouring countries serious anxiety, because its high hopes for a flourishing nuclear energy industry are not yet matched by high safety standards. The Bulgarian authorities intend that 40 per cent of the country's electricity should be nuclear-generated by the end of this decade, but the International Atomic Energy Authority (IAEA) in Vienna has grave doubts over safety aspects. These have been echoed by the environmental experts in the European Commission, who say that Bulgaria has built a number of nuclear power stations in seismic areas.

The focus of its concern is Bulgaria's chief nuclear plant at Kozlodui on the Danube, which produces 42 per cent of all nuclear-generated electricity in Bulgaria but dates from 1974 and is of the same Soviet design as Chernobyl. Like Chernobyl, it is without adequate protective shielding, and needs US$400m to be spent on safety equipment. The IAEA has warned: 'The seriousness of the situation should not be underestimated.' Across the Danube, Romania is growing concerned about the situation at Kozlodui, and says it has prepared civil defence plans against a 'radioactive explosion'.

Czechoslovakia also has ambitious targets for nuclear energy that must be qualified by serious concern over nuclear safety standards. The country plans that 12 Gigawatts of electricity should be nuclear-generated by the year 2005, but in the short term it may even have to reduce its output of nuclear power.

Neighbouring Austria is pressing for the closure of two 'unsafe' nuclear power stations at Janslovke Bohunice, even though they produce 27.5 per cent of Czechoslovakia's electricity. Austria is offering to help with direct subsidies for conventional power stations to replace lost output from Janslovke Bohunice, but is adamant that the two nuclear plants there must be shut down. Austria's environment minister, Mrs Marilies Flemming, has stated that 'an uncontrollable accident is possible at any time'.

Romania has been slower to embark on nuclear energy planning, and its first nuclear power stations are coming into service in the early 1990s. Its nuclear safety problems are therefore not so serious, although the EC Commission's environmental experts have warned that Romania, too, is building reactors in seismic areas.

Five reactors of 700 Megawatts each are to be built at what will be the major nuclear complex of Cernavoda, using Canadian, American and Italian technology. Romania's aim is that 6.8 per cent of primary energy demand, or 11-15 per cent of electricity, will be supplied by nuclear power in the year 2000, rising to 30-40 per cent of electricity needs by 2010.

The chief safety worry so far seems to be that Romania's plans for disposal of radioactive waste are still unclear. The EC Commission's concern that this should be clarified has been heightened by unofficial reports of uranium ore being disposed of in open fields near the city of Petru Groza.

Hungary has situated its main nuclear power stations on the Danube. It has two 440-Megawatt nuclear reactors functioning at the riverside site of Pakston, 100 kilometres south of Budapest. Both have been approved by the IAEA, although a planned enlargement with two 1,000-Megawatt reactors has been shelved because of heightened public anxiety over nuclear safety standards.

Poland has plans for only a limited nuclear power programme. The country envisages a maximum of 2,000 Megawatts by the year 2005, and 6,000 Megawatts by 2010. Poland's nuclear programme has been dogged by delay ever since it was first decided on in 1971, so its implementation did not begin until 1982. At that time the aim was to build 11 nuclear plants in northern Poland and derive 15 per cent of all energy from nuclear power by the year 2000. Because of technical and financial problems, the programme is now far behind schedule.

Poland's first nuclear reactor, generating 440 Megawatts, is due to become operational during 1991 at Zarnowiec, 10 kilometres inland from the Baltic Sea. Four reactors had originally been planned, but mounting public antipathy has combined with cost problems and seen their cancellation. In January 1990, environmental reasons also contributed to the cancellation of a major nuclear reactor project not far from the port of Gdansk.

The Baltic is also the favoured site of Eastern Germany's troubled nuclear power sector. Six new Soviet-designed nuclear plants are currently being built, but of the five nuclear reactors that have already been commissioned in Eastern Germany, four have been closed for safety reasons. They are all 440-Megawatt reactors at the Greifswald plant on the Baltic, and together they account for 10 per cent of Eastern Germany's electricity. It is estimated that it will cost some US$12m per reactor to instal adequate diagnostic and safety equipment.

Energy in crisis

The difficulties that beset nuclear energy in Eastern Europe are just a further setback when placed against the background of energy shortcomings and structural weakness. But nuclear energy represented an escape route that might have saved a number of these countries from serious energy shortages, were it not for the restrictions now being imposed in the interests of nuclear safety.

Eastern Europe will have to cope with its worsening energy crisis without the solution of an immediate boost in the volume of nuclear power. Governments in Eastern Europe and the USSR will have to tackle such fundamental issues as their artificially cheap energy prices to the consumer before they can hope to attract foreign investors into their energy sectors.

From the European Community's standpoint, a serious energy crisis in Eastern Europe would be a substantial reverse. EC and G-24 efforts to assist the new market economies could be cancelled out almost overnight by energy shortages.

It is wrong to lump together the countries of Eastern Europe, in energy as in other things. The European Commission's Constantinos Maniatopoulos is well placed to sum up their different outlooks: 'The Czechs, I think, will find solutions. Provisional ones at first, like interconnections, and then longer-term solutions. But other less industrialized countries will have a much tougher time adapting to the new energy situation; the Balkan countries in particular.'

Notes

1. *Energy Reforms in Central and Eastern Europe – The First Year*. Report by the United Nations Economic Commission for Europe, Geneva, 15 January, 1991.

2. Quentin Peel, *Financial Times*, 26 October 1990.

3. Report on EEC-USSR Cooperation on Energy, Commission of the European Communities, DG-17, 11 October, 1990.

4. *Monitoring European Integration – Eastern Europe*, published by CEPR, October 1990.

5. *Financial Times*, 26 October 1990.

10

Environment:

Cleaning Eastern Europe's Augean Stables

The scale of the crisis — 'Everybody's problem': the cross-border dimension — The cost of the clean-up — Why the West must invest — Business opportunities for Western companies — What the European Community is doing — The emergence of a longer-term strategy — What is the outlook?

'I stepped on a rock, and couldn't step over the little puddle of water. When I got back to the hotel, the dye came out of my shoe, my foot blackened and burned for three days', ruefully reported Ben Tisdale, an American pollution control expert, after a first-hand brush with the problem in Czechoslovakia.

Tisdale, president of an Alaska-based environmental company called Martech, had been visiting an abandoned Soviet military installation that was awash with unidentifiable substances thought to include sewage leaks, waste fuel, cleaning agents and chemical warfare components.[1] In short, the sort of noxious cocktail for which Eastern Europe is famous.

How high on the priority list should Eastern Europe's environmental clean-up be placed? Self-interest has prompted Western Europe to target air- and water-borne pollution and nuclear safety as problems for immediate attention. But what sort of impact can Western technology and limited amounts of finance make on an eco-disaster that stretches from Central Europe halfway around the world?

The European Community is anxious to help Eastern Europe and the USSR to come to grips with the pollution issue. From the start, there has been heavy emphasis in the EC's PHARE assistance programme on environmental projects. Now, the EC Commission is trying to develop a longer-term strategy that would address the deeply structural character of Eastern Europe's environmental problems.

In their role as coordinators of G-24 assistance, EC officials have come to realize that a more carefully structured approach is needed if the West is to make a real contribution. Allocating a few million dollars to selected environmental projects has limited value and risks being chiefly cosmetic. Above all, they concluded that the essential first step to be taken is to accurately map and measure the environmental crisis, for its dimensions are still a matter of guesswork.

Why is the EC attaching so much importance to the environmental issue? The chief reason is that pollution knows no frontiers, but there are also wider motives. In Bulgaria, Czechoslovakia and Poland the emergent democratic movements share their roots with Green activists. Progress in combating pollution commands much public support, and is an essential underpinning of democracy and political stability.

Making a dent in the environmental problem is going to be easier said than done. The damage is on a scale that beggars description, and it results from old-fashioned technologies and industries than cannot be replaced overnight. Many of Eastern Europe's power stations pump between six and eight times more sulphur dioxide into the atmosphere than a Western power station, and a single Trabant from East Germany is dirtier than a hundred much bigger BMW or Mercedes cars equipped with catalytic converters.

Nor is cleaning up Eastern Europe a straightforward problem of finding the necessary cash and throwing it at the problem. Some very difficult political choices lie ahead for both Western and Eastern governments. The situation is so serious that they can no longer choose between good and bad but between two evils. For instance, if Western Europe insists that its own strict nuclear safety standards must be observed in the East, will it be prepared to see many more power stations burning lignite?

Lignite is the high-sulphur brown coal that is so dirty that in parts of Poland and Eastern Germany motorists sometimes have to drive with their headlights on in broad daylight. Margaret Brusasco, in charge of international affairs at the EC Commission's Environment Directorate, says a major switch to lignite-fuelled power stations 'would be an environmental disaster'.

Eastern European governments will face many other hard choices. Confronted by rising inflation and unemployment, the temptation will be to delay environmental actions that will close factories and make their economic woes all the greater. And if Western countries wish to encourage the closure of the old-fashioned smokestack industries that are creating the pollution, they must be prepared to help with investment in clean new industries.

The scale of the crisis

Pollution on such a scale presents the Eastern European countries with a 'no-win' situation. They cannot afford to clean up, and they cannot afford not to. For the environmental damage is a huge burden on their economies.

In the first place, the outdated technologies that create pollution are uncompetitive in world markets. Worse, there are heavy costs to be borne in health care, lower farm output, reduced industrial efficiency and the spoiling of water supplies. Boris Porfiriev, a member of the Soviet Academy of Sciences, has estimated that the cost of the environmental catastrophe to the Soviet economy is akin to the amount of the country's defence budget.

In March 1991, Porfiriev told security experts who had gathered at the National War College's annual conference in Washington DC that he estimates the cost of Soviet pollution and natural resource degradation at 15-17 per cent of GNP, which is about the same as defence spending. Jessica Mathews, a vice-president of the World Resources Institute who was attending the conference, commented: 'While I found Mr Porfiriev's estimate to be staggering, none of the Russians seemed surprised by it. Those I asked guessed it was too low.'

The scale of the environmental crisis is almost unbelievable. The same conference heard testimony from another Soviet scientist, the distinguished biologist AV Yablokov. He said that over half the Soviet population now lives in environmental crisis areas. 'Every third man in those regions has a cancer and the average life expectancy is four to eight years shorter than in the developed countries.'

The situation in Eastern Europe is much the same. The total cost of environmental damage in Poland is estimated as equivalent to 10-15 per cent of GDP.[2] Different types of pollution typify different areas, but all countries share the human misery and economic burden that results from more than half a century of environmental damage.

The USSR

The most striking aspect of environmental catastrophe in the USSR is not industrial waste and casual pollution. It is the irreversible effects on the environment of the Soviet authorities' own development policies.

Ill-judged irrigation, forestry and farming policies are laying waste to a country that occupies one-sixth of the world's land surface. Over two-thirds of all arable land in the USSR is now suffering the effects of soil erosion. Even more dramatically, for a country whose forests stretch endlessly across thousands of miles, the USSR is losing its forests at the same rate as Brazil is losing its rain forests. In Siberia, 600,000 hectares are being cut yearly, and only one-third is replanted.

Irrigation schemes have wrought spectacular disasters. As a result of the large-scale drawing off of water for Uzbekistan's cotton fields, the Aral Sea – once the fourth largest lake in world – has shrunk in area by 40 per cent since 1960. Clouds of salt and dust from its exposed beds now rise 100 kilometres into the air. There is no more commercial fishing, and two-thirds of the region's animal species have disappeared. Similar, but less acute, difficulties have reduced fishing in the Azov Sea to 55 per cent of 1950 levels. The Black

Sea now receives less than half the water it should get from the Dnieper river, because of dams and industrial use.

Industrial pollution has also contributed to the disasters afflicting Soviet water resources. The Black Sea and the Azov Sea are both seriously affected by industrial waste as 25 per cent of the water that flows into them is from heavily polluted rivers like the Don, the Volga and the Ob. Lake Baikal, which contains 20 per cent of the world's fresh water, is suffering irreversible pollution from the Soviet pulp and paper industry.

Air pollution, on the other hand, improved slightly in the USSR during the 1980s. Industrial pollutants emitted into the atmosphere had been reduced to 64m tons by 1987 from 70m tons in 1980. But 50 million citizens are nevertheless reckoned to breathe air containing ten times more than the Soviet legal maximum for pollutants, let alone the levels recommended by the World Health Organization.

It is the scale of nuclear pollution that is the hardest to grasp. Boris Porfiriev's revelations to the US National War College conference in Washington DC included some astonishing comments about his country's nuclear safety problems. He spoke of a mysterious nuclear accident at Kyshtym in the 1960s, and of the dumping of over 1bn Curies of radioactive waste at Chelyabinsk. He said that the USSR's first plutonium facility there had casually discharged its waste into rivers and lakes that feed into the mighty Ob river basin.

As to Chernobyl, Porfiriev indicated that the aftermath is even graver than any official Soviet reports have so far admitted. He puts the number of people living in contaminated areas at 4 million, adding that 500,000 are now under permanent medical observation and that a further 100,000 people are likely to be evacuated.

Poland

Poland is generally reckoned to be the most polluted country in Europe. Now that the subject of environmental damage is no longer cloaked in State secrecy, Poles are beginning to take stock of an appalling situation.

Over half of Poland's river water is too acidic even for industrial use. The country's two major rivers, the Oder and the Vistula, are both heavily polluted, especially by saline water from coal mines. They both carry untreated waste to the Baltic Sea, where the coastline is now badly polluted. Two-thirds of the length of the Vistula is reckoned to be too corrosive even for industry, and by the time it reaches Krakow it is biologically dead.

Half of the Polish cities, including Warsaw, have no waste treatment systems at all. One-third of the country's industrial plants are also without water treatment equipment, and discharge their waste water without any filtration. Only 34 per cent of waste water in Poland is treated, and only mechanically at that. The result is not only serious pollution but also a chronic water crisis. Some 40 per cent of Polish households suffer from water shortages.

Soil contamination from toxic waste is another serious threat to health in Poland, and it has not yet been fully documented. Alarmingly high concentrations of lead, cadmium, zinc and arsenic are to be found in the soil of south-western Poland. In the Krakow area, 60 per cent of food produced may be unfit for human consumption as a result of soil contamination. Lead contamination in fruit and vegetables often exceeds World Health Organization recommended levels by a factor of ten.

The chief villain in Poland's environmental drama is brown coal. Because of its reliance on lignite as an energy source, Poland suffers devastating pollution from sulphur dioxide, and so to a lesser extent do its neighbours. In the short term, there seems no likelihood of a respite.

The United Nations Economic Commission for Europe has warned that Poland's emissions of SO_2 will continue to rise during the 1990s because the country relies on lignite and domestic coal for 80 per cent of its energy. A major filtration and smokestack scrubbing operation could be mounted, but it is unlikely to do more than slow the rate at which Polish air pollution is increasing.

Czechoslovakia

'We have laid waste to the soil, rivers and forests that our forefathers bequeathed to us, and we have the worst environment of all Europe today. Adults in our country die earlier than in most other European countries.' So said Vaclav Havel to the people of Czechoslovakia when he took office as President on New Year's Day, 1990.

The record bears him out, even though in Czechoslovakia as elsewhere in Central and Eastern Europe the seriousness of the environmental disaster is not yet fully apparent. But it is clear that the effects of pollution are cumulative. Infant mortality is not only twice as high as in Sweden or Japan, but is also 65 per cent higher in Czechoslovakia than it was in 1960.

Over 70 per cent of the country's forests are suffering the effects of acid rain, and the situation is particularly serious in northern Bohemia. Over two-thirds of major rivers are badly polluted, and almost one-third no longer support fish. Half of all arable land suffers from soil erosion due to poor farm methods.

Air pollution results mainly from the use of brown coal, and in the Prague basin sulphur dioxide levels are 20 per cent higher than the norms recommended by the World Health Organization. About 40 per cent of Prague's sewage is untreated, and even when it does receive treatment the resulting sludge is returned to the river Vltava. The federal government has set itself the target of building 111 urban purification stations and 37 industrial ones by the year 2000.

The greening of Czechoslovakia is a powerful political force in the country, for its 1989 revolution and the rise of Civic Forum was fuelled by the environmentalist movement. Both Czechs and Slovaks are increasingly anxious to repair the damage. There is a long way to go, for 75 per cent of toxic wastes are still stored dangerously or with inadequate protection.

Hungary

Hungary is only 'moderately' polluted, by Eastern European standards. Airborne pollution in the industrial belt that runs from the north-east of the country down towards the south-west affects about 11 per cent of Hungary's surface area and 44 per cent of its population.

Its water pollution problems are more serious. As much as 96 per cent of all surface water in the country originates from outside Hungary, and is heavily polluted with industrial waste and substances like oil and phenol. Hungarians contribute substantially to the problem, as only 46 per cent of the population have adequate sewage systems.

Soil degradation, caused chiefly by water and wind erosion, affects half of the total land surface of Hungary and the third of the country that is arable farming land. About one-fifth of the country is forest, and 30 per cent of its forests are affected by acid rain.

Romania

Atmospheric pollution is not as bad as elsewhere in Eastern Europe, because Romania burns comparatively little brown coal. But it is beginning to increase fast with industrialization, and the Romanians are beginning to introduce environmental control systems. German scrubbing technology is being used to clean two major coal-burning power stations.

Water pollution is the most serious of Romania's environmental problems, as only one river in five now provides drinkable water. Bucharest, for instance, has no waste-water treatment plant. Soil erosion is also a fast-developing problem, and now affects 5m hectares of farm land.

Bulgaria

The Green Movement played an important role in Bulgaria's recent political development. The country has the lowest levels of atmospheric pollution of all the Eastern European countries, because 50 per cent of its energy needs are satisfied by oil and another 30 per cent is nuclear-generated. However, industrial pollution, particularly from the country's metallurgical industries, is a problem. Half of the inhabitants of Bulgaria's seven largest cities are exposed to what EC Commission observers say are 'intolerable levels of pollution'.

Water pollution is serious, with 40 per cent of waste water going untreated. Bulgarians are alarmed that the Black Sea will be dead in ten years, but they are powerless to halt the pollution that pours in from the USSR. One-third of Bulgaria's forests are seriously affected by acid rain, and there is a growing deforestation problem.

Yugoslavia

Yugoslavia's chief environmental concern is its coastline, where further tourist development is threatened by serious pollution of the Adriatic. Domestic water quality is also poor in Yugoslavia, with only 10 per cent of domestic and industrial water being retreated.

Airborne pollution is a problem in the industrial regions of Yugoslavia, where brown coal is used. Another source of anxiety is soil erosion, as 25 per cent of the land area is affected by felling, over-grazing and deforestation.

Eastern Germany

The 'environmental union' of the two Germanies is going to take considerably longer than their political reunification. The target date that has been set is the year 2000, by which time it is intended that there should be little difference in environmental standards and conditions between Eastern and Western Germany. It will, however, be a struggle. The Munich-based IFO Institute has calculated it will cost DM 200bn during the 1990s to clean up East Germany.

Industrial waste and pesticides have 'killed' 30 per cent of Eastern Germany's water, according to German Environment Minister Klaus Topfer, and a further 25 per cent is undrinkable. Two-thirds of the water courses, and a quarter of all lakes, are more or less seriously polluted.

Water pollution is an especially tricky problem; water is in very short supply, and Eastern Germans have less than half as much per head as West Germans. The cost of completely solving their water pollution problems looks prohibitive. One estimate is that pollution of the Elbe could be halved for an investment of DM 30bn.

Eastern Germany's reliance on brown coal for its energy also conjures up the prospect of huge investment costs if West German environmental standards are to be attained. About 70 per cent of primary energy comes from 17 lignite-burning power stations. The East Germans plan to cut their yearly consumption of lignite from 320m to 200m tonnes by switching to Soviet gas.

'Everybody's problem': the cross-border dimension

How serious a threat is Eastern Europe's environmental catastrophe to neighbouring countries? And what tactics can be used to limit its cross-border effects?

Attempts to do just that started as long ago as 1975 with the launching in Helsinki of the Conference on Security and Cooperation in Europe. One of the areas the Helsinki process focused on was cross-border environmental damage, and by 1979 the talks resulted in the Convention on Long-range Transboundary Air Pollution. This has now been ratified by 31 states, including those of the EC.

By 1984 the ponderous mechanisms of the CSCE had yielded a pact on the evaluation and monitoring of air pollutants, and a special unit was set up with a yearly budget of US$1m. In 1985 the Helsinki talks produced a protocol setting the target of a reduction of sulphur emissions by at least 30 per cent.

This was not quite as ambitious as it sounds, because the base year was 1980 and the target date to be met is 1993. So far, 12 countries have cut their emissions by 30 per cent, and ten of them expect to attain reductions of over 50 per cent. But all are Western European nations whose airborne pollution is in any case far less serious. Poland, Eastern Germany and Czechoslovakia each produce more sulphur dioxide per head of population than any other country in the world.

In 1988, the CSCE process also resulted in a protocol on the reduction of nitrogen oxide emissions. The Eastern European countries signed it, but again there seems little chance that they will observe it. Meanwhile, another transboundary protocol, this time on waterborne pollution, is about to be unveiled.

The fate of the CSCE transboundary agreements so far raises some important questions. Czechoslovakia has begun to moot the idea of an 'Environmental Charter for Europe' that would lay down minimum standards, but would it be worth while? Having a target to aim at has some value, but not if the Eastern Europeans have no chance of hitting it.

The cost of the clean-up

Money is the major problem. The cost estimates of cleaning up Eastern European industry are far beyond those countries' means. A recent report entitled 'Energy for Tomorrow's World', by a World Energy Council study group, puts a US$200bn price tag on the cost of making both energy production and energy use environmentally friendly throughout Eastern Europe but not counting the USSR. It breaks down that figure into roughly US$40bn for the introduction of clean technologies, US$100bn to build 'environmentally acceptable' power stations and US$60bn to modernize energy use.

The report adds that as the USSR's energy sector is about five times greater than those of Poland, Czechoslovakia, Hungary, Romania and Bulgaria combined, the likely cost of cleaning-up the USSR's energy production and use is around US$1,000bn over the next two or three decades.

Even much more modest designs for overhauling Eastern Europe's airborne pollution come up with cost figures that look well beyond the reach of these countries. Bringing East Germany into line with West Germany is expected to cost DM 130-150bn by the end of the century. The Polish government estimates that desulphurization alone will cost US$1bn during that period. One third of Czechoslovakia's sulphur dioxide emissions could be cut at a cost of DM 1bn, whereas a really ambitious programme to reduce them by 80 per cent would involve modernizing the whole electricity industry at a cost of DM 45bn.[3]

Why the West must invest

There seems to be widespread agreement that the solution to the problem does not lie in waiting for Eastern Europe's governments to somehow find the money. As the UN Economic Commission for Europe commented in early 1991: 'The size of the challenge evidently exceeds financing and logistic possibilities, even assuming an upsurge of business relations with third countries.'

If the countries of Western Europe and Scandinavia are anxious to tackle the root causes of acid rain, then perhaps they will themselves have to shoulder the job of cleaning up the energy sectors of Central and Eastern Europe. The 'polluter pays principle' will have to be shelved.

This argument has been advanced by David Newbery, who heads the Department of Applied Economics at Cambridge University. He believes that it will be cheaper for 'downwind' Nordic countries to pay for abatement of air pollution by 'upwind' Polish industry than to spend their money on further reducing their own relatively harmless emissions.[4]

It is a view shared by Johannes ter Haar, a Dutch EC official who runs the PHARE environmental operations. Ter Haar says there is substantial evidence that the Scandinavians and EC countries such as Germany, Denmark, Holland and Greece would do better to invest directly in water technology and power generation than to try to stop waterborne and airborne pollution at the frontier.

Business opportunities for Western companies

'Where there's muck there's money' they used to say in Britain's grimy industrial north, and it holds just as true for Eastern Europe today. The region's environmental catastrophe carries the promise of rich business opportunities for Western clean-up specialists. Dealing with largely penniless clients means that there will be few easy pickings, but nevertheless a huge market awaits the most ingenious and the most persistent.

Eastern Germany is already giving a foretaste of the way things may soon develop throughout Eastern Europe. As many as 4,000 West German companies are reportedly seeking environmental control contracts of one sort or another, for the 'environmental union' of the two Germanies is creating an exciting new market for specialist companies who had saturated their domestic market in Western Germany. As Volker Hannemann, chairman of Ruhr-based specialists GEA, put it: 'The market for desulphurization and denitrification equipment was largely satisfied in West Germany about two years ago, and this makes the market in East Germany attractive.'[5]

Because of the rush to clean up Eastern Germany, the environmental control sector can look forward to renewed growth and prosperity. 'We estimate that profits for the 22 major German environmental firms could rise by 14 per cent in 1991', says Volker Riehm of Bayerische Hypothekenbank. Riehm has also estimated that environmental spending throughout the European Community will rise from 0.85 per cent of GDP at present to 1.5 per cent by the mid-1990s. In Germany, environmental spending is expected to grow by 6-8 per cent a year throughout the decade.[6]

How fast the environmental control market will grow in Eastern Europe is anyone's guess. Environmental consultants are already beginning to set up offices in Eastern European capitals, but much of the emphasis seems to be on ensuring that new investment projects such as hotels meet Western environmental standards. Some specialists, like Duncan Fisher who is the Eastern Europe programme director of the London-based Ecological Studies Institute, say that for the time being Western companies should concentrate on providing training for local people.

What the European Community is doing

The role that the European Commission has chosen to play is to prime the pump of the market mechanism. The funds being advanced under the EC's PHARE programme or by members of the Group of 24 are not enough to make a real impact on Eastern Europe's environmental damage. The hope is that EC-backed programmes will seed fully commercial projects.

The EC Commission is itself still trying to launch a coherent strategy that will enable Western European know-how to be harnessed to the problem. Its efforts began in 1990 with what in many cases was emergency assistance, such as hazardous waste disposal and nuclear safety measures. Within the next few years, the Commission's environmental experts believe they will have built up a framework of technological know-how and financial assistance that will be able to make inroads into Eastern Europe's pollution crisis.

The Community's financial assistance so far has been under the aegis of PHARE, and has been targeted at immediate short-term needs. The aim is to help Eastern European countries to develop their own environmental programmes, and to ensure that in future these will dovetail with EC environmental standards.

The EC is also taking a longer-term view of the issue, and special 'environmental chapters' aimed at developing a more strategic approach are being written into the association agreements. These chapters will reflect the Community's view that Eastern Europe's environmental crisis is inextricably intertwined with its uncompetitive and old-fashioned industrial structures, and that there will be little genuine improvement in environmental standards until Eastern European industries are streamlined.

There is no EC timetable for cleaning up Eastern Europe, but clear stages are beginning to emerge in the Commission's approach. The pattern has been that 1990 saw the launch of EC assistance, the submission of shopping lists by Eastern European governments and the joint selection of viable projects. 'It was an audit year', comments EC official Margaret Brusasco.

The EC's PHARE environment spending depends entirely on the priority that Eastern European recipient nations attach to the problem. During 1990 some, like Czechoslovakia, gave top priority to the environment. Others, notably Bulgaria and Yugoslavia, found themselves facing such a disastrous situation that the 'quality of life' was an irrelevance when set against economic survival, even though in Bulgaria's case environmentalism is a powerful political force. Instead, the Bulgarians gave priority to their PHARE requests for agricultural assistance, and Yugoslavia to restructuring the financial sector.

Czechoslovakia wanted 90 per cent of its 1990 PHARE appropriation to be devoted to environmental projects, and therefore received Ecu 30m for short-term measures that ranged from water and waste management to desulphurization, hazardous waste disposal and nuclear safety.

Hungary received Ecu 25m to improve its monitoring of both airborne and waterborne pollution and to help finance measures to improve the country's waste disposal systems, to regenerate the ecosystems of lakes and rivers, to cut atmospheric pollution and support an environmental training effort. For 1991, Hungary has said that it wants only half that level of environmental assistance from PHARE.

Poland, on the other hand, boosted its 1991 PHARE assistance on environmental projects. In 1990, the Poles had allocated much of their PHARE money to agriculture, and received only Ecu 22m for environmental control. East Germany received Ecu 20m under PHARE in 1990 for short-term help in the upper Elbe valley and to help fund the development of its new environmental strategy, and Bulgaria received Ecu 3.5m to upgrade its air pollution monitoring methods.

The emphasis of PHARE's environmental efforts in 1991 is much more on training. At the same time, PHARE assistance has been enlarged to include joint projects that will group the European Comission's efforts with others being mounted by G-24 countries, by the European Investment Bank, OECD and the World Bank.

Margaret Brusasco stresses that for 1991 the problem has been to define a medium-term strategy. 'That has not always been easy', she adds, 'as the environment is a sensitive domestic political issue in Eastern European countries.' Meanwhile, the EC Commission has begun to clarify its own thinking about the sort of help that best suits the Eastern Europeans' problems. 'We think importing know-how is better than simply receiving aid', Margaret Brusasco says, and cites the example of Poland's request for the patents to manufacture fluidized bed boilers and sulphur gas scrubbers for tall chimneys, rather than import the equipment.

The EC was more than happy to devote PHARE funds to buy the patents for the Poles. 'Instead of selling them end-of-pipe technology, we are helping them to re-launch their market economy. The Poles will be able to sell the equipment they manufacture all over Europe', says Margaret Brusasco. 'We hope the Polish example will be a pilot for the Czechoslo-vaks and the Hungarians.'

The main aim of EC policies is to encourage what officials call 'coherence' in the way environmental projects are developed with PHARE money. 'We want recipient countries to work out coherent programmes linked with industrial

204 / Eastern Europe and the USSR: The Challenge of Freedom

development stretching years ahead', Brusasco explains. Brussels is also anxious that Western companies should not try to cash in on the region's backwardness. The Commission is working on a Code of Conduct that would try to prevent the sale of outdated environmental control technology to Eastern Europeans.

The emergence of a longer-term strategy

Looking still further ahead, Commission officials are aiming eventually to put the EC's environmental efforts on a quite different footing. Brussels is urging a major change in the Community's approach to Eastern Europe's pollution crisis. It says the present system of preparing lists of projects is not the answer, even though it may give the impression of a concerted programme.

The argument is that while the project-by-project method may look good to EC governments, it is in fact a rather piecemeal way of tackling the crisis. Top officials in the Environment Directorate say that a more thematic approach is needed. This would involve laying long-term plans for overhauling Eastern European infrastructures and industries, and for measuring much more accurately the scale and nature of the environmental damage.

PHARE official Johannes ter Haar admits he is worried that the EC risks imposing environmental control strategies without regard to the economic upheavals involved. In other words, he is saying that the modernization of Eastern Europe's industrial base cannot be divorced from the cleaning-up process.

The idea that environmental policy must be closely integrated with the many other policies that affect business and industry is a new departure in Commission thinking. It is applying the same approach to the environmental policy proposals that it is presenting for the Community itself in its 1992 Fifth Action Plan for the Environment, a five-year blueprint for the EC.

Ter Haar also believes that the problem still needs to be properly analyzed and measured. 'Consistent analysis is needed in order to get consistent solutions', he comments. EC environment officials are therefore urging an ambitious baseline survey of Eastern Europe's environmental disaster.

The survey would consist of six national studies, each using the same criteria, that would build up a scientific picture instead of the present one which is largely anecdotal. 'Our main problem is finding the qualified personnel to carry out the study', ter Haar adds. 'If we had it two years from now, we could achieve a lot.'

The EC is now suggesting a three-year programme for setting up the structures needed to run this more thematic approach to Eastern European environmental problems. It would have three elements, the first of which would be the setting up of a basic framework to establish methodology, training procedures, and the development both of a database and of links with environmentalist organizations throughout Eastern Europe. Its second element would be to research the most cost-effective solutions; the third would be to harness appropriate technologies to the region's problems.

EC officials are also proposing that this more thematic approach should be adopted in parallel with the Community's present project-based efforts. Plans are afoot to make Yugoslavia a pilot project for the new approach, because establishing a framework of strict monitoring, higher standards and tougher Codes of Conduct could make an immediate impact on the country's spoiled tourist resorts. The snag is the cost, as the World Bank estimates that US$5-6bn would be needed to implement the plan.

What is the outlook?

Two principal factors will determine the speed with which Eastern Europe's eco-disaster is cleaned up. The first is the Eastern Europeans' determination to close down old-fashioned polluting industries, whatever the unemployment cost. The second is the willingness of Western companies to invest in the modernization of Eastern Europe.

The social and economic impact of abandoning Eastern Europe's 'rust-bowl' industries will be dramatic. Developments in Eastern Germany are showing how severe the effects can be when tough environmental standards are imposed. The fate of the Buna and Leuna chemical plants, whose activities date back to 1916 and are based on the local lignite fields, is creating a political furore. Pollution controls are to cut the combined workforces of the two complexes from 45,000 to 22,000 people, and tempers are running high.

It remains to be seen whether Eastern European countries will act with the same determination. After all, they do not have the imperatives of German reunification to drive them. For newly democratic countries facing the rigours of transition to market economies, it will be hard to shut down factories on environmental grounds. This is especially true of 'dirty' industries, because on the whole they are large employers.

The deciding factor will be the interest shown by Western capital. If Western investors are prepared to put money into power generation and manufacturing plant that is both more efficient and environmentally friendly, then Eastern European governments will no doubt rally to the cause.

The EC's PHARE programme is far from being the only source of environmental help for Eastern Europe. The Scandinavian countries are involved in a number of projects centred on northern Poland and on rivers running into the Baltic. There are several projects mounted by the United States – notably its effort to save the mediaeval city of Krakow from the effects of acid rain. Canada is also active, and a number of EC countries such as France and Germany have major bilateral programmes with Poland.

The next step will be to shift the emphasis from government-funded support to private investment. Thousands of specialist Western European companies are showing interest in the PHARE programme's environmental projects, and the aim must be to create purely commercial deals. Eastern Europe's environmental clean-up has to become a sound business proposition.

Notes

1. 'Eastern Europe: The World's Greatest Polluter'. In the October

1990 issue of *Europe*, the monthly magazine of the EC Commission representation, Washington DC.

2. 'Are the Costs of Cleaning up Eastern Europe Exaggerated? Economic Reform and the Environment', by Gordon Hughes. Centre for Economic Policy Research discussion paper No 482, London, November 1990.

3. *Energy Reforms in Central and Eastern Europe – The First Year.* Report by the United Nations Economic Commission for Europe, Geneva, 15 January 1991.

4. 'Acid Rain', by David Newbery. Centre for Economic Policy Research discussion paper No 442, London, October 1990.

5. *International Herald Tribune*, 16 February 1991.

6. *Ibid.*

11

Debt:

Avoiding the Latin America Debt Path

The Latin America syndrome — Each country has different debt problems — Helpful ways the West can structure lending — The Polish debt write-off as a pilot for Eastern Europe

---

Parisians are justly proud of the Pont Alexandre III that spans the Seine not far from the Invalides. But French diplomats, who can admire its lines from their desks in the Foreign Affairs Ministry on the Quai d'Orsay, may recall uncomfortably that the bridge is a monument to the pitfalls of Russian debt. It was a gift to the French people from Tsarist Russia, and marked the Russians' gratitude for a huge loan in 1888 that was the first of many to finance the railways as they began to stretch across Siberia. The graceful wrought-iron bridge later came to be a constant reminder of the way that debt can sour a friendship. In 1918 the Bolsheviks announced they would not honour Tsarist debts or pay compensation for property that had been nationalized. Western bankers and their governments at once froze all credits to the USSR. To this day, France and other nations who bought Tsarist bonds continue to demand their repayment. The 7bn gold francs that France claimed in the 1920s is today put at 140bn francs, and the French are by no means the only creditors still holding 'railway bonds'.

Today, the debts of the USSR and, indeed, of all Eastern Europe, are causing fresh concern. Although already deeply in debt, these countries need loans and other forms of financial assistance on a massive scale if they are to become market economies. But their creditworthiness, as far as the West's commercial banks are concerned, is in most cases virtually zero.

'For all practical purposes', comments the Organization for Economic Cooperation and Development (OECD) about the USSR's borrowing situation, 'the USSR is no longer able to raise funds in the syndicated Eurocurrency or external bond markets.'[1]

The USSR is by no means the worst off. Market analysts say it is a 'moderate debt' country, with a debt mountain that is a good deal less daunting than those of countries like Hungary, Bulgaria and Poland. Since the mid-1980s, Eastern Europeans have seen their debt commitments soar to foreign governments, banks and institutions like the World Bank and the International Monetary fund.

The commercial banks are the most sensitive barometer of confidence in Eastern Europe, and 1990 saw a marked change of mood among international bankers. The surge of commercial lending that had taken place during the euphoric days of 1989 went sharply into reverse. In the first nine months of 1990 the commercial banks' lending to Eastern Europe dropped almost US$7bn, having increased by over US$9bn the year before.

In other words, the commercial banks are getting edgy – after all, they hold the bulk of the outstanding loans to Eastern Europe and the USSR. In contrast to much of the Third World debt that is government-to-government, the big European, Japanese and, to a lesser extent, US banks are heavily exposed in Eastern Europe.

By the autumn of 1990 these banks were owed US$86bn in loans to the USSR, Bulgaria, Hungary, Czechoslovakia, Poland, Romania and Yugoslavia. German banks held 20 per cent of the debt and Japanese banks 18 per cent. These loans by the commercial banks added up to a very substantial part of the US$123bn debt that the OECD calculated for the region by the end of 1990.

The result is a growing reluctance by the Western banks to get in any deeper. Official aid rather than private credits will be critical to the success of Eastern Europe's economic reform effort, observed the Basle-based Bank for International Settlements (BIS) in February 1991.

The BIS, which links the central banks of the West, added in its dry banker's fashion that 'the prospects for the private provision of financial credit from abroad, even in modest amounts, are not at present very bright'.

The debt problem goes wider than the banks' growing uneasiness. It extends also to industrial corporations both great and small that have found they have become involuntary creditors.

Eastern European countries, and above all the USSR, have been failing to pay their suppliers. Exporters in Germany and the United States alone were owed at least US$1bn in unpaid deliveries to the USSR by mid-1991. By some estimates, Soviet trade-related debts could even be over US$5bn.[2]

Doing business has become considerably more risky than in the days when contracts were fixed through the ponderous mechanisms of the State trading organizations. Then, payment was assured; now, however, the word is getting round that Soviet companies and others elsewhere in Eastern Europe simply do not pay their debts.

Eastern European debt raises major policy issues for Western nations, and most of all perhaps for the European Community. Decisions taken by Western governments will determine how much more debt Eastern Europe can take on, and under what conditions.

Just like a bank manager, the West will have to judge whether the borrower's business plan is basically sound, or whether the interest charges of a bigger loan will bring about the collapse of the whole enterprise.

Unlike a bank manager, though, the West cannot foreclose. The overall strategy of integrating the new democracies of Eastern Europe into the European market economy would be seriously imperilled by a credit freeze. Nor can the West let Eastern Europe be dragged down by the weight of its debts. Even if loans were to be pegged at present levels the size of the debt will grow inexorably. In 1990, when private lending dried up, the total amount of Eastern European and Soviet debt grew by more than 13 per cent because of interest charges that keep mounting.

Western governments will need to work out a more coherent debt strategy regarding Eastern Europe and the USSR. They will have to help the borrowers to decide what level of debt servicing costs their export industries can sustain with hard-won foreign currency earnings. At the same time, the West must agree to more generous lending policies if Eastern Europe is to build up a more dynamic industrial base.

The major question that faces the West is what level of debt 'forgiveness' should be accorded to Eastern Europe. In the wake of the decision in March 1991 to write off a major part of Poland's existing foreign debt, the hot topic in financial circles is the sort of deal that should be cut for other countries – in Eastern Europe, of course – but also throughout the developing world.

Other question-marks over the future shape of Western policy towards Eastern Europe debt are legion; should the European Community, for instance, issue guarantees that will help the USSR and others to raise money privately from banks and the capital markets? If so, should these guarantees cover all of the loans, or rather less than that?

Then there is the issue of conditionality. Should strings be attached to loans? Poland's case for a major write-off of its debt was greatly bolstered by the determination with which it has implemented its tough economic austerity plan. A system for rewarding unpalatable reform measures with easier credit conditions could help to accelerate Eastern Europe's transition to becoming a region of market economies.

The Latin America syndrome

Debt is arguably the biggest single factor arresting economic growth in the Third World today, and it is essential that Eastern Europe and its creditors should not repeat the mistakes that have been made there. Of all the world's debtor nations, those of Latin America have suffered the most needlessly from Western debt policies that were short-sighted and ill-considered.

In the 1970s, the major international banks – many of them from the US – saw rich lending opportunities in Latin America. The glut of petro-dollars to be recycled in the wake of successive OPEC oil price increases fuelled the banks' lending spree. Little was imposed in the way of controls on these loans to borrowers in comparatively unstable Latin American economies. The result was that often the foreign loans to many of these countries did not stay within the borrowers' economies. Instead, the funds were spirited out of Latin America and reinvested privately in the international capital markets.

This phenomenon of foreign loans that financed massive capital flight rather than growth has been particularly serious in Mexico, Chile and Argentina. These countries have contracted huge debt burdens that must be serviced and eventually repaid with foreign exchange, but they have not received the industrial goods and investments that the loans were intended to pay for.

The saga of Latin America's debt problems has since become all too familiar. The major Western banks now deeply regret their open-handedness in the 1970s and early 1980s, and their balance sheets bear witness to a succession of defaults on interest payments.

A game of brinkmanship has ensued in which the debtors aim to stave off their bank creditors without losing their eligibility for World Bank and IMF assistance. However, the upshot has been that the Latin American economies that 25 years ago were seen as far more promising than those of South-East Asia are now widely regarded as being trapped in a vicious circle of debt and low growth. Even Brazil, with a sophisticated industrial base that has been acting as a magnet to foreign investors, looks condemned to economic stagnation by the costs of servicing a foreign debt that is more or less the same size as for the whole of Eastern Europe and the USSR.

For the Third World as a whole, the weight of the debt burden is stifling growth and depressing living standards. Julius Nyrere, the veteran leader of Tanzania, calculates that there is now a US$30bn net transfer of resources every year from the world's poor nations to the rich ones.

The interest payments on loans to the Third World, that now stand close to US$1.5 trillion, or almost three times as much as in 1980, are crippling the developing nations' attempts to develop new industries.

Nyrere points out that this debt spiral is counter-productive for the industrialized Western nations, whose exports to the Third World are falling. 'The developed countries' exports to the South', he told a UN-backed meeting of international bankers in 1989, 'were about US$150bn less during the three years 1984-86 than they were during the previous three years. The poverty of his customers causes the poverty of the shopkeeper.'[3]

The knock-on effect of the international debt crisis as it has got out of hand has been to depress the volume of new loans to developing countries. Lawrence Summers, the World Bank's chief economist, has forecast that during the five-year period 1992-96 the world's poorest countries will be receiving only US$2 per head of population in transfers from the industrialized nations, compared with US$9 (in current prices) per head back in the latter 1970s.

Preventing Eastern Europe from being drawn into a similar pattern of debt and depression will require imaginative policy-making. So far, though, Third World borrowers have come to look on Eastern Europe as yet another begging bowl in the competition for scarce funds.[4]

Each country has different debt problems

The debt problems of the countries of Eastern Europe are very varied, which will make it all the harder for the EC and for the World Bank and IMF to draw up a cogent new debt strategy for the region.

The nature of their debts is often very different, as are the elements that determine their creditworthiness. Poland's debt, for instance, has been mostly to foreign governments, whereas that of Hungary is owed much more to private bankers. As to creditworthiness, there are substantial differences between the Eastern Europeans themselves and between them and the USSR, whose collapsing economy is to some extent buttressed by gold reserves and oil exports.

The USSR

It would be wrong to present the USSR as an irresponsible spendthrift. In its heyday as a superpower, when the country was anxious to export communism worldwide, it advanced development loans to many Third World countries. It is currently owed about US$120bn in largely irrecoverable loans to socialist states like Mongolia, Cuba and Vietnam and to the Third World.

The reality is that these credits cannot be counted against the USSR's own foreign debt. According to Ernst Obminsky, the Soviet Foreign Trade Minister, it reached US$60bn at the end of 1990, which meant it had doubled since 1985, and is still rising. Moscow's debt has became a major problem. It will not only be a further constraint on the country's economic policy options, but will also shape much of the USSR's future relationship with Western governments.

The burning question is how big the Soviet debt will grow. Non-payment of interest is already beginning to swell the principal amount owed, and because of the paralysis gripping the Soviet economy the country is in the throes of a balance of payments crisis that means there is little or no foreign exchange to settle debt interest charges.

Looking on the bright side, the USSR's debt, at about US$200 per capita, is quite modest. So too is the ratio of its debt to its yearly exports, the measurement that bankers most often use to judge a country's creditworthiness. On that measurement, the USSR's figure of 139 per cent compares very well with Bulgaria's 468 per cent, Poland's 418 per cent and an Eastern European average for 1990 that was 292 per cent.

Sadly, these figures do not tell the whole story. The truth is that the Soviet government and its State-owned agencies have become badly strapped for cash. All the major Western financial institutions have noted with growing concern that the USSR has been running down its foreign currency deposits in the West at an unprecedented speed. The inevitable conclusion is that it is using these reserves to pay the interest on its debts.

In short, the USSR is living off capital and not income. The country's export earnings are proving inadequate to finance the interest payments, so it is running down the foreign currency holdings that it has traditionally regarded as almost sacrosanct. In the first six months of 1990 they dropped by US$6bn, which was 40 per cent, and by the end of the year had slipped to below US$5bn. 'Contrary to the USSR's long-standing policy of maintaining very high levels of deposits in Western banks', the OECD observed in February 1991, 'its reserves are now well below minimum acceptable levels.'

The USSR's ability to borrow more to cover its liquidity crisis is very limited. Between 1982 and 1988 it enjoyed access to comparatively cheap capital from the international financial markets. Now that source of funds has dried up.

After 1988, as the country's economic weaknesses became more apparent, Soviet borrowers were offered increasingly unattractive terms. By the early 1990s they no longer had much access at all to these markets. In 1988 the USSR had been able to borrow US$2.7bn on the international markets; in 1989 it raised US$1.8bn and by 1990 only US$290m.

The effect of the USSR's seven-year fling in the international capital markets has been to change the nature of its foreign debt. In the early 1980s two-thirds of its debt was to governments, and now it is to banks.

Officially guaranteed loans to the USSR accounted for only 22 per cent of the foreign debt by the late 1980s. Unguaranteed loans by the banks and the holders of Soviet bonds now represent a major proportion of the teetering debt mountain. In short, the USSR has gone the way of Latin America.

And, like Latin America, it has even developed a version of the capital flight phenomenon. A growing share of the country's hard currency is being held outside the USSR by Soviet companies. Even though in late 1990 the Soviet government introduced a hard currency levy to compel companies to sell it 40 per cent of their export earnings so that it could service the foreign debt, the companies are salting money away in overseas bank accounts.

The signs are that the USSR is heading for a Brazil-style tussle with its creditors; its outlook is one of endless and bitter negotiations with the commercial banks grouped in the 'London Club' and with creditor governments in the 'Paris Club'.

German banks have already begun to react sourly to the USSR's worsening debt crisis. Hilmar Kopper, head of the leading Deutsche Bank, has ruled out any new lending to the USSR unless backed by a 100 per cent guarantee from the Bonn government. 'For us, the USSR is a problem country', he says.

Germany's bankers have already lent $11bn to the USSR, and although much of that is backed by partial guarantees from Bonn, about US$4bn is totally unsecured. The position of the big French banks is reckoned to be even worse. Only one-tenth of French loans have government guarantees, leaving the exposure of the French banks at US$6bn.

The Western bankers can be expected to demand tough terms of any debt reschedulings the Soviet authorities may propose, but it is possible that they will not be the country's most vociferous creditors. The former 'satellites' of Eastern Europe are also substantial creditors to the USSR.

As part of the switch to hard currency trading between former members of Comecon the USSR pledged to repay these loans, but by mid-1991 had still not done so. Some extremely tetchy negotiations have been taking place over the hard currency rate at which the USSR will settle its transferable rouble debts, and over repayment schedules. The Czechs have been told they must wait until 1996 to be paid, but the pressure on Moscow from other Eastern European countries is fierce. Settling its accounts with debt-ridden Eastern Europe may yet be the crunch in the USSR's own liquidity crisis.

The Soviet government has two sources of foreign currency to help stabilize its debt problems. The first is oil, where output and exports continue to fall off alarmingly, and the second is gold. Although officially the level of Soviet gold reserves is still meant to be a 'State secret', they are thought to stand at 2,000 tonnes.

The USSR is second only to South Africa as a gold producer, and its gold reserves are widely believed to represent an escape hatch from its debt problems. In fact, Western gold experts say that it is unlikely that the USSR could swell its normal foreign sales of about 200 tonnes, worth US$2.5-3bn, by much more than a further US$1bn without badly weakening the price of gold. Set against the country's scheduled repayments in 1991 of US$11bn, that will not go very far.

The upshot is that there is no easy escape from a Soviet debt crisis that could shake the world of finance to the core. The limited room for manoeuvre now available to the Soviet government is clear enough. What is much less clear is the sort of role the West will play.

The official line from the West has been that until the various political factions in the USSR agree to implement austerity disciplines as part of a transition plan to a market economy, there will be no financial help from Western governments.

A study of the USSR's economic difficulties, prepared at the request of the Houston summit in mid-1990 between the seven top industrial nations, recommended that until a clear Soviet economic strategy emerges the West should limit itself to humanitarian aid and technical assistance.[5]

But it is far from certain that the West will be able to stand off from the USSR's deteriorating debt position. The country's inability to service its debt grew steadily more evident in 1991, with the likelihood that Western banks will be dragged willy-nilly into the crisis.

They in turn will be putting pressure on their governments to bail out the Soviets. As the USSR is not a member of the International Monetary Fund, an *ad hoc* international refinancing package may have to be assembled in the place of the more usual IMF stand-by credits.

Poland

Poland exemplifies the political nature of the debt problem, and of its solution. The country accumulated US$49bn in international debts by early 1991 as a direct result of its tense political relations with the West in the early 1980s.

In March 1991, when Poland's political relationship with the EC and the United States had become very positive, it was 'forgiven' about half of the money owed to foreign governments.

Poland's debt had reached crisis proportions because of the stand-off between the West and the communist military government led by General Wojciech Jaruzelski. When his government introduced martial law in 1981, Poland found itself ostracized by the West. Its response was to cease paying interest on its official debt, while continuing to service its loans from Western commercial banks.

The effect was a snowballing debt to the Western governments that rapidly overtook the country's commercial debt and left it far behind. By the beginning of the 1990s the principal amount of the debt to foreign governments had doubled, and accounted for almost three-quarters of the total amount owed. Because of its interest payments default, Polish debt soared to US$1,100 per head of population. The annual interest owed on it had grown to the equivalent of 49 per cent of Poland's yearly export earnings.

By 1990, as the economic austerity plan introduced by finance minister Leszek Balcerowicz began to bite, Poland was emphasizing that its efforts to establish a market economy were being neutralized by its huge hard currency debt. The Polish government appointed a chief debt negotiator, Janusz Sawicki, to shuttle between the Western capitals and persuade Poland's creditors that they were in danger of killing off a goose that might yet lay golden eggs.

Sawicki's task was to explain to Poland's official creditors that Warsaw would like to resume the payment of interest on its loans, but that to do so would court economic disaster. If it paid interest on all of its accumulated official debt it would have a balance of payments gap over the next three or four years of US$5-6bn a year, equivalent to 4 per cent of Polish GNP. Extra IMF support would not be enough and it would virtually have to blockade itself against imports. In the process, it would jeopardize Poland's drive to streamline its industries.

Sawicki's tactic was, as he put it, 'to play the quartet'. Moving between Warsaw, Paris, London and Washington his aim was to reconcile the interests of Poland with those of the governments grouped in the Paris Club, the commercial banks in the London Club and the IMF in Washington.

By mid-March 1991, after weeks of 'on-off' newspaper headlines that testified to the trickiness of the negotiations, Sawicki brought off a deal that Poland's creditors themselves described as 'extraordinary'. Although not going as far as the 80 per cent write-off that Poland had been demanding for its US$33bn official debt, the creditor governments agreed to a two-stage debt forgiveness plan that by 1994 will mean a 50 per cent reduction.

During the first phase, which is to last for three years, creditors will have the option to cut the debt by 30 per cent – by forgiving principal, offering below-market interest rates or by transforming interest payments into principal and then offering low interest rates. When the second stage begins in 1994 creditors are due to reduce the debt by a further 20 per cent.

The pact gives Poland a breathing space, but little more. It underlines the Western governments' collective approval of the way Poland is tackling its economic difficulties, but it does not point the way towards a new financing strategy that would help Poland's transition to becoming a market economy. It is a welcome development, but it does not seem to be a blueprint for a more positive longer-term relationship between Western creditors and the debtor nations of Eastern Europe.

Hungary

The enthusiasm and success with which Hungary has embraced the market economy tends to disguise the precariousness of its financial situation. Of all the countries of Central and Eastern Europe, Hungary is the most heavily indebted. Some analysts say it is 'insolvent'.

In the latter 1980s, when Hungary's first faltering steps into 'Goulash capitalism' were the envy of her Comecon neighbours, the country's external debt was growing at a runaway speed. Between 1984 and 1989 it more than doubled to reach US$20bn, or US$2,000 per head of population.

Opinions differ over the seriousness of Hungary's indebtedness. Daniel Cohen, an expert on debt issues, has argued that Hungary's situation is alarming. He finds Hungary scores worse than any other Eastern European country, and is almost twice as debt-ridden as Poland, Bulgaria or Yugoslavia. 'While half as indebted as Poland in absolute terms', comments Cohen, 'Hungary has a population that is about four times smaller.'

He also uses the measurement of a growth-adjusted burden of debt that is designed to reflect the Eastern European countries' low growth problems. 'By this measure, Hungary is insolvent. Its growth-adjusted debt is one of the largest in the world, larger than Bolivia and equivalent to the Ivory Coast', Cohen commented in an analysis prepared for the EC Commission in early 1991. 'Poland and Bulgaria, while also large debtors by this measure, find themselves in better company, in the vicinity of Chile or Ecuador.' He adds: 'This will sound surprising, perhaps, to the extent that Hungary is viewed as one of the better risks in Eastern Europe, essentially for the naive reason that it has never rescheduled its debt.'[6]

Certainly, it is not a view shared by Hungarian economists. Laszlo Csaba has put the case in Hungary's favour. 'Hungary, in spite of many difficulties, has always met its international commitments. Demands for debt relief were expressed during the election campaign in the spring of 1990, but the present Hungarian government and the coalition parties did not act in those terms.' He went on to say: 'Last year (1989), the country's debt service burden exceeded 40 per cent of export earnings, and it will be no less in the coming years either. Nevertheless, this level of servicing can be met, though not easily: indeed, under adverse conditions in other years (1982 and 1986) it was even higher (more than 60 per cent), and still Hungary did not reschedule.'

Csaba also commented: 'There is no economic emergency, no financing crisis, especially since, with the passing of pre-election uncertainty, the larger part of the deposits withdrawn in the first three months [of 1990] have again been placed in the National Bank.'[7]

By 1991, however, the Hungarian government had begun to look more carefully at the prospects for alleviating its debt burden. In the wake of the Polish debt forgiveness deal, some political leaders in Hungary began to cast around for a similar arrangement that could ease the foreign exchange costs of servicing a debt that by March 1991 stood at US$21.5bn.

The problem is that 75 per cent of Hungary's debt is to commercial banks, so a Polish-style write-off by the Paris Club banks would reduce Hungary's interest charges by only a small amount.

An imaginative solution has nevertheless been put forward by Gyula Horn, former foreign minister and chairman of the Hungarian parliament's Foreign Affairs Committee. He has suggested that Hungary's debt to the commercial banks should be taken over by governments, and that the task of converting this more volatile private debt into a more manageable official debt should be assisted by the setting up of a new international fund.

For the present, Hungary's access to the international financial markets for further funds now looks to be diminishing. 'Even if Hungary continues to have access to bond markets', noted the OECD in February 1991, 'no net increase in private market funding seems probable. The country will therefore be obliged to seek considerably more credit from official sources.'

In addition to the US$1.6bn loan granted at that time by the IMF to help ease Hungary's transition to full currency convertibility and the establishment of a market economy, the OECD pointed out that 'among the other sources of finance that will be providing increased flows are the World Bank, the International Finance Corporation, the European Investment Bank and the European Community.' Hungary's credit needs, meanwhile, have been put at US$3bn a year by Laszlo Bekesi, the finance minister.

Czechoslovakia

The financial conservatism of the communists has left Czechoslovakia with an enviably clean slate on its external debt. Its debt rose from a negligible US$3.5bn in 1985 to almost US$8bn in 1990, and its debt at about US$450 per head of population is about one-half that of Poland and one-quarter that of Hungary.

It is also a substantial creditor. Communist Czechoslovakia's eagerness to sell arms to Third World nations led it to advance considerable sums to potential buyers. It is owed US$5.5bn in generally unrecoverable hard currency loans.

Czechoslovakia's standing in the international capital markets is therefore sound. But the country's economic difficulties as it struggles to establish a market economy mean that private bank lending is unlikely to increase very much.

'The share of official creditors is likely to rise', the OECD has commented, 'as borrowing requirements increase in 1991 . . . Overall, the country will need to borrow heavily in 1991, but adequate resources would appear to be available if the authorities' commitment to reform is sustained.'

Bulgaria

Bulgaria is the nearest Eastern Europe has yet come to the Latin America syndrome. The story of its foreign debt and the moratorium it declared in 1990 on the payment of its interest charges sounds a warning bell for Eastern Europe as a whole.

Along with the rest of Eastern Europe, Bulgaria borrowed over-enthusiastically during the latter 1980s. Having withdrawn completely, for internal political reasons, from the international capital markets between 1980 and 1984, Bulgaria returned to them in 1985 with gusto. Its net indebtedness shot up from a mere US$1.6bn in that year to US$6bn in 1988 and US$10bn in 1989.

At first, Bulgaria's new government tried to tackle the debt servicing crisis by drastically curtailing imports. But an 8 per cent drop in imports predictably failed to make much of an impact on the country's US$1bn a year trade deficit, and by early 1990 Bulgaria was left facing the prospect of US$2bn in hard currency interest payments that year and a continuing balance of payments crisis.

In March 1990, the Bulgarian Foreign Trade Bank announced that it was suspending principal payments on its US$11bn foreign debt, and then in June it stopped interest payments too. Western banks responded with their own moratorium on further credits to Bulgaria. They also granted Sofia a 90-day freeze on payments, which has since been rolled over a number of times as the search for a solution to the Bulgarian problem continues.

Talks have been taking place sporadically ever since. The Paris Club of sovereign creditors agreed in April 1991 to reschedule Bulgaria's fairly modest official debt of US$1.8bn over ten years, beginning with an initial six-year grace period. The more thorny problem has been the US$8.6bn owed to the private banks grouped in the London Club.

A consortium led by Deutsche Bank has been discussing the possibility of a major rescheduling of Bulgaria's private debt. Henning Christophersen, the Dane who is EC Commissioner for Economic and Financial Affairs, called in mid-April 1991 for Bulgaria to be accorded similar debt forgiveness to Poland, but the picture is complicated by the Bulgarians' own ambivalent attitude to a debt write-off.

The Bulgarian government fears that a debt forgiveness agreement with the major commercial banks might have the unwelcome side-effect of slowing the country's economic reform drive. Ivan Kostov, Bulgaria's finance minister, has indicated that Sofia's concern now is that a solution to the debt issue could remove Bulgaria's incentive to push through radical economic reforms. 'We have never discussed the elimination of the debt . . . not even among ourselves', he remarked during the inaugural meeting in London of the European Bank for Reconstruction and Development.[8]

Nevertheless, a solution to Bulgaria's debt moratorium deadlock is urgently needed. The effect of the banks' freeze on new credits has been to accelerate the fall in Bulgaria's industrial production. In 1990 it fell 10 per cent and for 1991, according to Atanas Paparizov, the Bulgarian foreign economic relations minister, the economic collapse is so great that the country's GDP will fall by 30 per cent.

So it is that Bulgaria has ended up in a situation that is grimly familiar to many Latin American and Third World debtor nations. It can go neither forward nor backward. It can get no new credits from the banks until it pays out hard currency that it does not possess and, even then, in future it can expect only official loans.

Romania

Romania's is a case of virtue unrewarded. With no foreign debt to speak of, Romania is nevertheless considered to be one of the worst credit risks in Eastern Europe. The story of Nicolae Ceaucescu's obsession with wiping clean all Romania's external debt is well known. In 1982 the country was forced to reschedule its fairly modest foreign debt when the USSR's involvement in Afghanistan triggered a crisis of confidence throughout Comecon. From that time on, the Ceaucescu regime swore to eliminate foreign borrowings at virtually all costs.

When he fell from power the task was complete. In 1989 Romania's external debt was a mere US$500m and the country's hard currency reserves stood at a healthy US$1.8bn. Unfortunately, the effort involved in clearing the debt failed to strengthen either the Romanian economy or its foreign trade position.

The Ceaucescu years were marked by the dictator's 'export or die' policies and by his virtual ban on imports. That has since given way to rising domestic consumption, a steadily mounting import bill and a trade gap that is running at about US$2bn a year. With the Romanian economy in bad shape, the only hope seems to be foreign credit. Commercial banks have made it plain that Romania must look for this from governments and the IMF.

Yugoslavia

Looking back over the 1980s, Yugoslav government officials ruefully confess that their country's debt experience contains some useful lessons for Eastern Europe as a whole.

'The investments we made using the funds borrowed abroad did not generate large enough profits to wipe out that debt', comments Mikhailo Crnobrnja, Yugoslavia's ambassador to the European Community, and adds: 'This is a lesson for the 1990s. External financial aid has to be aimed at boosting efficiency enough that the debt can be serviced and repaid.'

The 1980s saw a determined struggle by Yugoslavia to get its foreign debt back on to an even keel. At its peak, Yugoslavia's external debt stood at US$25bn, and interest payments on that were mopping up 43 per cent of the country's export and tourist earnings of hard currency. Now, after repeated reschedulings and a stern IMF stabilization programme, the country's foreign debt is under control.

Yugoslavia's external debt was painfully clawed back to around US$20bn by the late 1980s, and at the end of 1990 had been further reduced to US$16bn. Before the Yugoslav crisis erupted into violence in mid-1991, the Belgrade government had hoped to have cut it to US$10-12bn.

Helpful ways the West can structure lending

Western governments and the leading banks of the industrialized countries must, in concert with the Eastern Europeans themselves, devise a debt strategy that will ensure that the region avoids the Latin America route. What such a strategy should look like is far from clear.

There seems to be widespread agreement, though, that the West will have to be cruel to be kind. It was misplaced generosity, coupled with a lack of control and supervision, that created the Latin America and Third World debt nightmares. Eastern Europe, say the experts, would benefit most from a system in which Western credit is strictly linked to economic reforms.

'I would suggest that the strategy of the Western nations should be to reduce Eastern Europe's debt, but I must add the warning that a really hefty write-off would be unsound', says Yugoslav ambassador Mikhailo Crnobrnja, who is himself a former banker. 'There would no longer be such a strong motivation for the Eastern European countries to streamline as fast as possible.' As to further lending by the West, Crnobrnja adds: 'I would be tight on the credit side, but very generous with technical assistance.'

There is a growing consensus among Western economists that Eastern Europe cannot be left to lurch from one debt crisis to another. If it is, warn the analysts, the debt problem will cancel out all the efforts by the EC and others to help Eastern Europeans make the grade as functioning market economies.

Jeffrey Sachs, the 'grand young man' of US economic thinking, who in his mid-thirties is not only a professor of economics at Harvard but also a prominent adviser to Poland and Yugoslavia, speaks for much of the Western academic community when he urges an ambitious programme of debt relief and additional finance for restructuring.

Sachs believes that Eastern European countries urgently need grants and loans that will build up their hard currency reserves enough to help them to stabilize their exchange rates and make their own currencies fully convertible. He points out that while the IMF has been pursuing precisely such a policy, the amounts available to it are far too small.

He also favours a dramatic cancellation of most of the debt owed by Eastern Europe to both governments and banks. 'The debts should be reduced cleanly', he says, 'not in a long drawn-out battle.'

Sachs warns that a failure by the West to wipe the slate almost clean would be short-sighted in the extreme. 'Any attempt to collect these [debts]', he comments, 'would subject Eastern Europe to financial serfdom for the next generation; a plight that would be particularly bitter since the debt is a legacy of communist mismanagement, over which the public had no control.'[9]

The Polish debt write-off as a 'pilot' for Eastern Europe

Agreement among economists on a debt strategy is one thing; getting politicians and bankers to put it into practice is quite another. The Polish debt write-off has triggered a general reappraisal of the whole issue of debt – in Eastern Europe and throughout the developing world – but it has also highlighted the different attitudes that Western governments have to debt forgiveness.

Japan was uncharacteristically outspoken in its condemnation of the Polish write-off. Japanese officials have made it plain that Tokyo feels that debt forgiveness encourages irresponsibility among debtor countries, sets an unwelcome precedent, and is being used by the United States as a way of rewarding certain countries for political rather than economic reasons. Tokyo has indicated that debt write-offs may prejudice Japanese banks against advancing further loans.

France has also expressed reservations about the way the Polish write-off was structured. The US government decided to set an example to other creditors by writing off 70 per cent of its debt, while the Paris Club opted for 50 per cent. The US debt was a comparatively small US$2.9bn, made up chiefly of farm trade credits, but the French government fears that the US's generosity is misplaced.

'This begs the question, "Are bilateral deals going to proliferate or will we retain a multilateral framework?"' complained Pierre Beregovoy, France's finance minister, shortly after the Polish deal was struck. He pointed out that for debtor countries the risk is that without the collective discipline of the Paris Club some creditors will not want to grant much in the way of concessions. 'Debtor countries have an interest in multilateral solutions', he emphasized, 'because while some creditors may be able to offer a bit more, others often want to do less.'

The roundest criticism of all over the terms of the Polish deal has come from the commercial banks. They apparently see it as the first step on the slippery slope to worldwide debt forgiveness that could lead to a collapse of the international financial system.

Horst Schulmann, managing director of the Washington-based Institute of International Finance, which promotes the views of the major commercial banks, has condemned the Polish write-off as 'foreign aid through the back door'. He believes that the pressure on banks to match the Paris Club terms of at least 50 per cent forgiveness, coupled with interest arrears from debtor nations that in the six months to March 1991 soared from US$18bn to US$27bn, is in fact choking off the flow of bank credits.

Referring, as Horst Schulmann also did, to the Polish write-off as a 'moral hazard' that poses a threat to the international financial system is unlikely to strengthen the banks' case. But the point about bank lending being severely discouraged by debt write-offs is inescapable. Unless an across-the-board system of debt forgiveness can be negotiated that ensures that the banks as well as the debtors are equally and fairly treated, governments' efforts to restructure international debt will come to nothing.

The idea of a concerted attempt to restructure the world's debt problems is a familiar one. In 1985, James Baker, the US Secretary of State who was at that time President Ronald Reagan's Treasury Secretary, put forward a US$30bn plan for tackling Third World debt.

The Baker Plan's requirement that the banks should shoulder US$20bn of that burden meant that it was never properly implemented. The cudgels were taken up again, though, by Nicholas Brady, Baker's successor as US Treasury Secretary, in March 1989. The Brady Plan aims at a 20 per cent debt reduction that links write-offs with economic restructuring. By mid-1991, however, out of the 19 developing countries eligible for debt forgiveness under the plan, only Egypt, Mexico, the Philippines, Costa Rica, Venezuela and Morocco had negotiated deals.

Getting the world's creditors and debtors to agree on a debt strategy is not proving easy, and until progress is made on the Brady Plan there seems little hope that a special strategy will emerge for Eastern Europe.

The effort to hammer out a common position between the Western creditor governments is making some progress, but too often falls victim to domestic political pressures that push it off track. The lending policies of EC member states vary wildly. Some countries, notably Germany, concentrate on export credits that will benefit their own industries. A common EC position remains elusive, as the Community's competence does not extend to such matters as sovereign debt.

Although not a debt forum, the Group of 24 offers a framework within which an Eastern European debt agreement might eventually be worked out. So far, though, G-24 has done little more than focus attention on the very different attitudes of its European and non-European members to the debt issue. The 'Europeans only' attitude of the US towards Eastern Europe's problems has been particularly marked on the debt question, where US banks have little exposure.

The United States, having urged Polish debt forgiveness on a lavish scale, raised eyebrows when it responded to a G-24 proposal that it should contribute to a US$1bn loan to Czechoslovakia with an offer of only US$15m. Washington has been similarly unresponsive in its support for G-24 macroeconomic assistance loans for Hungary, Romania and Bulgaria.

For the Eastern European debtors, meanwhile, weighed down with interest payments that in several cases gobble up as much as half their precious export earnings, the outlook is bleak. The capital needs of Eastern Europe over the four years 1991-94 are being reckoned at about US$80-90bn, and there is clearly no hope of that coming from the banks and the financial markets.[10]

The cry among Western politicians and business leaders has been that Eastern Europeans must let the market work. Eastern Europe has been told repeatedly that there is no middle way and that no hybrid form of 'market socialism' can ease the transition to becoming market economies. But the Western nations should not swallow their own rhetoric.

The funding of Eastern Europe's economic rebirth cannot be left to the markets. Governments and supranational institutions like the EC Commission, the IMF and World Bank must fashion a system that injects capital into the Eastern European economies.

Debt forgiveness must be just one element in a strategy as wide-ranging as the Marshall Plan that helped to re-launch the economies of Western Europe in the wake of World War II.

Notes

1. 'OECD Financial Market Trends'. Special feature on the international financial situation of the Central and Eastern European countries, Paris, February 1991.

2. *The Economist*, 9 March 1991.

3. United Nations World Scientific Banking Meeting, Dubrovnik, 7 June 1989.

4. Annual Report for 1990 of the Asian Development Bank, Manila.

5. 'The Economy of the USSR: A study undertaken in response to a request by the Houston summit'. Prepared by the IMF, World Bank, OECD and the European Bank for Reconstruction and Development and published in December 1990.

6. *The Solvency of Eastern Europe*, by Daniel Cohen, CEPREMAP, Paris and CEPR, London, January 1991.

7. 'Gearing Up for the Economic Future', by Laszlo Csaba. In No 119 of *The New Hungarian Quarterly*, 1990.

8. *Financial Times*, 17 April 1991.

9. 'Eastern Europe's Economies', by Jeffrey Sachs. *The Economist*, 13 January 1990.

10. Jonathan Wilmot of Credit Suisse First Boston to a Euromoney conference on international finance markets, Geneva, 28 February 1991.

12

Assistance:

A 'Marshall Plan' for Eastern Europe?

The calls for a 'Marshall Plan Mark II' — Western assistance so far — What the Western nations are spending — The aims of a concerted strategy — Some of the blueprints being advanced — What a concerted plan for Eastern Europe might cost — Why 'throwing money' may not be the answer — How EC assistance could be refined — The outlook for Western aid

---

Barely six months before he rose to address a packed audience of eminent persons at Harvard University, Jiri Dienstbier had been a stoker shovelling coal into a furnace in the Prague metro system. The events of autumn 1989 that came to be known as Czechoslovakia's 'velvet revolution' catapulted him overnight from dissident obscurity to become his country's foreign minister and President Vaclav Havel's loyal associate.

In May 1990, Dienstbier travelled to Harvard with a vital message. His purpose was to appeal for a Western aid strategy that could put Eastern Europe back on its feet. It was no accident that he had chosen the hallowed precincts of Harvard University just across the Charles River from Boston, for it was at Harvard that US Secretary of State George C Marshall, 43 years earlier, had launched his famous plan to rebuild the ruins of post-war Europe.

On 5 June 1947, Marshall had publicly revealed the true state of the European economy, and outlined a US government assistance scheme that he believed could give it a substantial boost. Despite two years of peace, he explained, economic life in Europe was still stubbornly refusing to take off again.

The situation he outlined was in many ways remarkably similar to that of Eastern Europe today. Although six years of war had not destroyed factories and machinery on the scale that had at first been feared, Europe's industries were nevertheless in very poor shape.

The wartime years had that meant there was no new plant and equipment, no modernization and precious little maintenance. Consumer goods industries had often been converted to producing military items. Returning them to their original uses when investment funds were so very scarce was proving easier said than done.

Housing was a major problem, of course, because of the widespread devastation. Europe's battered roads and railways also made travel and the shipment of goods difficult and expensive. Trade between the formerly prosperous European nations had all but dried up. The culprit was not just the physical difficulties of exporting and importing goods but the financial constraints on doing business.

It was the era of the 'almighty dollar', and dollars were desperately scarce in Europe. The Western European nations' own currencies were as soft and unconvertible as those of many Eastern European countries now. What trade there was between European countries in those grim post-war years was strictly controlled by governments whose chief concern was not to run a trade deficit of any size.

The breakdown of the business structure in Europe, Secretary Marshall announced at Harvard, had become complete. The economies of Western Europe were starting to collapse and, worse, were threatening to send their unwelcome shock waves back across the Atlantic to the US. Unless steps were taken at once to rescue Europe, this time economically, the United States would eventually suffer too.

His answer was the Marshall Plan, or to give it its official name, the 'European Recovery Program'. It turned out to be a concerted four-year attack on Europe's most fundamental economic problems, and its effect was electric. US dollars were used as the seed money for a European Payments Union which helped to re-launch international trade between Europeans, and special attention was given to improving the productivity of Europe's old-fashioned factories and to encouraging the transfer of trade from government ministries to private companies.

Between 1949 and 1952, the Marshall Plan pumped almost US$20bn into Western Europe. In all, 16 countries were involved in the scheme – the USSR and its new Eastern European satellites having declined on the grounds that it constituted a form of US economic imperialism. Its mixture of financial aid for infrastructural spending and trade-related measures gave the Western European economies a kickstart that put them back on the road to recovery.

At today's prices, the US aid programme was equivalent to something like US$200bn, for the United States was transferring 1.3 per cent of its GNP into the effort. Over 80 per cent of the money was in grants, not loans. As an act both of generosity and far-sighted statesmanship it still towers over the figures now being talked about for Eastern Europe.[1]

The calls for a 'Marshall Plan Mark II'

A latter-day version of the Marshall Plan was more or less what Jiri Dienstbier appealed for at Harvard in the spring of 1990. His initiative reflected the widespread hope throughout Eastern Europe that Uncle Sam might be persuaded to wave his magic wand over their economic difficulties just as he had over those of Western Europe almost half a century before.

Dienstbier's plan was fairly modest, yet practical. He proposed that US$16bn should be advanced to Central Europe over three years via the European Bank for Reconstruction and Development (BERD), which at that time was still being set up. His idea was that the BERD would credit these funds to the USSR in order to enable it to buy industrial goods from Czechoslovakia, Hungary and Poland.

These three countries would, in turn, use the hard currency payments from the USSR to modernize their own industries, 'which means', pointed out Jiri Dienstbier, 'that they'll spend it in the countries providing them with the money'.

The core of the Dienstbier Plan was that the BERD would coordinate and supervise the USSR's use of the funds, and thus ensure that they were not poured away in fruitless attempts to prop up State-run industries. The plan also reflected Vaclav Havel's view that the USSR is the key to the problem of re-launching Eastern Europe.

In February 1990 President Havel had spelt this out to a joint session of the US Congress. 'You can help us most of all', he told his listeners, 'if you help the USSR on its irreversible but immensely complicated road to democracy.'

At first, Dienstbier's appeal made newspaper headlines around the world (which is more than could be said for that of Marshall himself; it was at first widely ignored by both the US and international press). But as the months slipped by it faded from view. The Dienstbier Plan, along with the many other suggestions for a 'Marshall Plan Mark II' that could tackle Eastern Europe's problems, had failed to fire the imagination of the public or the politicians.

It is nevertheless an idea that continues to be hotly debated among economists and international civil servants. The sheer scale of Eastern Europe's crisis is believed by many Western policy analysts to demand a more concerted and generous response than has so far been the case.

In May 1991, Czechoslovakia returned to the offensive. When President Havel was invited to the German city of Aachen to receive the annual Charlemagne prize for international relations, he called on Western nations to give 'generous help' comparable to the Marshall Plan. He said this would enable the former communist states of Eastern Europe to 'rejoin the path of Western civilization, culture and values'.

President Havel is not the only leader to urge a major assistance programme. In January 1990, EC Commission President Jacques Delors had suggested that something like US$23bn a year would be needed in Community finance for Eastern Europe over the coming five to ten years. He told the European Parliament that US$17bn a year might come from the EC as aid to underpin economic reform, with a further US$6bn or so in loans.

Gianni de Michelis, the Italian foreign minister, proposed that the EC should allocate US$15bn a year to assisting

Eastern Europe, which would involve setting aside 0.25 per cent of Community GNP. He also believes the same amount should be injected into the poorest countries of the Mediterranean, and that another 0.5 per cent of the EC's GDP should be allocated to Third World aid.

Zbigniew Brzezinski, formerly President Jimmy Carter's national security adviser and a prominent Polish-American with a keen interest in Eastern Europe's development, has advocated a capital transfer from the West of US$25-30bn. This, he believes, is needed 'to prevent the region's slide into political and economic chaos'.[2]

Western assistance so far

One reason that the West has been slow to embrace the idea of an ambitious Marshall-style initiative is that it is widely thought that enough is already being done. There are over 40 different Western organizations involved in giving financial and technical assistance to Eastern Europe, and the impression given is that a major aid effort is under way. Yet the truth is that very little grant aid is getting through to Eastern Europeans, who feel they are being exhorted by the West to become capitalists without capital.

Another reason for the lack of enthusiasm is that there is comparatively little public pressure on Western governments to step up their financial assistance. Where there has been a strong lobby, such as the US's Polish community, the result was the Bush Administration's backing for Polish debt relief.

Otherwise, although Eastern Europe's problems attracted the fickle support of the general public in the West during the heady revolutionary days of 1989, public attention has since been distracted elsewhere. Perhaps only a serious crisis in Eastern Europe can recapture it.

Broadly speaking, there are three types of assistance to Eastern Europe, and three groups of aid donors and lenders. Assistance comes in the form of macroeconomic assistance, which is money to bridge balance of payments gaps and to support currency convertibility. There is also technical and infrastructural support and, third, there are export credits which enable an Eastern European country to buy the goods of a particular country with funds loaned by its banks.

The three main sources of funds for Eastern Europe are: first, the Washington-based Bretton Woods institutions – the International Monetary Fund together with its sister organization the World Bank; then the European Community, which commits money both at an EC level and in the national programmes of its 12 member states; finally, the Group of 24.

The three types of assistance and the three groups do not, however, match up very neatly. The IMF concentrates on providing finance for macroeconomic adjustment and the World Bank specializes in infrastructural development and project finance. The EC also concerns itself with project finance through its PHARE programme, which was launched in 1989 to aid Poland and Hungary and has subsequently been extended to most of the other Eastern European countries.

The EC-level effort also includes the activities of the Luxembourg-based European Investment Bank, which has a long history of funding infrastructural projects in under-privileged regions of the EC and which is now starting to fund development projects in Eastern Europe.

Then there is the G-24 effort, which is coordinated by the European Commission and is a framework for national and institutional activities in Eastern Europe. Its grants and lending activities are intended to complement the EC's PHARE programme and dovetail with the Bretton Woods institutions. Its work includes making macroeconomic adjustment loans.

Since May 1991 the G-24 framework has also included the new London-based European Bank for Reconstruction and Development (BERD), which is due to channel funds into private investment in Eastern Europe and which sees itself as partly a development bank and partly a merchant bank.

In other words, there is a profusion of official aid agencies, many of them with overlapping responsibilities. The decision by the G-7 Western economic summit in July 1989 that the EC should coordinate Western assistance to Poland and Hungary marked a positive step towards rationalizing these different efforts, but the West has stopped short of forging them into a single strategy. In July 1990, the G-24 countries decided against the idea of a general fund for Eastern Europe.

It was scarcely surprising that they should do so. Pushing so many different bureaucracies into a new vertical structure would have been a superhuman task. Brussels' coordinating role goes some way to limiting confusion, but probably not far enough. As Bimal Ghosh, coordinator of the Committee on North-South Issues, observed ruefully from Geneva: 'Inevitably, the multiplicity of international and regional agencies, including the newly-established European Bank, the divergence of interests and priorities among the donor countries and, not infrequently, their individual desire for visibility and aid-based leverage in the recipient country will continue to limit the EC's coordinating role.'[3]

What the Western nations are spending

Putting a global figure on the amount of Western aid extended to Eastern Europe is not made easy by this fragmentation. By mid-1991, though, the headline figure for both development loans and outright grants from the industrialized countries of the world to Central and Eastern Europe stood at around US$42bn. But it is a total arrived at by adding together a bewildering variety of apples and oranges and it must be stressed that nothing like this sort of money had at that point found its way into the Eastern European economies.

According to EC Commission figures, which have been calculated in Ecus, a grand total of Ecu 35bn had been committed by G-24 nations, the Community itself and other sources ranging from the IMF and World Bank to the oil-rich Gulf States. Of that, Ecu 22.9bn was designated as 'assistance', and was broken down into Ecu 13.8bn in grants and Ecu 9.1bn in loans or credits. A further Ecu 12bn is attributed to organizations like the European Investment Bank (EIB), the European Coal and Steel Community (ECSC), the World Bank and IMF.

The apparent emphasis on grants rather than loans does not stand up well to closer scrutiny. Of the Ecu 13.8bn described as grants, Ecu 8.2bn is accounted for by the share capital of the BERD that G-24 nations and the EC are subscribing. Other EC Commission analyses show that bilateral assistance by countries in G-24 and the EC divides evenly into one-third for export credits, one third for macroeconomic assistance and one-third for technical assistance and infrastructural investment.

Commitments by G-24 at that time stood at about US$23bn, of which half was from the EC and its 12 member states and two-thirds from Europe when EFTA is included. The figures broke down into US$8bn in outright grants, US$1.7bn in loans from the EIB and ECSC, US$11.4bn in capital for the BERD and US$2bn in bilateral loans and credits.

These figures give an exaggerated impression of the size and impact of Western assistance to Eastern Europe. In reality, of course, the BERD had not begun lending in earnest at that point, and many of the other funds were still unspent or unlent. It must be said, too, that the proportion of genuine grants does not compare well with the Marshall Plan, in which less than 20 per cent of the funds were loans and the balance was grants.

This criticism cannot, however, be levelled at the EC's PHARE programme. 'Over 99 per cent of our funds are grants, not loans', emphasizes Tom Garvey, the tough-minded Irishman in charge of PHARE. The programme is the centrepiece of the European Community drive to direct EC-level help to Eastern Europe. It was set up in 1989 with a budget for 1990 of Ecu 500m; for 1991 that was raised to Ecu 820m and for 1992 raised again to Ecu 1bn.

PHARE's aim, Garvey explains, is to bring about systemic change in Eastern Europe. Its funds are being directed towards problem areas such as inadequate banking systems and non-existent telecommunications that are a major barrier to foreign investment. As well as tackling the root causes of Eastern Europe's economic difficulties, PHARE spending is also intended to concentrate on immediate crisis areas such as environmental pollution and industrial training.

Unlike macroeconomic assistance, in which a billion dollar loan can be transferred to a country's central bank at the stroke of a pen, spending PHARE money is a lengthy and labour-intensive process. Setting up the structures needed to inject money, technology and education into Eastern Europe's ramshackle economic structures is proving far more difficult than many experts anticipated.

The aims of a concerted strategy

If a Marshall Plan Mark II for Eastern Europe were ever to get off the ground, its chief purpose would be to introduce some sense of order and strategic thinking to the situation. The financial transfers involved should be only an element of a strategy that ranges from streamlining industries to regenerating trade.

The West's present assistance effort has been launched with commendable speed, but it is nevertheless too piecemeal and haphazard. The effort to bring Eastern Europe into the global market economy will take at least a decade – more likely two – and that time-frame demands a more sophisticated approach than the present proliferation of assistance programmes.

It is probably a mistake for advocates of a more carefully structured and comprehensive Western assistance programme to refer to the original Marshall Plan. To call on a formula that is almost 50 years old raises obvious objections. One of the most often-heard is that the Marshall Plan was aimed at countries that were already market economies, and therefore a Marshall-style effort would be unsuitable for Eastern Europe.

This overlooks the fact that the Marshall Plan was originally proposed for both Eastern and Western Europe, until Stalin rejected the whole idea. Furthermore, the Eastern European economies' transitional problems as they struggle to become market economies make a wide-ranging aid strategy even more attractive as it would address their profoundly structural difficulties.

Too often, the use of the term 'Marshall Plan' wrongly gives the impression that it would involve slavishly following the same methods as the original. Even the potential recipients of assistance from a Marshall Plan Mark II sometimes jib at the name. 'I'm not sure I like re-heated dishes. The Marshall Plan was that, at that time', comments Jan Kulakowski, Poland's ambassador to the EC.

The name of the Marshall Plan is most frequently invoked because it communicates simply and clearly the idea of a much more ambitious assistance programme than anything so far envisaged. It has become a shorthand way of describing a new approach that would both boost present levels of financial assistance and link that funding with policies to encourage trade and revitalize Eastern Europe's industries.

Some of the blueprints being advanced

A variety of blueprints for a more integrated Western assistance strategy have been put forward. None of them has yet become established as the leader in the field, and indeed many of them share a number of common ideas. They give an indication, though, of the options open to Western policy makers when fashioning a more strategic approach to helping Eastern Europe.

Plan 1: Creation of a Marshall-style 'overlord' organization

The United Nations Geneva-based Economic Commission for Europe has not put forward a formal proposal to this effect, but its chief economist, Paul Rayment, has set out the broad lines of a plan that draws heavily on the Marshall Plan experience.

Rayment's thinking is that the United Nations ECE, which during the Cold War years was the only institution that straddled the East-West divide in Europe, should provide the central administration of a Marshall-type effort for Eastern Europe. It should play the role that was played by the Organization for European Economic Cooperation (OEEC). Rayment adds that any latter-day OEEC should self-destruct at the end of a five-year mandate.

The job of this new administrative body would be to prepare an economic recovery programme for Eastern Europe that would clearly set out the timetables and objectives to be met. It would set economic reform targets such as currency convertibility for the various countries, and it would also plan the correct sequencing of these to help these countries to achieve their reforms in the best order.

The plan would also consist of contingency plans that could help the Eastern European countries to overcome setbacks to their reform programmes. A system of technical assistance would be devised in which economic advisers from the Western donor nations would be seconded to Eastern Europe to help supervise implementation of the programme.

One of the functions of such an elaborate and carefully structured plan, Paul Rayment points out, is that it provides a realistic framework for the Eastern Europeans' own expectations. 'It is a far better alternative to their present vision of economies that seem to be hopelessly sliding backwards', he says.

Plan 2: 'Good ideas from the past'

Susan Strange and Stuart Holland, professors at the European University Institute in Florence, have set out a number of lessons that can usefully be drawn from the Marshall Plan years.

- *A limited lifespan* for whatever agency might be set up to administer a recovery programme for Eastern Europe.

- *Self-allocation.* As with Marshall aid, it should be left to the recipients of assistance to decide on the distribution of funds.

- *A multilateral payments system* that could provide Eastern European countries with a vital halfway stage on their way to full currency convertibility. The Marshall Plan launched the European Payments Union with a float of US$350m to break down the currency restrictions that were severely blocking trade. The EPU ran from 1950 to 1959 and provided a central hard currency fund that enabled Western European countries to resume trade and settle payments with one another on a monthly basis. It had an immediate effect on trade between these countries, which until then had become bogged down in unworkable barter arrangements.

- *Privatization targets.* Under the Marshall Plan, Western European governments were encouraged to withdraw from wartime State trading. They had to report monthly on whether they had met their agreed privatization targets. A similar device could help to speed Eastern Europe's drive to privatize.

- *Positive trade discrimination.* Europe's weaker economies were allowed, during a transitional period, to discriminate against the United States and in favour of each other. A principal aim of the Marshall Plan was to encourage Europeans to trade freely with one another, and the US therefore tolerated measures that gave European companies an edge on their US competitors.

- *Counterpart funds.* The recipients of Marshall aid dollars agreed to set aside an equivalent amount in local currency that could be spent on such projects as infrastructural development and urban renewal. Some counterpart funds have been set up in Eastern Europe, notably a Polish agricultural fund, but a more systematic approach could be taken.

- *Investment guarantees.* Companies investing in Eastern Europe should be able to cover themselves against political risk. A version of the World Bank's Multilateral Investment Guarantee Agreement (MIGA), which was designed with unstable Third World countries in mind, should be developed for Eastern Europe.

Plan 3: A coordinating body that would focus on debt

Attila Szilassy, a Hungarian-born economist, has proposed the setting up of a Central European Information Centre (CEIC) to coordinate, as an advisory body to the European Commission, the efforts of the 40-45 Western institutions and government bodies now involved in aiding Eastern Europe.

Szilassy proposes that debt management should be the 'central axis' of what would be a G-24 effort. He suggests channelling a major part of Western assistance through the new European Bank for Reconstruction and Development (BERD). He says the BERD could buy up Eastern European countries' debts in the secondary markets at 40-50 per cent of their nominal value, and thus subsidize commercial banks' exposure.

In a second step, BERD 'would forgive half the nominal value of the debt, thus restoring its original value'. The BERD would make a one-time investment of Ecu 8-9bn that would be used partly to wipe out the more unstable of Eastern Europe's debts and partly to finance infrastructure, joint ventures and other investments.

Plan 4: A 'non-Marshall Plan' for Eastern Europe

A scheme put forward by Michael Palmer, until recently the head of research at the European Parliament's secretariat in Luxembourg, calls itself a 'non-Marshall Plan' that adapts itself to the different conditions of Eastern Europe in the 1990s.

Its first priority would be to introduce realistic pricing and genuine currency convertibility. Recipient countries would launch a joint appeal to the West for 10 to 15-year funding in the form of grants, not loans, and would prepare coordinated 'shopping lists' for financial and technical aid.

Grant aid would be aimed at bringing about radical improvements in transport and telecommunications and in the environment. Loans would be used to finance currency stabilization measures and balance of payments support.

Plan 5: A 'plan of plans' for Central Europe

A strategic plan that brings together the assistance requirements of Poland, Czechoslovakia and Hungary and their absorption capacities is being researched by a team of the Institute for East-West Security Studies team based at Stirin Castle, 25 kilometres outside Prague.

The project is chaired by former French Prime Minister Raymond Barre and is led by a Polish economist, Krzysztof Ners. Its aim is to analyze the assistance so far given to Central Europe, to look at the three countries' economic reform programmes and transition targets and to study the problems they are having over absorbing assistance.

It tries to assess the dimension of a future plan and to judge the institutional barriers in both Eastern and Western Europe that must be overcome. Finally, the project considers the timing of a strategic assistance programme for the Central

European region, its appropriateness and the touchy issue of conditionality.

What a concerted plan for Eastern Europe might cost

Economists have been arguing for years over whether the Marshall Plan really saved Western Europe, or whether the European economies had begun to bounce back anyway. What nobody disputes, however, is that the Marshall Plan was an excellent business investment for the United States.

By helping to pull Europe into a faster growth path, the United States ensured that its own economy would prosper from the increased trade opportunities. The same must be said of Western Europe's efforts to help the East. The question is not whether the EC and EFTA countries can afford to assist Eastern Europe, but whether they can afford *not* to.

On present showing, the economies of Eastern Europe face a grim future. At best, most of them will stagnate during the 1990s, as they struggle to break out of the vicious circles created by their command economies. At worst, they will descend into crisis and chaos. A Western aid and assistance strategy that can step in and help to turn these economies around is vitally important to maintaining stability in Europe. And if it were to succeed in expanding the Eastern European economies, then Western Europe would benefit too.

There could be a major and positive impact on the Western European economies from boosting those of Eastern Europe, says the Observatoire Francais des Conjonctures Economiques in Paris. It reckons that Eastern Europe's successful transition to becoming market economies could boost Germany's GNP by 3.5 per cent by 1993, and that of the rest of the EC by 1.5 per cent. The Banque Indosuez has estimated that the OECD countries as a whole would derive an extra 0.5 per cent yearly growth from the opening up of Eastern Europe.

Before reaping any rewards, Western Europe must first make the necessary investment. What, then, are the needs of Eastern Europe and what are the sums of money under discussion in the West?

When EC Commission President Jacques Delors outlined a US$23bn yearly transfer from the Community to Eastern

Europe he based his calculations on the amount that is currently being spent within the EC on helping its depressed regions. That would in fact be substantially more than the original Marshall Plan. According to the UN's Economic Commission for Europe, if the Marshall Plan's average spending of US$3bn a year is adjusted upwards to today's prices, but downwards because Eastern Europe's population is much smaller than the 16 Western European countries that were assisted, a comparable present-day figure would be US$42 per head per year.

On that basis, a Marshall Plan Mark II would cost about US$5bn a year if it were aimed at the six countries of Central and Eastern Europe, and US$16.5bn if the USSR were included. Delors's suggestion was in fact for an effort that, financially at any rate, would be three times greater than the Marshall Plan itself.[4]

If, on the other hand, the yardstick were to be the donor nations' ability to pay, then a Marshall-style commitment by Western Europe would yield a breathtaking US$200bn a year in transfers to Eastern Europe. That is what a commitment equivalent to 1.3 per cent of those countries' combined GDPs would add up to, whereas the UN ECE's figure of US$16.5bn a year works out at only 0.1 per cent of the combined EC, US and Japanese GDPs.

Comparisons with the late 1940s risk being both misleading and fruitless. A better idea of the sums that the West should spend on a future Eastern European Recovery Plan can be gleaned from the financial and infrastructural needs of the countries concerned.

Much revolves around the definition of 'needs'. In December 1990 Jacques Attali, the President-designate of the BERD, put the financial needs of Eastern Europe and the USSR at US$2 trillion. Earlier in the year he had put those of Eastern Europe alone at around US$1 trillion.

He was clearly not talking about investment levels or aid targets, but rather the degree to which these economies must grow if they are to become integrated with those of the industrialized world. The money needed for a recovery programme would be a much smaller amount that would serve to prime the pump of Eastern Europe's economic rebirth.

A glance at Eastern Europe's infrastructural needs gives an indication of the sort of spending that will be required. They exceed by far the funding currently available from the EC and G-24. The World Bank says that for telecommunications alone Eastern Europe needs US$60bn over the next ten years. That may be a modest estimate, for the Bonn government has revealed that it will be spending almost US$30bn on modernizing and extending Eastern Germany's telecommunications networks over the six years to 1997.

Telecommunications are just a small part of the financial needs of these countries. Modern roads, railways, housing, industrial streamlining, environmental cleaning up and control, higher energy costs, agricultural efficiency and the burden of servicing foreign debt are all costs that these countries cannot meet unaided.

The true costs of their transition towards becoming market economies is only now emerging. The 'financing gap' that faced the six Eastern European countries in 1991 was about US$20bn, with Soviet needs being put by the IMF at about US$20-30bn more if food credits and debt service needs are added in. Some of this money has been found in extra lending by the IMF and G-24, but much of it must be covered by 'adjustment' in Eastern Europe. The danger is that economic transition is being hampered by a desperate shortage of funds.

Why 'throwing money' may not be the answer

Despite the arguments in favour of a concerted recovery programme, the idea of another Marshall Plan is hanging fire. There are profound reservations in the West about the effectiveness of a massive financial transfer.

The fear is that until Eastern European countries have definitively made the switch to becoming market economies, financial aid will cushion the shock of transition and in many cases could actually delay the process. Western cash, say the opponents of a more generous aid programme, will enable

Eastern European governments to go on subsidizing employment in their inefficient State-owned industries.

The former German Democratic Republic offers an example both of the scale of spending that an all-out financial aid programme for Eastern Europe would involve, and of the perils of 'throwing money' at the problem.

Between 1991 and 1995 some US$700bn is due to be injected into the economy of Eastern Germany, which has a population of about 16 million people. If that amount were to be scaled up to match the total population of the six Eastern European countries it would add up to something like US$5 trillion. But there is mounting criticism in Western Germany that this money will fail to accelerate Germany's economic union and that much of it will be wasted.

Eastern Germany is now being held up as an example of the difficulties of pouring in financial assistance. Much of the money is said to be going straight into social security payments to people who are being made redundant by plant closures. The ex-GDR is becoming even more of a wasteland as jobs are switched from East to West.

André Leysen, the Belgian industrialist who heads Agfa-Gevaert and is the only non-German to be a board member of the *Treuhandanstalt* that is handling East Germany's privatization drive, is in no doubt that a major financing effort is very risky. 'There should be *no* Marshall Aid-style money', he says. 'It'll be sucked into the old system.'

How EC Assistance could be refined

The setting up of a Marshall-type plan for Eastern Europe would, nevertheless, be an important political signal, especially if some sort of Soviet element were included. Quite apart from making Western assistance more coherent and transparent, it would show that the West's early enthusiasm and support for these countries' efforts to become democratic market economies remains undiminished.

But to set such a recovery programme in motion takes time, even if the political support were to be there. For the time being, the streamlining of the EC's PHARE programme and the G-24 system as a whole would be a useful first step.

The European Community's PHARE programme could be a pilot for a wider and more concerted effort by the Western nations. Although the sums involved in PHARE are comparatively modest, it has concentrated on developing a 'hands on' approach, in which EC officials play an active role in developing projects, rather than merely administering the spending.

The EC's launch of PHARE has been an impressive effort. The EC Commission is, contrary to popular misconception, a tiny bureaucracy and its response to Eastern Europe's needs has been swift and efficient. But EC officials believe that experience already suggests a number of changes.

Tom Garvey, who heads PHARE, believes that one area in which the programme can be improved is to change the requirement by EC member states that money should be committed in the same budget year. Officials running PHARE projects complain that it is absurd to have to commit funds so hurriedly. They maintain there should be at least a two- or three-year commitment period if a wider strategy is to be developed.

There is also a view inside the European Commission that a separate EC programme with its own task force should be set up to deal with humanitarian assistance, and should be endowed with separate budget lines.

EC officials argue that a time limit of perhaps five years should be set for PHARE. Deadlines for ending PHARE assistance could be integrated into the framework of the three Central European countries' EC association agreements. This would help these countries to get away from what Eurocrats call the 'dependence culture' of EC aid.

The outlook for Western aid

It is hard to believe, given the long haul that lies ahead of Eastern Europe, that Western assistance will not be both improved and enlarged in the years to come. On the other hand, it is equally hard to see the present fragmentation of efforts being centralized into a single assistance programme.

When George Marshall launched his European Recovery Program, the United States was the undisputed economic and military victor of World War II. With Europe in ruins, it was natural that the US should set up a single administration to administer aid that was coming from a single source. Today, conditions are very different.

Each of the industrialized countries has its own development aid programme, and its own commercial aims embedded in its aid. The most prominent feature of Western assistance to Eastern Europe is the level of tied aid. The countries of the European Community are vying with one another to offer assistance that is firmly tied to export contracts. Germany, France and Italy are particularly prone to aid that is all too close to exploitation.

Nor do the EC member states' national aid programmes dovetail very neatly with Community-level efforts. EC officials sometimes complain that in the G-24 framework they receive better cooperation from non-EC nations such as the US and Canada than from the member states themselves.

Persuading Western governments to pool their resources into a single Eastern European effort looks an impossible task. It is made no easier by the independent roles of the IMF, the World Bank and the EC Commission, and now the BERD, or European Bank as it styles itself. It is hard to imagine any of these players ceding their independence to a new central authority.

So much for the pressures against a new and imaginative initiative. There are also compelling reasons why the governments linked in G-24 should think again about the shape and scope of their aid to Eastern Europe.

To begin with, there is the greater visibility that a combined aid effort would have. It is important for Eastern Europe's vulnerable new democracies that they should feel part of an enlarged community (with a small 'c') of European nations. A much more high-profile and recognizable assistance programme would go a long way towards that.

A combined programme would also entail greater transparency. In other words, it would mean the end of the arithmetical games that at present make it so hard to establish how much is being spent, and of that how much is loaned and how much given away. A more transparent system might also push the Western nations into being more generous and far-sighted.

Then there is coherence. The PHARE programme and the G-24 coordination effort have gone some way towards rationalizing assistance for Eastern Europe, but the overwhelming impression remains of fragmented, and too often competing, national or institutional programmes. Above all, there is little feeling that more general economic assistance measures such as trade financing and promotion are being fitted into a wider scheme.

The challenge is to integrate the Eastern European nations into a wider Europe. The financial and technical assistance these countries receive is part of this transition process. A more coherent aid strategy in which the EC plays a central role is essential if the Eastern European economies are to be part of the European Community, either as full members or associates.

The Marshall Plan's chief feature was that it used its funds to establish new systems in Europe. Trade flourished and factories were modernized, and it was the resulting prosperity that enabled Europeans to rebuild their roads and houses.

Eastern Europe is grappling with the even harder task of fashioning new economic structures. The free market system is strange and alien to most Eastern Europeans. That does not diminish the case for a much more imaginative and ambitious Western aid strategy that would be on a par with the Marshall Plan. It strengthens it.

Notes

1. 'Economic Reform in the East: A Framework for Western Support'. In the Economic Survey of Europe 1989-1990 of the United Nations Economic Commission for Europe, New York, April 1990. See also *Assistance to Reforms in Eastern Europe*, by Attila Szilassy for the Netherlands Institute for International Relations' Clingendael Institute, February 1991, and *An Eastern European Economic Rehabilitation Programme?*, by Susan Strange and Stuart Holland, European University Institute, Florence, March 1990.

2. 'Towards a Trans-European Commonwealth of Free Nations', by Zbigniew Brzezinski, *International Herald Tribune*, 8 March 1990.

3. 'Money Can't Buy Reform', Bimal Ghosh, *European Affairs*, Winter 1990-91.

4. *Economic Reform in the East: A Framework for Western Support*, UN Economic Commission for Europe, New York, April 1990.